Flight into Freedom and Beyond

Flight into Freedom was originally published in 1988.
Flight into Freedom and Beyond (first published in 2002)
contains an additional 24-page chapter
covering the years 1987–2002.
This revised edition (first published in 2007)
also contains a new postscript
following Eileen Caddy's death in December 2006.

Also by Eileen Caddy

books

Opening Doors Within

God Spoke to Me

The Living Word

Footprints on the Path

The Dawn of Change

The Spirit of Findhorn

double meditation CD

The Small Voice Within

DVD (by and about Eileen Caddy)

Opening Doors Within

all published by Findhorn Press
available from your favourite bookshop
or directly from www.findhornpress.com

Flight into Freedom and Beyond

Eileen Caddy

with Liza Hollingshead

This new edition first published in the UK by Findhorn Press 2002
Revised 2007 (additional postscript)

ISBN 978-1-899171-64-4

Cover design by Damian Keenan
All photographs © Findhorn Foundation Visuals Departement 2002

Printed and bound by Bookwell, Finland

3 4 5 6 7 8 9 10 11 12 13 12 11 10 09 08 07

Published by
Findhorn Press
305a The Park, Findhorn,
Forres IV36 3TE
Scotland, UK
Tel +44-(0)1309-690582
Fax +449-(0)1309-690036
eMail info@findhornpress.com

Introduction

I FIRST CAME TO the Findhorn Foundation for a weekend in 1974. I was not a 'spiritual type' but I certainly was looking for something. Having left my home in South Africa with an overwhelming sadness at the separation in every aspect of that society, I dreamt of an idyllic utopia where everyone had a common unity and purpose. What power that could generate! I didn't know how to create the harmony I longed for in my world, so I went looking for it.

My first impression of the community growing at Findhorn was that the 150 people I met there also wanted to live in harmony, and were setting about creating it themselves. So I stayed for a weekend . . . then a few weeks . . . then a year, which stretched to ten . . . and more.

What appeared at first glance to be just a group of nice people living happily together turned out to be much more. The community lifestyle was very busy – delicious vegetarian meals were produced twice a day in the spotless kitchen, the community centre was kept immaculate, there were gardeners digging, planting and weeding in the lovely flower and vegetable gardens, and other people worked in the craft studios or the Publications department, which had a darkroom and printing press and had published several books. The community was also about to break ground to build a new Hall to accommodate their ever increasing numbers. And there was something special about the place I couldn't define – a kind of magic.

In my quest for harmony I had set one foot on a path which was to lead me into worlds far beyond my dreams – towards a new understanding of Self, and of the very purpose of life.

One of my first steps along this path as a new member of the Findhorn Community was to clean Peter and Eileen Caddy's bungalow each morning. Only years later did I learn that I was there only because Eileen Caddy was recovering from a major operation. With my South African background I had assumed a servant was the least the founder members of this community were entitled to!

I was honoured to do the job, and astonished at the way Peter and Eileen included me in whatever conversation happened to be going on in the bungalow. My eyes and ears were opened as I listened to snippets of conversation about the inner workings of the community, both spiritual and practical – about an important special meditation meeting to 'ground the forces of light' or the equally important noon arrangements for the community van to take everyone for a swim at the beach to keep the body as healthy as the soul.

My spiritual education began at the hearth, under the eagle eyes of Peter and Eileen. "You have to learn to love where you are and what you are doing before you can move on", either one would say to me. "Don't leave even a speck of dust. It must be perfect. God made us perfectly, so only perfection is good enough for God. No sweeping things under the carpet!"

That applied to human relationships in the community too. People's openness impressed me – they were willing to share their deepest thoughts, fears or dreams with each other without reservation. Eileen would tell me about a difficulty in her relationship with Peter or share with me her most recent personal triumph as I dusted the semi-precious stones and crystals on the shelf. And God was so normal. Everyone seemed to accept without question that there was life, and spirit, in everything – even in those stones on the shelf.

Peter and Eileen's outward appearance as a conventional middle-aged English couple belied the fact that they, with their friend Dorothy Maclean, were the founders in 1962 of a spiritual community, which was on the crest of a new wave of thinking more often associated in those years with the flowering hippy movement. Eileen, the perfect lady, always carefully and elegantly dressed, with her white hair set and curled, was quiet, composed and maternal. Peter, tall and robust, with his ruddy, healthy, round face and tanned, balding head fringed with white hair, exuded energy and dynamic positivity. Dorothy Maclean had already left to live in the United States when I arrived at the community. At our first meeting several years later she impressed me as an intelligent and direct woman with a refreshingly commonsense approach to life, particularly the spiritual life.

Every evening Eileen changed into a long evening dress and high-heeled shoes and walked the hundred yards to the community centre for dinner. In those days Peter and Eileen insisted that everyone changed for the evening meal, which was served by candlelight at the tables. It was a gracious and pleasant tradition that Peter and Eileen kept alive for many years, resisting the informality that came with the young Californians.

As time went by and I moved on to other work within the community, I often popped in to see Eileen and we'd spend half an hour catching up with each other. We have always had an easy rapport, and our relationship has been blessed with a mutual appreciation, although at the same time we have always seen clearly each other's weaknesses as well as our strengths.

Eileen introduced me to the idea of God within. She had a way of sharing her own faith that allowed me to consider it might apply to me too. If ever I had a problem or needed direction in my life, she would gently turn me within to find my own answers. Her faith that God exists within inspired me to be still and listen for myself.

We first started working on Eileen's life story in 1976. It was to go out in conjunction with another book, a more 'esoteric' history of the Foundation, supposedly to give the more personal angle. Eileen was feeling very vulnerable at the time and wasn't very enthusiastic about the project, but because Peter thought it was a good idea she went along with it.

My first step was to read through all the messages she had ever received from her inner voice since 1958. Some of this 'guidance' had already been published, God Spoke To Me being the first of several books. In addition, however, there were dozens of small notebooks of messages recorded in her tiny writing which were of a more personal nature, given specially to Eileen to help her grow through each event in her life. None of these had ever been typed out before.

As I read, I began to trace the threads of a course in spiritual education. Step by step Eileen had been given one simple lesson at a time. Her inner voice was so personal, with all the lessons connected to every-day events, that it was difficult not to imagine a benign father-figure watching over a beloved child, repeating her lessons over and over until she had grasped them. Then would come an experience to test her and a comment on how she had done: "Well done, My child, you see how that worked"! or "Whoops! Not quite. Try again."

Once one lesson was learned, she was given a new one, taking her deeper into herself, challenging her more. It was the most exciting reading – all the more so because I found the guidance consistently applied to my own life at that very moment. I was, in a way, receiving the same spiritual education as Eileen. If that could happen with me, why not with everyone else who read it? All I needed to do was edit it and tie it in with what was happening to Eileen in her life at the time and we would have a fascinating story.

For weeks – months – Eileen and I met every day and talked and talked. I also asked Peter for his version of events, which was sometimes quite a different story! I started the first draft of what was to be a biography of Eileen Caddy. I had written a couple of chapters when work stopped – someone had told Eileen she should be writing her own life story. She did not feel ready to do this, partly because it would bring her too close to some still painful memories, and my own energy and enthusiasm to continue with the book dissolved. I put all my notes in a box, certain they would come in handy some day.

Several years later, Eileen wrote to me from New Zealand to say she had an inner prompting to write her autobiography at last and she asked me to help her. I was thrilled.

This time our enthusiasm for the project was equal. Eileen willingly wrote down everything she could remember from her early childhood to the present. Her guidance messages helped to jog her memory, and then she told and retold to me all she could remember that related to her spiritual unfoldment. No matter how painful the recollection, she allowed me to question and probe until both she and I fully understood the significance of a sequence of events or a relationship. Then I collected all our notes and began to shape this *Flight into Freedom*.

The project was full of challenges, not the least of which was to represent the picture truly from Eileen's perspective and resist the temptation to inject my own interpretation of events. I hope I have succeeded. Jokingly I have said that while Eileen is a channel for God, I am a channel for Eileen!

After working so closely with Eileen Caddy for so many years, my overriding experience is of her immense courage and faith in God. No matter how great her fear, no matter how strong her resistance to change, if she is told from within to do something, she does it. At the beginning, when her faith in God was negligible, her belief in her own worth was even less. Over the years I have watched her faith in herself grow as her relationship with God has developed from a hopeful belief into a firm knowledge that God is within.

Eileen's love for humanity is awe-inspiring, as is her willingness to continue to change and grow not just to benefit herself but, more importantly, to help all of humanity. Her life and her inner connection with God demonstrate that we can create anything we wish through the power of our thoughts, the power of our love, the power of spirit. If this story has anything at all to offer us, it is that Eileen Caddy has revealed a way for each of us to create our world in harmony.

Liza Hollingshead
Findhorn, 1987

2002 Edition Postscript

IT HAS BEEN THE greatest privilege to know Eileen Caddy as a friend, mentor and surrogate mother since I was 24 years old. She has seen me through the all vicissitudes of my adult life, helped me with difficult relationships, watched my son grow to be a man, and supported me in my work in the world. Always she has been constant in her advice: never dwell on self-pity, forgive, be positive and move on, and serve the good of the whole. She has inspired me to stretch and to grow, and to trust the divinity within that is the guiding force in my life. She has taught me, through her own example, how to find deep satisfaction in life by serving a higher purpose, and how to bring peace to my world through the power of love.

I have not yet heard the voice of God speak to me as clearly and directly as she does, nor have I written dozens of books with thousands of inspired and inspiring messages in them. But Eileen's conviction that each one of us has the ability to turn within and hear the still, small voice gave me the confidence to trust the promptings of my soul and of my heart which led me to spend my whole adult life in the Findhorn Community and to my work supporting the orphans of Kitezh Community in Russia.

Over the years, I have witnessed Eileen's unrelenting commitment to work on herself, to work through her personal setbacks and emotional disturbances in order to bring more love and peace into the world. This has consistently been her aim and her desire. She is a very private person, and yet she stretches herself to accommodate and embrace the needs of others. It took great courage for her to speak in public, yet she did it many times. She grappled with her human nature, her jealousy, pain and feelings of rejection, until she changed and came to a place of love and unity with everyone. She did not give up. She sees everything as service to God, and is willing to share the intimate details of her personal story in the hope that by doing so, it will help others.

As we completed the epilogue together, Eileen's 'last word', I had a personal realisation that remains with me. So many times Eileen commented on how blessed she is in her old age. She has everything she could possibly need or wish for, and yet she has never earned a penny in her life! When I reflected on Eileen's working life, I understood that her job was simply to meditate. Nothing more. Of course she was mother and wife as well, but her life's work, in the world, was to be still and hold the spiritual energy steady while so many others rushed about being busy. As a result, all her material needs were indeed taken care of in mysterious and remarkable ways. Like many of us, I work long hours to satisfy my need to make a difference in the world, and to survive materially. What if I were to spend those same hours in meditation instead? Would God perhaps take care of me too? A thought to ponder – as I rush back to my computer to answer another email!

I am deeply grateful for this opportunity to write *Flight Into Freedom (and Beyond)* with Eileen, to be party to her innermost thoughts and to put them together in this story. My wish for you, the reader, is that the spirit of Eileen Caddy and her life's work will inspire you as much as it has inspired me.

Liza Hollingshead
Findhorn, 2002

~ 1 ~

In a vision I was shown a fledgling learning to fly,
Its first efforts were very feeble
but as it used its wings more and more,
they became stronger
until it found the freedom of flight
and was able to soar to great heights
and fly great distances without any effort.
I heard the words:
'Faith comes with practice.
Live by faith until it becomes rocklike and unshakable
and find the true freedom of the spirit.'

I TOOK A DEEP BREATH and looked out at the sea of faces before me. *Four thousand people.* All looking at me, waiting expectantly for me to speak about peace. I felt the butterflies in my stomach and had the absurd memory of a friend who told me it was all right to have butterflies as long as they were flying in formation! For a second I stood immobile. "Please God, help me," I whispered quietly. "I said I could only manage to do this with Your help." It worked. I began to see all those thousands of people as my family and I was no longer afraid. I felt a great wave of love for every person in that hall in India and I knew that all I needed to do was share with them what was in my heart.

"How easy it is," I began,

. . . for each of us to say 'Of course I want universal peace, but there's nothing I can do about it. After all I am only one person. I'll leave it to the politicians. So what do we do? We hide in our little shells and allow the issue of the peace of the world to fade into the background because we feel powerless.

What can I as one individual do about it? Where does my responsibility lie? I can talk about universal peace, but that won't bring it about. I can write about it, send out pamphlets and go on protest marches, but that does not create peace. We can even have large conferences among nations about peace, but they don't make it happen.

We all long for peace and yet we go about it in the wrong way. Instead of starting at the top, we need to start at the foundations. As we think, so we are. As a nation of people thinks, so it is. If its outlook is aggressive or defensive, it will surely create war. When there is jealousy, greed, hatred at the heart of a nation, no amount of talking about peace will bring it about. Change the thinking, the consciousness of a whole nation and you will see its foreign policy change too. The world can only be saved from destroying itself by a change of consciousness. This cannot be brought about by lecturing people, or criticising governments. It is not other people who need to change, it is we ourselves.

Universal peace starts within each individual. It starts within me and you. It is like a stone thrown into a pool of water. The ripples spread out and out, but they start at the very centre.

We can start doing something about it right now. Let's look within our hearts. What is happening in our own lives? In the family? With the people we work with? What will happen as a result of the angry row I had yesterday with my husband? What about the person you met last week whom you swore never to speak to again because she refused to see your point of view? This is where peace breaks down, how wars begin. Until we can bring harmony into our everyday lives and learn to love the people around us, how can we hope to bring universal peace into the world? It's love and understanding and tolerance that bring peace.

We can each become part of the disease or part of the cure. It is up to us. There is so much negativity in the world. All you have to do is pick up a newspaper or turn on the television to be bombarded with negative and destructive thoughts. Your reaction to these is vitally important. You can absorb them and allow them to weigh you down until you become part of the negativity around you, or you can fill the situation with your love and help to transmute it.

Negativity is like a dark cloud that can envelop you unless the light within you is strong enough to dissolve it. Let your light shine forth at all times. The more of us who do this and see its importance, the more quickly will all negativity and darkness disappear, and peace reign on earth. So let there be light and more light within each one of us.

A person of peace does not resist war, but practices peace. If we take sides, we practice attack. Defensive retaliation is responsible for war, for we are at war in our minds. We cannot fight for peace. We cannot know the nature of peace until we have arrived at peace in our own hearts. And the way to do this is by ceaseless prayer. It is what I call the 'inner work' which all of us need to do, not just now and again, but constantly. That is what will bring peace.

To understand the true meaning of peace, look away from outer appearances – close your eyes and be still. Still your senses, breathe deeply. Allow peaceful thoughts to flow into your consciousness. Allow your heart to fill with love and gratitude. Pour your love out into your world, visualising it whole and joyful and peaceful. Let us practice peace by starting the day in a peaceful frame of mind, awakening with peaceful thoughts that we carry into our daily lives.

There can be no unity without love. Love is the key that opens all doors. Love is the balm that heals all wounds. Love is the Light that lightens the darkness. Love draws together, makes whole, creates oneness. Love makes us want to give and give – of our talents, our service, our lives. Love makes life worth living.

Where there is love there is peace. When we love one another we will no longer stand back and criticise other people's way of life, their religion, rituals, beliefs, traditions. When we are at peace within ourselves, we will no longer try to change others, and we will no longer be frightened of our differences.

As we relax and allow peace to fill our hearts and minds and we *feel the oneness of all, we go beyond the outer to the very heart where there is no separation at all. And as we make these changes in ourselves, we will find they have taken place in those around us as well.*

When we are at perfect peace within, all conflict will disappear and we will see humanity through the eyes of love. We will know that we are indeed all one in God's sight. For God is Love. Let us remember that as we think, so we are; as we think so we create. We are indeed co-creators with God.

There was a moment's hush. Then the applause rose into a crescendo and I clung to the podium, staring at 4,000 upturned faces.

How could it possibly be me standing before this vast crowd of people – in India of all places?

TWO MONTHS PREVIOUSLY, opening my mail in the small caravan that is my home at the Findhorn Foundation in Northern Scotland, I had found a letter inviting me to speak at a big international Peace Conference in India. In my recent prayers and meditations I had affirmed that I wanted to change and grow spiritually and that I was willing to do anything to bring this about. But this was too much! Go to India? Alone? I couldn't possibly, I decided, and declined the invitation.

Then something strange happened: my back seized up. It was so painful I had to go to bed for several days. As I lay in agony, I searched within myself for the cause of the problem, or at least a clue to finding some relief. All I got was, "Go to India." "How ridiculous," I thought, "It's a long way and I don't have the money for the air fare. Anyway, I don't have anything to say – and I can't possibly travel to India on my own." My list of reasons not to go was endless. But the pain in my back persisted . . .

Finally, in desperation I stopped resisting and agreed to go to India. "But I can't do this on my own," I thought. "I'm going to need God's help to get through this one."

As soon as I had made my decision and sent off the letter of acceptance, the pain in my back eased, and everything began to fall into place; the tickets, money for expenses, even the right person to travel with me. I realised this trip must be right and that my resistance had given me the pain in my back.

The Peace Conference was much bigger than I had expected. To travel all that way to attend such an event was a big enough hurdle for me to overcome, but when I got there I was told that I was, in fact, a guest of honour, and I was asked to give the opening blessing as well as a talk. It was an ordeal just to walk up the long flight of steps to the platform and to cut the cord of flowers, with the crowd pushing and shoving behind me. The fact that I managed to give a coherent talk made me realise yet again that of myself I can do nothing, but with God's help I can do all things.

TO LEARN TO TURN WITHIN for God's guidance has become the purpose of my life. One of the most visible results of this was the founding of the Findhorn Community in 1962, which was based entirely upon the guidance I received from God within. When I went to India in 1984, the community was 22 years old, and had grown from a small family group living in one caravan into a community of 250 resident members, who host approximately 3,000 guests each year. It is still situated on the same caravan park where it began, but now the community owns the land and is beginning to expand into new forms of relationship with the local area. In spite of its expansion, it has maintained the integrity of the original group, and remains a spiritual centre dedicated to living in harmony with all life forces on the planet. At the core of the members' beliefs is still the conviction that God, the creative life force, is present within everything and everyone, and that it is possible, even essential, to bring harmony and peace into all aspects of life. What started as a few 'cranks' doing something outlandish and suspect, has grown into a place of substance and stability that is a symbol of hope to many people in the world.

I decided to write this book because I believe deep down we all long for freedom – the freedom and joy of the spirit. My life is about moving into that state of being. I learned to listen to God within me the hard way – through disbelief and resistance to change, growth and new ideas. Now that I have found a freedom of the spirit, it is so glorious I wonder what all my resistance was about.

I hope that as you read my story you will discover that, just as I have moved through seemingly impossible situations and emerged triumphant with God's help, you can do it too. I have dedicated my life to the very highest, come what may. I tell my story in the hope that you may learn something to make your path towards finding yourself and your own inner God easier and more joyful. If there is anything in my life of value to you, I offer it with love.

~ 2 ~

You cannot hope to grow spiritually unless you are prepared to change. Those changes may come in small ways to begin with, but as you move further and further into the new, they will become more drastic and vital. Sometimes it needs a complete upheaval to bring about a new way of life. It is necessary at times seemingly to be cruel to be kind, to cut out the old to reveal the new. So resent not the tremendous changes which are to take place, but be prepared for them and flow with them to help speed them up.

I WAS BORN, the second child of four, in 1917 in Alexandria, Egypt, into an extremely happy family. We lived on the outskirts of the city in a large and spacious home surrounded by a beautiful garden with palm trees and a long rolling lawn where my parents gave outdoor parties. They entertained a lot, as my father was a director of Barclays Bank, DCO.

I adored my father; he was my hero. We shared a deep love and under-standing and I often helped him in the garden or went fishing with him, sitting for hours as quiet as a mouse beside him on a rock. But my greatest joy was to ride with my mother in the horse-drawn carriage to visit him in his office at the bank, where I sat and watched him work. I saw that he always had time for the people who came to see him, and he treated everyone the same, no matter who they were. His love and respect for his fellow human beings was obvious. I longed to be like him when I grew up.

Even as a small girl I was moved by the love my parents had for each other. My mother was quiet, frail and very lovely. Her life centred around my father and she was utterly dependent on him. He was warm, vital and energetic, playing rugby, tennis and cricket, getting up early every morning to ride his horse, and yet also caring tenderly for my mother when she was ill with one of her migraine headaches. She for her part supported my father fully. Even though she disliked their busy social life because she was so shy, she was a gracious hostess. The seeds of love were planted in my heart not by words but by the way my parents lived their lives together. This early experience of love had a deep impact on me and made me want a happy marriage like theirs.

On Sundays, instead of going to church, we went to the beach. As a boy my father had been forced to go to church three times every Sunday and he vowed he would never make his children do the same. Nevertheless, he was a deeply spiritual man and it showed in the way he treated both his family and everybody else.

I was 6 when the calm of my childhood was disrupted for the first time. My parents told me that my brother Paddy and I were to go to school in Ireland. We were attending a small school down the road from our home, which was run by a cousin, and I loved it there. Now we would have to travel a long way across Europe to join hundreds of noisy, strange children in an unfamiliar place. The schools in Egypt were considered unsuitable for British children, but they couldn't have had a worse effect on me than that of leaving home. My parents wanted Paddy to go to my father's old school and preferred to send both of us rather than have him travel alone. They considered schooling a very important responsibility, and although I knew they sent us away for the best reasons, I was absolutely miserable.

The first goodbye is still vivid in my memory. It was the end of a family holiday in Switzerland, and my Irish aunt, who had joined us, was taking us back with her on the train. I stood dejectedly on the station platform while my father bought us Swiss chocolate from a vending machine to try and cheer us up. It worked until the train gave its final signal to leave and we really had to say goodbye. I felt as if the world was coming to an end. I leaned out of the window as the train drew out of the station, sobbing hopelessly, waving a wet handkerchief to the solitary couple standing on the platform. I cried for hours and my aunt could do nothing to console me.

When we got to Ireland, my brother and I went to different schools. Mine was huge and full of noisy boys and girls. I was terrified. I started making myself ill every morning so that I wouldn't have to go, until my aunt realised I was unhappy and sent me to a smaller school. I lived with her until I was 11 years old, returning to Egypt each year during school holidays. The journey took five days by train and boat and, although Paddy was the eldest, I was responsible for looking after the passports and the other two children when they grew old enough to join us.

Even worse were the boarding schools that my sister Torrie and I went to. I don't know why we changed schools so often, but each time I seemed to fall further behind, and my blocks against academic learning increased. I loved handwork, but felt very inadequate about my poor learning ability, especially in comparison to Torrie, who did well at everything. I was jealous of her from the day she was born, when I had to share my father's love with her. She stayed home when I first went to school, she had fewer school changes and later went to college to become a teacher while I went only to domestic science college.

The only happiness I experienced away from home was the time I spent with my aunt. We had a close, loving relationship, and I became very attached to her. It was she who introduced me to my first religious education. Because she loved going to church on Sundays, I went with her. Sunday School, however, I disliked, because I had to go alone. Being with my aunt awakened a deep yearning within me to know more about God. She taught me to say my prayers and read me stories from the Bible which I enjoyed. To my surprise, I found it quite easy to remember the catechism and verses from the New Testament. But even though I grew to love the Bible, I was never attracted the Church itself, and when it was my turn to be confirmed with the rest of the children my age at school, I refused. I wouldn't do it just to be like everyone else.

When I was sixteen, Torrie and I were at a boarding school in England. One evening the headmistress called me into her study. I stood in front of her desk, wondering what I had done to merit this unexpected attention.

"Sit down, dear," she said. I perched on the edge of the chair apprehensively. "Have you heard from home recently?"

"I had a letter from my father last week," I replied.

"I'm afraid I have very bad news for you," she said sympathetically. "This came for you an hour ago."

She handed me a telegram. It read, in bold, bleak letters: EILEEN AND TORRIE JESSOP. DADDY HAS DIED SUDDENLY OF PERITONITIS. FUNERAL ON MONDAY. LOVE MUMMY.

I couldn't believe my eyes. Daddy dead? That was impossible! I had seen him only a few months before, full of energy and life. Someone with such vitality didn't die. I said nothing. I couldn't even cry. Somehow I felt my father's presence with me even more strongly than before. I remembered the last time I saw him – I was standing on the platform waving goodbye as his train pulled out of the station. We had parted this way so many times before, there was no longer any sense of loss or grief. We'd see each other again next holiday. His death seemed the same sort of parting. I felt he had gone to some distant shore and I knew I would see him again someday. It was just a matter of time. I felt a tremendous flow of love towards him as if he were physically present next to me.

When I went to Egypt to be with my mother, I saw a profound change in her. It was as if her life force had drained away. My father was her whole life and without him she had nothing to live for. I knew immediately that I was to look after her; it was almost as though my father himself had asked me to do so. Happily I left school and settled into taking care of my mother and my younger brother, Rex.

As a result of a diving accident Rex suffered from epileptic seizures. He was quite dependent on my mother and adored her, as she did him. In an attempt to find help for him, my mother became interested in Christian Science, believing that the power of positive thought would cure her son's malady. I don't know whether it did Rex any good, but it did provide my mother with a spiritual anchor after my father's death. She was keen for me to become a Christian Scientist too and, although it didn't interest me much, I kept her company by reading the Bible with her and accompanying her to church.

As my mother was advised to send Rex to a Christian Science home in England, she decided that we all would move to live there as a family. Only a year later she fell seriously ill with meningitis. I nursed her at home as long as I could, but as I watched her deteriorate I felt she had no desire to live. I sat with her thin hand in mine, telling her we would go back to Alexandria as soon as she recovered, but I knew she never would. Only two weeks after she became ill, my mother died. Although I wondered what would become of us all, I couldn't be sad for her. Her body was just a shell; her essence, her real self, had passed on to be with my father, where she wanted to be.

In the space of two years I had experienced the death of both my parents. Because I continued to be so strongly aware of my father's presence, I had a profound sense that death is nothing more than taking off an old coat, casting it aside and stepping through a doorway into another place. Death held no fear for me, no horror. I saw it so clearly. Four years later Rex died too. He had been so close to our mother that when she died it seemed he just wanted to join her.

I was nearly nineteen years old, with no idea what to do next. I enrolled in a domestic science college, and although I did well on the practical side, I could not come to grips with the theory. I found a job as a cook until Paddy suggested we buy a roadhouse with our inheritance and run it together. I agreed, although in my heart I longed to meet a man who would marry me and take care of me for ever. We bought a roadhouse near an RAF station in Oxfordshire. Although we were run off our feet, we enjoyed the lively social life that resulted from living close to the airbase. By the time war came, I had met an RAF officer who asked me to marry him. I was tired of being on my own, struggling through life, so I accepted. Andrew Combe and I were married on 13 May 1939.

I was never 'in love' with Andrew, but I did love him. He gave me the home, children and security I had been longing for, so for the most part I was content with our life together. He was tall and good-looking in his uniform, and had the distinction of making the first long-distance flight to Australia in a single-engined bomber, which made him quite a celebrity.

Andrew was a big man, and loved big things – cars, boats, houses. I liked little things. He was also domineering and held very strong opinions, but I didn't mind because I felt secure with him. I lived in his shadow as my mother had lived in my father's. And then I began to have babies. While the war was going on I had three children one after the other, and I was content. The fourth was born in America, and the last back in England. Everything else came second to them.

After we were married Andrew discovered Moral Rearmament. It became an obsession with him and he insisted that I become involved. As I had done with my aunt and my mother, I went along with him to make him happy and to keep the family together, although I personally did not feel attracted by MRA. I participated in their 'quiet times', when everyone sat and listened inwardly and then wrote down what they 'heard'. Each person was expected to produce something from these quiet times, and if they didn't the others would help them 'unblock'. I couldn't relate to any of this, particularly since I had no 'guidance' to write down. Although I felt a hypocrite, I pretended to hear something then wrote down the first thing that came into my head to avoid having my inner world investigated.

When I was staying with an MRA group in America, I was taken into a little room and asked to 'give my life to God'. I just couldn't do it. It didn't come from my heart. Committing myself to God was something I'd have to do with every atom of my being, and I knew I just didn't experience what they expected of me. I felt as I had when I refused to be confirmed in the Church at the age of 11.

I was a simple person with a simple Christian training and outlook. I had seen how much my aunt loved her Church, and I longed for the same contact with God. Somehow I couldn't find it except in rare instances – in the silence of a church as I arranged the flowers, or at an early morning communion service where I was the only person present besides the minister. I felt it was important to make the effort to get up early to take communion. Afterwards I always felt good. I never knew why. Attending church on Sundays was not the same at all. I needed to be still and quiet. I knew nothing about meditation then but it was as if I needed to be on my own in a church to think about God.

Because Andrew was away a lot of the time, and he was engrossed in MRA, bringing up the children was mostly left to me. I didn't mind as I loved them dearly and my life was thoroughly wrapped up in them. During the war years in London, even though there were heavy air raids, we never went into an air raid shelter. When we heard the bombs dropping and the guns in the park firing at the German planes, my son Richard would say in a sleepy voice, "Mummy, must those guns make all that noise? I want to go to sleep." I stayed very calm and he and his sisters were never frightened. Some nights the bombs dropped very close, and I wondered what we would find outside in the morning, but I never believed we would be hit. I had great faith that we all had a part to play in the future, and that nothing would touch the family.

I included the children in everything I did. Often I had three of them in the kitchen helping me prepare a meal. One would be on a box near the sink peeling potatoes, one would be mixing the filling for a treacle tart and another would be helping with the stew. It always took longer that way, but we all enjoyed it and the children learned so much it was worth the extra trouble.

I enjoyed my children immensely. There was always someone's birthday coming up, and we had a different kind of party for each one every year. It was fun stretching my imagination to think up new ideas. I loved fancy dress parties. We made our costumes together and had a great time going round the house looking for things we could use to dress up in or use for props. A shoe polish tin became a clock for the white rabbit and an old black skirt turned into a highwayman's cloak.

As Andrew wasn't home much, I had to discipline the children myself, even though it made me feel ill to have to smack any of them. But I learned to wait until I was calm before I did it. Then I could explain why it was necessary, and it was more effective. Although I never enjoyed doing it, I felt that both love and discipline were essential in bringing up children. Without learning to respect a firm 'no' a little one would soon take over the entire household, and we'd all be unhappy.

From London we moved to America for a few years and then to Iraq. It was there that Jennifer, my eldest daughter, fell ill with polio. I was distraught, and prayed as I had never done before. Polio was the dreaded disease of the time, and many people never recovered from it. After two months in hospital Jennifer looked like a skeleton. She could barely raise her arm to feed herself. One day as she sat pathetically beside the swimming pool I wondered whether she would ever swim again. Then she informed me that she was going to swim a mile. I so much wanted her to succeed, and yet I was afraid because I had been told to let her take things very quietly for a long time. As she slid into the water for the first time and started swimming weakly, I didn't take my eyes from her. I continued to pray. What a triumph when she eventually succeeded in swimming her mile! My heart overflowed with gratitude and I wondered whether my prayers had helped.

The children gave me an excuse not to participate more than I had to in the social fife that was so much a part of living on an RAF station. Like my mother, I didn't enjoy the cocktail parties and hectic social life and, like her, I put a good face on it and adopted a gracious manner, hiding my shyness. The MRA code forbade all its members to drink alcohol and the women were not allowed to wear any make-up at all, which made me feel awkward in the company of other RAF wives. It was no use arguing with Andrew about it as he insisted on adhering to the MRA code to the letter. I submitted, to keep the peace, and dutifully went out with him only when I had to.

After we had been in Iraq for some time, Andrew introduced me to a young man he thought might be a potential member of MRA. His name was Peter Caddy. Andrew was impressed by an article on moral leadership Peter had written in the RAF journal. I liked Peter. At the talk on archaeology where we first met, I was impressed by the pertinent and intelligent questions he asked. There was something about his lively interest in everything that intrigued me.

From then on Peter became a frequent visitor to our home. He always dropped in to see us when he was in Habbanya, and I was flattered that even if there was no one else at home, he would stay and talk to me.

On several occasions, as we sat on the verandah while I did my mending, Peter told me extraordinary stories. I listened quietly, although I did not understand half of what he was talking about. But I encouraged him to tell me more. Something deep inside me resonated with what he was saying, although I did not realise it at the time.

He said he was a member of a group studying ancient mysteries and spiritual truths, and that he had been taught by a Master of wisdom. He also said God is within each one of us, within everything. That seemed outrageous to me. They never told us that in church. So much of what Peter said contradicted the orthodox religion I had been brought up with but I did not argue or interrupt him because he sounded so knowledgeable, and I didn't know very much about it anyway.

One day Peter told me about his first spiritual lesson, when he was a young boy. "My father, who was a strong-willed disciplinarian, had been ill for sometime," he said. "He had consulted doctors, homeopaths, osteopaths, anyone who might be able to rid him of his rheumatoid arthritis. Eventually he heard about Lucille Rutterby, a spiritual healer who was also a trance medium. My father took me with him to the first meeting. An American Indian chief spoke through her, which impressed me no end. Then I was asked if I had any questions. I asked, 'How can I win tomorrow's boxing match at school?' Everyone laughed, but the Indian chief continued to speak through the medium. 'Look him straight in the eye, and you will know when he is about to hit you.' I tried it and it worked! From then on I knew that the spirit world existed, because I had practical confirmation."

I didn't know what to make of this. Obviously Peter wasn't lying, but it was all rather odd, if captivating. I had never met anyone before who had anything to do with psychics, spiritualism and the occult. When he told me about spiritual masters on 'higher levels' who worked through people to impart spiritual knowledge and healing, and mentioned names like Koot Humi, Morya and Hilarion, I was mystified.

Although Peter had a reputation as a playboy, our talks showed me a completely different side of him. He was attractive, dynamic, active and positive. He was serious too – and unconventional; he didn't mind that his ideas conflicted with what was generally accepted in society. I felt he was a spiritual person, although I didn't really know what the word meant. 'Religious' was not the way to describe him. I knew he didn't go to church, but I sensed a commitment to something spiritual that I didn't understand.

I liked Peter's directness. He had a clear look in his eye, and called a spade a spade. Although he showed consideration for me, which I enjoyed because I had so little of Andrew's attention, there was nothing romantic about our relationship. Peter's manner was so matter-of-fact that there could be no question of that and, besides, I was married with five children. I enjoyed having a good friend.

One time when Peter stopped in to see us on his way from Akaba, he hobbled into the house with his foot in a plaster cast.

"What on earth have you done to yourself?" I asked him.

Slightly embarrassed, he replied, 'I was underwater diving in the Persian Gulf and I stepped on a sea urchin. The doctor couldn't get the tiny spines out, so he put my foot in this plaster to keep my heel off the ground in the hope they will work their way out. It's very painful."

"Can I try a remedy my Greek nurse used on me when I was a child?" I offered. "She loved to eat sea urchins, and we used to go out collecting them. Whenever we got spines in our fingers, she rubbed in olive oil which dissolved them."

"At this point I'll try anything," Peter said.

So I did exactly what I remembered my nurse doing to me, and it worked. Within a matter of days the pain was gone, and Peter was able to walk easily. He was delighted.

"The plaster certainly cramped my style," he joked, as he dashed off again. "Thanks a lot!"

Peter was always going off on trips. He was constantly on the move, taking advantage of his time in the RAF to explore the world driven by his peculiar sense that nothing happened by coincidence, that everything was part of the plan for his life. One of the qualities I most admired in him was his unfailing positivity. "There's no point in indulging in negativity," he often remarked. "We've been given a marvellous life to live. Why waste it with doubts and fears?" He tackled the most impossible tasks, and never took 'no' for an answer, with the result that he seemed to be able to accomplish anything he set his mind to. He attributed this to his training in positive thinking with his 'Master', the teacher who gave him his early spiritual training. It reminded me a little of my mother's Christian Science teaching of healing by positive thinking or mind over matter.

When Peter heard of a monastery high in the mountains of Tibet that was supposed to be the ancient seat of Eastern spiritual teaching, he decided to lead a party on the 350-mile trek in search of it.

"It was part of my spiritual training to make that trip," he told me afterwards. "Even though I was told it was inaccessible, that it was impossible to get transport for the men and supplies, that it was an exceptionally difficult climb, I was determined to find it. And we did. I managed, by sheer persistence and perseverance, to engineer the trip. The other officers were amazed," he added with sly pride. "They never thought I'd pull it off.

"It took us fifteen days of arduous climbing to reach the monastery at Gyantse. The abbot was a great soul, humble yet with a marvellous sense of humour. It was a magical place and the discipline of the monastery was admirable, but I felt it belonged to the past. The customs were stylised and it was clear to me that it was of the old order, not the new. I had thought Tibet was the centre of spiritual world government, but I came away knowing that this was no longer true. I also knew that it was not where my future spiritual path lay."

"You must have been disappointed," I said sympathetically.

"Not in the least!" Peter exclaimed. "The purpose of the journey was to test me on positive thinking and perseverance, to put the theory I have learned into practice. Besides, I learned something very important: the power that has been held for hundreds – thousands – of years by hidden teachers in the faraway mountains of Tibet has been released to the world and I have a part to play in the direction of these energies. I've been told that I have been prepared for lifetimes for this work, and this is part of my final training.."

"Lifetimes – what do you mean?" I asked, puzzled.

"My past lives."

"Do you mean to tell me that you honestly believe you have lived before?" I asked him in astonishment.

"Of course," he replied casually but with conviction. "I've been told so by several people who are sensitive to higher levels of awareness."

"But Peter," I protested mildly, "that goes against everything the Church teaches."

"Well the early Christians believed in it," he replied," but in 500 AD they decided to cut out all mention of reincarnation from the Bible to reinforce the importance of the Church. There are still references to it if you look, though. The point is that reincarnation makes perfect sense. Otherwise, what's the purpose of spiritual growth? If you're only going to live once, there's no point in learning from your mistakes. If a soul is given different opportunities in various lifetimes to progress and learn, it will return to serve God and humanity. We are part of a much bigger picture than just our little lives here on earth."

What Peter was saying sounded blasphemous to me, and yet he spoke with such certainty that I dared not argue with him. Besides, I was afraid he'd think I was stupid and ignorant.

Not long after that, Peter came to visit me again. As we sat on either end of the sofa, he said. "I've had the most extraordinary experience I must tell you about." He could hardly contain his excitement. "When I was in Jerusalem last week I had a prompting to walk to the top of the mountain overlooking the city. As I lay on the ground at the top it came to me that you are my other half! It was the nearest I've ever experienced to actually hearing an inner voice." He looked at me expectantly. I glanced up from my mending, half expecting him to be teasing me, and when I saw his bright blue eyes staring at me with such intensity, I burst out laughing.

"Peter, you can't be serious," I protested. "With a husband and five children, I'm an unlikely other half. Besides, you're married as well!" He looked so crestfallen that I laid my hand on his arm and said more gently, "Peter, what is to be, will be. Let's leave it at that, shall we?"

I never mentioned the conversation to Andrew. Although I felt no emotional involvement with Peter, I was afraid Andrew would misunderstand. Anyway, Peter had been so objective, so unemotional, in telling me his story, it was difficult to see how it had anything to do with my marriage. There was no romance, no flattery, no passion. Peter was thoroughly down to earth.

Peter did, however, keep in touch with me and it was clear by now that it was a relationship with me he was pursuing, not with my husband. When I went with the children to the RAF summer camp up in the hills to escape the heat, Peter sent me packages of books with people who were passing through. Sometimes Andrew brought them, and since he never asked about them, I assumed he wasn't interested.

One time, however, Andrew was given a parcel for me which contained some photos Peter had taken of me and the children, and a letter. For some reason I suddenly didn't want to read it to Andrew, so I disappeared into the bathroom and read it alone. Then I tore it up and flushed it down the lavatory. I still don't know why I did it, as it was not a love letter at all. It contained nothing but sixteen pages of Peter's thoughts on those strange esoteric subjects he had spoken to me about. But I was suddenly afraid. I thought Andrew might label it black magic. Perhaps he would prevent Peter from visiting me. I realised those visits had become important to me but I couldn't talk to Andrew about it because I was sure he wouldn't understand. I felt very alone. All these strange new ideas were churning in my mind, and I had no one to discuss them with.

The last Christmas we were in Iraq was a particularly busy one, and we were involved in a round of parties that never seemed to end. One night, as I was getting dressed to go out, I was suddenly tired of wearing such plain, dull clothes, with no make-up or anything, just to fit in with Andrew's Moral Rearmament code. Rebelliously, I put on a touch of lipstick and face powder, something I had not done for years. I appeared and said brightly, "Are you ready to go?"

Andrew took one look at me and scowled. "Take that muck off your face, Eileen! You know I won't have you wearing paint on your face." Something in me snapped.

"I will do no such thing!" I retorted. I could hardly believe I had dared to oppose Andrew like this, but I'd had enough of his domineering.

"Eileen, I insist you go and wash your face. And hurry up, or we'll be late."

We stood glaring at one another, in a deadlock of wills. I held out.

"All right, then I won't go." I said. "You can go on your own." And I went to my desk and started to write a letter.

Andrew sat there in stony silence. I wasn't angry with him, but I was determined not to give in to being forced to do things against my will. The time ticked by and Andrew glanced uneasily at his watch. By midnight he realised that I meant what I said, that I had no intention of going out on his terms. Reluctantly he relented.

"Have it your own way," he said gruffly. "We'd better go now or our absence will cause comment."

When we arrived at the dance, very late, Andrew withdrew into a group of his friends and became engrossed in a conversation about MRA. Peter came over and asked me to dance. He commented on the tense look on my face and chuckled when I told him what happened. "Let's go and have a drink," he suggested. "What will you have?"

"A John Collins," I replied rebelliously. "I don't care if Andrew disapproves!"

Peter grinned, enjoying playing conspirator in my little bid for freedom. I felt exhilarated by my small step towards independence, and had a marvellous time, dancing, laughing and joking until the early hours of the morning. Peter was wonderfully attentive, giving me just the boost I needed. I felt attractive and alive for the first time in years.

I DIDN'T SEE PETER for months after that. Andrew and I reached an uneasy compromise and life carried on as usual. When Peter next visited Habbanya, he was full of a 'chance' encounter he had had in the Philippines.

"I asked God to let me stay in Habbanya, you know, after that marvellous evening with you, but to my surprise my aircraft took off as scheduled," he told me, bubbling over with excitement. "I had an introduction to a major and his wife in the Philippines, so I looked them up. When I knocked at the door an older, white-haired lady opened it. Her son-in-law and daughter were not home yet, so she asked me in for a drink. I couldn't believe it when a couple of minutes later I found myself telling her, Naomi, all about my experiences in Tibet. We found that we had much in common spiritually, and I also discovered she was a channel for higher levels of consciousness!"

"You mean like the medium you went to when you were young?" I asked cautiously.

"No, not exactly. Like my wife, Sheena, she's sensitive to higher, more refined levels of awareness. She acts as a channel for some of these beings of power I have told you about. When she told me that, shivers ran up and down my spine. I knew this was a very important meeting." Peter went on, his words tumbling over each other. "We meditated together, and Naomi channelled a message from a great spiritual being who told her that she and I had been together in many lifetimes, and that we had been drawn together from opposite ends of the earth for a specific work."

I made no comment and went on with my sewing. That part of Peter's world was not mine. I had nothing in my own experience of life to judge it by, so I just listened to him, and put the slight feeling of disquiet to the back of my mind.

Towards the end of the summer of 1953, Andrew's tour of duty in Iraq was coming to a close. He decided to send me and the children home to England in time for the beginning of the new school year, planning to join us later. He fixed a date for us to travel, and when Peter heard about it he said he would try to get a seat on the same plane at Tripoli so that he could help me with the children. I had an ominous feeling that if I got on that plane something awful would happen. I could not put my finger on what that might be, but I felt strongly enough to try to persuade Andrew to change the date. I couldn't tell him of my premonition, as it sounded foolish, and he brushed my request aside. The night before we left I lay awake with a sinking feeling in my stomach. The next day we left Habbanya. Peter was in Tripoli to meet us. He had arranged everything for our stopover, complete with a vase of beautiful flowers in my room. We spent the day by the pool, and the children were all over him. In the evening he arranged for someone to look after them while he took me out for dinner. We drove along the beach front in a horse and carriage, and Peter treated me to a delicious meal. It felt good to be taken care of so well. Peter was the perfect gentleman, with no hint of any inappropriate emotion. I relaxed.

Although he had been told that the plane was already 2,000 lbs overloaded, he was determined to get on it. It was my first experience of the power of Peter's positive thinking. He arrived at the airport next morning to discover there was one seat left, which happened to be next to me. So we sat together all the way back to England, and he kept the children amused. When we arrived at Lyneham RAF base, he had his car, a white Lagonda, waiting to take us to our house in Cheam. Peter then returned to London to his wife, Sheena.

Some weeks later, Peter rang to invite me to dinner and a show with him and his wife. It was my 35th birthday. I accepted gladly. At the last moment Sheena was unable to go as she had a migraine headache, so Peter took me by himself.

That night I fell in love for the first time in my life. My heart was full to bursting with love and tenderness and Peter, too, was visibly moved by the intensity of our feelings. Yet a part of me wanted to reject it. It didn't seem possible that I, a married woman, had fallen in love with a married man. But at the same time it felt as though it was meant to be. I knew without a doubt that I was to be with this man, and now I knew, too, what he had meant by us being two halves of one whole.

Peter took me home and we spent the night together. For the first time in my life I felt utterly complete. I was committed to whatever life with Peter Caddy had in store with me, without considering for a moment what that might mean. I was helpless to resist this love that engulfed me.

My first thought was for Andrew. I had to tell him at once. No matter how shocking it might be, I had to have everything out in the open. Peter was strangely unconcerned about Sheena. "We haven't lived together as man and wife for some time," he said. "I've kept her fully informed about everything, and she has confirmed that you are my other half." This I could not cope with. It made no sense to me at all. I wrote to Andrew to ask him for a divorce. I was reeling with the intensity of my love for Peter and I had to be with him.

I also needed to tell my family what had happened. Peter arranged for Sheena and a woman friend to stay at the house with the children for a few days while Peter drove me north to see my aunt and my sister. My family was horrified, and my brother-in-law took an immediate dislike to Peter. Then came a phone call. It was Andrew. "As soon as I got your letter, I returned to England on compassionate leave," he said. "I found two strange women in my house so I turned them out. Eileen, you've destroyed everything. What you've done is shameful. So stay away from here. You'll never set foot in my house again! And stay away from the children – you're unfit to be their mother."

I was dumbfounded. I had told the children I'd be away for only three or four days. I thought the divorce would be a gradual process, that Andrew and I would talk and work it all out. The suddenness of the break devastated me. I just didn't know where to turn.

Peter took me back to London, to Sheena's flat, where I couldn't stop crying. Sheena was obviously becoming impatient with me, so Peter suggested we drive down to Glastonbury for a few days. I didn't care where I went, and clung to Peter as if he were my life support system. Life had suddenly become a nightmare.

GLASTONBURY IS AN ANCIENT TOWN, which has long been associated with Britain's mystical past. Some believe that it has connections with King Arthur, while another legend tells that Joseph of Arimathaea in his travels brought Jesus there as a child. The town is dotted with holy wells and sacred sites, and I had often heard Peter refer to it as a place of special power. I, however, was in no state to care about any of this and simply allowed Peter to lead me around.

One of the places we visited was a quiet sanctuary for prayer and meditation. As I entered it, the peaceful atmosphere steadied me a little. The room was plain, with several chairs placed in a circle and a few unfamiliar pictures on the walls. I sat down, still numb with the pain of the past 24 hours. Just a few days before I had had five beautiful children, a husband and a home with everything I ever wanted. And now, nothing.

It was all my fault. I wanted my children, yet I had left them – all because I was in love with Peter, this extraordinary, powerful man. Never had I known love like this. My heart contracted as I looked at him across the room, sitting next to Sheena. But then I shuddered again at the thought of what I had done. How could I – of all people – have got into this predicament? I had always had such proper ideas about marriage. The idea of divorce shocked me; to sleep with another man was unthinkable. And yet I had done it.

When it happened, all I knew was that I was in love for the first time in my life and I had to be with Peter. And now my punishment was to be parted from my children. I had never thought for a moment that I would lose them. They would think I had deserted them, lied to them. Was Penny crying? How on earth would Jennifer cope? She was only 14. I could hardly bear to think what they were going through.

And now what was I doing in Glastonbury, in this sanctuary? As I sat there and allowed the atmosphere of the room gradually to penetrate my distress, it reminded me of the early-morning, empty churches I had loved when I was younger. I began to pray, in the only way I knew, talking to God as if He were a person who could hear me. I saw the face of my father, kind, strong, loving, and I wished he was with me. He would understand and tell me what to do. From the very depths of my heart I called out for help. I had no one but God to turn to.

"Be still and know that I am God."

The voice was quite clear, and I turned to see who had spoken. It couldn't have been Peter or Sheena, and there was no one else in the room. The voice was inside my head. Was I going crazy? I sat very still, rigid with fear, my eyes tight shut. The voice went on: "You have taken a very big step in your life. But if you follow My voice all will be well. I have brought you and Peter together for a very special purpose, to do a specific work for Me. You will work as one, and you will realise this more fully as time goes on. There are few who have been brought together in this way. Don't be afraid, for I am with you."

When we came out of the sanctuary, I said shakily, "I had a peculiar, terrible experience in there. I heard a voice speaking to me. It was inside me. I'm afraid I'm going insane." I told Peter and Sheena everything, expecting them to dismiss me as a neurotic. Instead they listened intently.

"This is marvellous, Eileen!" was Sheena's response when I finished. "It confirms everything. Now I'm certain that God brought you and Peter together."

I was appalled. To me there was nothing to be excited about. "Tell us again the words that you heard," Peter urged.

"Be still and know that I am God," I repeated slowly. "I recognise those words. I've read them somewhere in the Bible."

Peter and Sheena were convinced that I had heard God's own voice. I wasn't at all sure, and yet if I accepted what I heard, it must be the voice of God. The more I thought about it, the more concerned I became. I remembered the people God spoke to in the Bible. But those were special people with special tasks to do. Why should He speak to a woman who had left her husband and children to 'live in sin' with another man? And yet here was this very clear voice telling me to listen and all would be well in my life. My thoughts kept turning to the Ten Commandments. The word 'adultery' plagued me. The voice said I was doing the right thing, but how could all be well?

Peter said Sheena was to be my teacher, as she had been his. I didn't understand Sheena. How could she say she was happy Peter and I had 'found each other', when he was her husband? She must be jealous of me, underneath the surface, and sooner or later she would try to get Peter away from me. I was terrified of her and felt I couldn't trust her. But I had nowhere else to go. So with only my love for Peter to nourish me, and this strange voice whispering in my head, I stepped into the most frightening time of my life.

~ 3 ~

My beloved child, try to see a pattern running through everything that is happening just now. Every experience, every vision, every revelation comes from Me and is given for a specific purpose. You may not see the reason at the time; you may wonder at the strangeness to the point of doubting your own sanity. Learn to go with it all. Resist absolutely nothing. Be afraid of nothing. Your faith in My word is being tested; you have to find where your security lies. Nothing matters but your relationship with Me. Put your whole life into My hands. I am your only security. Let Me be your guide and know that no matter how devious the road, everything falls into place perfectly. My love for each of you is so great that I will do anything to ensure that you are indeed firm in your complete loyalty to Me and to nothing or no one else.

SOON AFTER OUR VISIT to Glastonbury Peter returned to his post in the Middle East, leaving me in Sheena's charge. I felt utterly abandoned. Sheena was a strong and powerful woman, and she terrified me. If I'd had somewhere else to go, I would most certainly have turned tail and run. But I was trapped. Besides, the voice kept confirming that Sheena was my teacher.

My aunt, my brother and my sister, who were all the family I had, were shocked that I was having 'an affair' with Peter and strongly disapproved of my leaving Andrew. The way we had been brought up simply did not allow for such a thing. In their eyes, and in those of society, I was the guilty one and Andrew was within his rights, however hard that might be on me.

Even I felt I was guilty. I was deeply shaken by the idea that I was 'living in sin', but once I had fallen in love with Peter I had burned my boats. There was nothing for me to do but stay in London with Sheena and do whatever she told me. I was an outcast, at the mercy of Peter's wife.

Sheena was a good-looking woman, taller than I was, with dark hair and lovely eyes. I remember her as serious, and very severe, especially with me. She gave the impression of being aloof, of standing apart from others, and yet she had a powerful influence over the people around her. Peter loved her deeply and would have done anything in the world for her. Their meeting was one of those strange coincidences that seemed to fill Peter's life. He was travelling by train to London and found himself sitting opposite Sheena, who was reading *The Aquarian Gospel of Jesus the Christ* by Levi, a book that Peter had just recently read himself. They struck up a conversation, discovering they had a great deal in common. Peter then began visiting her regularly in her flat at Lupus Street and joined the group of followers that was growing around her.

Sheena had a mission in life: to transform the world through love. Although I never felt that love, I believe it was there, because I saw her help people in their search for spiritual truth. As more and more were drawn to her, Sheena's role as spiritual 'teacher' developed. She never gave people advice but encouraged them to discover their own inner direction. This she did with me too. She was firmly convinced that God is within each of us, that we are an expression of God. Her 'training' was to reinforce our faith in this inner God and to encourage us to follow it in our lives.

In my case Sheena was faced with terrific resistance. I had not come to her of my own free will, nor was I searching consciously for the meaning of God in my life. I wasn't even sure it was God's voice I continued to hear. Least of all did I believe that the vivid visions I was beginning to have were divinely inspired. For all I knew they may have been the work of the devil or caused by my emotional distress. The only reason I was there was Peter.

For a large part of the time I stayed with Sheena she was ill and I had to look after her and prepare her meals. She was very demanding.

Everything had to be perfect and she insisted on absolute punctuality. One day I was in a hurry trying to get her meal ready on time. I prepared a tray with a lightly boiled egg, an avocado pear and some thin slices of bread and butter, and took it upstairs to her room.

Sheena sat up in bed and looked at the tray. "You have not spread the butter to the edge of the bread," she said impassively. "Take it away and do it properly!"

I took the tray downstairs, fuming, and obediently spread the butter to the edge of the bread. I brought it back to her.

"The egg is overcooked. It should be boiled for exactly four minutes. Cook me another one."

When that was done to her satisfaction, she asked, "Where is the lemon for the avocado?" I trudged downstairs a third time to find a piece of lemon.

Finally she was satisfied and ate her meal. I deeply resented her treatment of me, but she simply said, "Let this be a lesson that when something is worth doing, it's worth doing perfectly. God creates everything to perfection and we have to learn to do the same." After that I tried to do everything as perfectly as I could – but more out of a desire to evade Sheena's sharp tongue than to be like God!

During this period of my training, I was expected to spend time listening to the inner voice three times a day, at 6 a.m., 12 noon and 9 p.m, The early morning session I did alone and then I had to share what I had recorded with Sheena as soon as she was awake and having her breakfast in bed. Most mornings she called me to her room at 11 o'clock and made me sit and see if I could receive anything from my inner voice for her. At noon I meditated on my own and again in the evening. Sheena insisted that I record everything I experienced, whether visions, dreams or words, and then share it with her. To begin with I heard many different voices and was confused. Sheena said to me "Listen for the very first one you heard in Glastonbury. Try to ignore any other voice and just focus on that one, and gradually you will find the others will fade away. This is why I want you to record everything you hear. Then I can help you to discriminate, until there won't be the slightest shadow of a doubt which voice is the voice of God, and you will follow no other."

Sheena was obsessed with punctuality. If ever I was a moment late, she would scold me. She could get very angry. "You are late for your appointment with God," she frequently said. "It is very disrespectful of you to be late for it. It's more important than anything else you have to do in your day. No matter what happens, you must never be late."

This dressing down upset me so much that all I wanted to do was to go off by myself to have a good weep. Instead Sheena said unsympathetically, "Pull yourself together and stop feeling sorry for yourself. Be more aware of what you are doing and then this will not happen again. Now sit down and open yourself to listen to God's voice."

After I had been through this interchange a few times, I learned my lesson and became extra careful to be on time, even a few minutes early. It taught me punctuality and soon I discovered that my meditation time had become more important than anything else.

Before I appeared on the scene, Sheena had received her own messages of guidance, but once I was there she seemed to stop and, relied on me instead. There were others who were working with her in the same way, including Dorothy Maclean, a Canadian who was living in London. Sheena and Dorothy had known each other for many years and had worked in Intelligence together during the Second World War. Dorothy was a nice person but we were as different as chalk and cheese. I felt inferior to her, as she was an intellectual with friends who were artists and writers. Had it not been for our mutual association with Sheena, she and I would not naturally have chosen each other as friends.

Dorothy had been attracted to work with Sheena of her own accord. She loved and respected her, and her experience of Sheena as a teacher was quite different from mine. She was not afraid of Sheena and responded to her demand for self-discipline with dedication and enthusiasm. Often after work she dropped in to spend time with Sheena, sharing her guidance or just talking while I prepared the evening meal. Sometimes the two of them ate their meal in Sheena's room while I had mine downstairs. It all depended on how things had been between Sheena and me that day. I still couldn't see any good in her, whereas Dorothy loved her and she loved Dorothy.

In spite of all his efforts in meditation, Peter never received guidance in the form of hearing an inner voice – apart from that one time on the mountain in Jerusalem. His guidance came through his intuition and he was training himself to be instantly obedient to his intuitive promptings, however bizarre they might seem. While Sheena encouraged him to continue listening for the inner voice, at the same time she reinforced the value of following his intuition which was, she said, an equally valid connection with God's will.

I never knew what Sheena's mood would be when I went upstairs with her breakfast. I had to wait until she tinkled on the phone connecting my room with hers, as she did not like to be woken up in the morning for breakfast. Some days she was as sweet as honey with me; other days everything I did was wrong and she reprimanded me severely. I grew to dread the tinkle of that phone. It could come at any time of day or night, and I had to go immediately, dropping whatever I was doing.

"You need to be on duty twenty-four hours a day," she told me. "God needs you to be ready and willing to listen and obey to do whatever is needed. Never question what you area asked to do. Just act immediately and you will see later why it was so important."

Frequently in the evenings, or late at night, she would summon me to her bedside and ask for healing. I had no idea what I was meant to do, but I knelt by her bed and held my hands over her body as she instructed. At times I had to stay that way for hours, with my arms aching and my eyelids drooping, desperately trying to concentrate and keep awake. If ever I dozed off or let my hands rest on the covers, Sheena rebuked me sharply. She never let me get away with anything. I learned very soon that it just wasn't worth standing up against her or ignoring the phone, as she would vent her fury on me without the least compunction.

Many times after one of these exhausting night time sessions, I would go to my room downstairs seething with indignation and resentment. "She's making me do all these things just to torture me," I complained to myself. "I'm not going to stand for it another minute. I'm leaving, and she can butter her own bread to the edges. I don't want to give her healing, I don't want her to be my teacher! I hate her! I hate her!" And I'd sob my frustration into my pillow lest anyone heard me and came to investigate. Then the logical part of my mind would take over again: "But where would I go? Auntie – no, she certainly would never dream of having me now that I've abandoned all the children. Nor will Torrie or Paddy. They all think I've behaved disgracefully. They'd try to make me go back to Andrew and

I couldn't stand that. Besides, I have no money. I couldn't even catch a bus out of London if I wanted to." Finally the sickening reality would hit me again: "If I left here Sheena would make absolutely certain that I never saw Peter again. I couldn't stand that, not after all I've been through to be with him. I daren't do anything that would cause me to lose him."

So I gave Sheena complete power over me. I was utterly dependent on her because I thought I had nowhere else to go and that she could separate me from Peter whenever she felt like it. I struggled on and grudgingly did what I was told, but without any goodwill or appreciation for the fact that she was a sick woman who needed my help, and feeling no love or appreciation in return for nursing her day and night.

I'm certain now that it was my resistance to everything that made it so painful. One time I was so overwrought that my right arm became paralysed for over a week. It was obviously psychosomatic but very frightening. Another time I had a vivid dream from which I awoke crying. I dreamt that pus was flowing out of my mouth and I was in great pain. I told Sheena, as I had to tell her everything and she explained that it was all the poison coming out of me, that I was being purified and the dream had come to prepare me. Three days later a boil swelled up in my mouth and after about a week it burst and the pus flowed out, just as it did in my dream.

I just longed for the times when Peter was back on leave. Sheena became less demanding of me, and it was bliss to be with him. I dreaded his going again. His visits were always too brief and without him I felt there was no purpose to my life. He was the only person in the world who loved me. But I was never able to confide in him about my difficulties with Sheena, as he refused to hear any word against her.

"Sheena's the most loving person I have ever met," he said. "I trust her totally and you should too. In the five years I lived with her I always found that she knew everything I was thinking and feeling and that she was always right."

"Well, I don't think she's very loving," I grumbled. "She's always criticising me and telling me I'm not good enough."

"That's because she is an adept at using the sword of truth," Peter replied. "She used it on me too to destroy my ego, my little self. It slices away all illusion. It's very effective – but it can be devastating."

Sheena was able to teach Peter through love, because he would have gone to the ends of the earth for her. Since I was so resistant to Sheena, however, and there was no love between us, anything I learned was because I was so afraid of her.

After several months of this Sheena announced that I had become too dependent on Peter. "You are not putting first things first,," she said. "You and Peter are putting your relationship before God and I cannot allow you to do that. You had better not see each other for a while. Besides, it's time you stopped thinking about yourself and your own problems and started giving to others."

My worst fear was realised. I was heartbroken, but Peter never questioned the wisdom of Sheena's decision, and cheerfully returned to his post in the Middle East.

While Peter was away, Sheena arranged for me to stay with a young couple who had a small baby and very little money. I had a room in the attic. It was sparsely furnished with an orange box for a dressing table and it had a roof that leaked. They were very kind to me, however, even though they were struggling to make ends meet, and I grew quite fond of them. I loved the baby and began to relax and open up a little.

The next time Peter came back he didn't stay with Sheena but somewhere on the other side of London. I had no idea where. One day I went for a walk in Battersea Park to be by myself and try to sort out my feelings. I was sitting on a bench in the depths of despair when I looked up to see Peter walking towards me.

"Peter, you found me!" I cried ecstatically, hugging him. "How did you know I was here?"

"I didn't, "Peter replied, slightly surprised. "This morning I suddenly felt compelled to walk through Battersea Park, so I caught a bus here. Where I've been staying is a long way from here, but I've learned to act on these inner promptings, so here I am."

I sighed with contentment. This was surely a sign that we did belong together. If God wanted it, we would always be drawn together like iron filings to a magnet.

Peter moved into my attic for the rest of his leave and it was there that a detective came to bear witness to my adultery with Peter so that Andrew could divorce me. He arrived early one morning and we showed him up to our little attic room where he could see Peter and I had been sleeping together. It was a sordid and humiliating ordeal.

Not long afterwards I discovered to my horror that I was pregnant. I was appaled. At that time, in the mid-1950s having a baby out of wedlock was the ultimate crime against decent society. And a divorce from Andrew was still a long way off.

Peter was away again, so I wrote to him, wondering what on earth he would say to this turn of events. He was delighted! Sheena was thrilled too. Then she told me about the miscarriage she had had when she was still married to Peter, which prevented her from ever having children. "Of course," she said, "this baby you're going to have is the one I should have had." I felt the distaste rising in my throat but remained silent. I had nothing to say.

SOME TIME BEFORE THE BABY was born, Peter and I drove to Glastonbury again. This time I was happier than on our previous visit, knowing that I was with the man I loved and that the child I was carrying had been conceived in the purest love. The fact that I was unmarried still troubled me, however, and when we went into St Patrick's Chapel near the Abbey, I knelt to pray. I received a wonderfully calm, reassuring message, so I asked God what the baby's name should be. "His name shall be Christopher Michael," I was told.

"But what if it's a girl?" I queried. The words were merely repeated. So that is what he was called. Sheena wanted us to add John, but I was clear that God had given me his name and nothing should be added or taken away.

When the baby was born, Sheena was away in Ireland and Peter came home to be with me, Christopher, my sixth baby, had the most wonderful birth of all my children. For the first time I had the child's father with me throughout the birth, and we brought Christopher into the world in purest love. Peter gave me the strength and support to give birth to the baby with no trouble at all, helped by a doctor and a district nurse.

I was utterly content and at peace.

When Christopher was six weeks old, Sheena rang Peter to suggest that I come to Ireland to show her the new baby. As Peter was about to leave again for the Middle East, he thought this was a good idea. I dreaded it. I never knew what might happen when I was with Sheena. But I obediently did as I was told and packed a case for a few weeks away. Sheena was thrilled with Christopher and loved him from the moment she saw him. To begin with she was friendly to me and I thought our relationship had changed, but as the days went on she became moody and silent. However, she couldn't spend enough time with Christopher. He brought out the softer, more loving side of her, so I happily let her bath and change him and take him out for walks in the pram.

I'd been there a few weeks when Peter phoned to say he had forty-eight hours' leave and wanted to meet me in Dublin. I was in a quandary. I had not yet weaned Christopher and yet I desperately wanted to see Peter. To attempt such a long journey by bus for just a weekend with a baby seemed ridiculous, so when Sheena suggested I wean him onto a bottle and leave him with her, I accepted her offer gratefully. Because I was in a hurry, I weaned him too fast and suffered from mastitis for several days, but I was driven by blind determination to see Peter again.

Peter told me he had put in his resignation from the RAF. He wanted to live for God alone, trusting that our every step would be guided. Meanwhile, until then, he had to be back in London at the Air Ministry, so he persuaded me to go with him. He asked Sheena to bring Christopher to London.

The ensuing months are a confused, nightmarish blur in my memory. When Sheena returned to London, she refused to have me in her flat and wouldn't allow me to have Christopher back or even see him. "You're not fit to be a mother," she kept saying. I began to understand what she meant when she had said that Christopher was really her child. The thought of losing him drove me crazy. Peter didn't help much. He didn't mind Sheena having Christopher for a while.

"She won't keep him for ever," he said mildly. "There's no need to worry about him; Sheena feels that she has a deep spiritual link with him and he'll be quite safe with her. She told me that she'll keep him until you've learned to put God first in your life."

I went to stay at Dorothy's flat and Peter, now out of the RAF, went back to Ireland at Sheena's suggestion, where he found a job as a cook in a small hotel. It seemed to me that we were all living at Sheena's whim.

Nobody seemed to mind in the least, though – except me. Peter did what Sheena said, no matter how I felt, and abandoned me once more to her crazy ways. I tried again to see Sheena to get Christopher back, but she wouldn't open the door to me and whenever I telephoned, she just put the phone down.

I couldn't stand it any more. I decided to put an end to it all. I got hold of a bottle of sleeping pills and, when I was alone in the flat, I drew the curtains and put some cushions by the door to prevent the gas from the oven escaping. As I was about to swallow the tablets and turn on the gas, the front door bell rang. I ignored it, but it rang and rang. Finally curiosity got the better of me and I went to open it.

"Paddy! What are you doing here?" I cried.

"I came up to London for a wedding and I got hold of your address," my brother said, giving me a warm hug. "I just wanted to see how you are."

I burst into tears, clinging to his shoulder, letting out all the pent-up misery and grief I had harboured over the past months. "I've had it, Paddy; I've had enough," I sobbed. "I'm just going to end it all. My life isn't worth living and I just can't go on any more."

He held me at arm's length and looked me straight in the eye. "Eileen, you're a fool! Don't be ridiculous. You'll do no such thing. Now go and get your things. I'm taking you home with me."

We went back to the farm where he was working. Paddy and his wife were looking after my five children, because Andrew was away so much, so he found me somewhere to stay nearby. I longed to see my children again, but Paddy would not allow it until Andrew had given his permission. Andrew also had a cottage on the farm where he stayed when he was on leave and he happened to be home when I arrived. After a few days he relented. Although I made it clear that it was the children I had come back to and not him, I think he hoped I would change my mind and take up our old life again. I had no intention of doing that.

What a reunion the children and I had! I had been away from them for three years and they had all changed and grown up so much. Penny, who was two when I left, did not know me, but with the older ones it was as if we had never been apart. As we started to get to know each other again, Andrew's hopes were raised and he even took me house-hunting one day. I knew in my heart of hearts that I still wanted to be with Peter, but I couldn't see any further than my nose and had no idea what the future would bring. All I was clear about amidst the confusion was that I would not have my life run by Sheena again.

When Peter heard that I had gone back to my children, he thought that meant Andrew as well. He rushed back from Ireland and got in touch with me. He couldn't come and see me openly, as neither my brother nor Andrew would allow it, so I made excuses to go to the village and phoned him in London from the public call box. I couldn't understand why he was so upset, since it was he who had gone off and left me alone. He tried all his powers of persuasion to get me to leave and join him in London but I refused. I couldn't face Sheena again and I didn't want to leave my children. But I did miss Peter terribly. I ached to see him but didn't dare. When I asked how Christopher was, Peter told me Sheena was looking after him and he was just fine. My blood boiled. *Never* would I let her interfere in my life again.

One morning after the children had left for school and I was alone in the house with my sister-in-law, Peter arrived. I was shocked at his appearance. He was thin and gaunt and his hair had turned quite white since I had last seen him. He looked even more ashen and dishevelled having spent the night in a ditch opposite the house, waiting for everyone to leave.

"Peter, what on earth has happened to you? What are you doing here?" I cried, my heart filled with joy at being with him again, yet shattered at his appearance.

"I've come to fetch you," he said.

"You must be crazy, Peter. I can't come with you and leave the children again."

"Eileen, you must. You don't realise how important this is. By running away from your destiny you are building up serious karma for yourself, and I can't fulfil God's plan without you. We have to be together or both our lives will be a complete waste." To my astonishment, his voice was choked with tears. "There's much more at stake than just your happiness and mine. We have important work together, spiritual work that cannot be done by any others. I can't do it alone. I must have you with me. We are spiritual partners. God has brought us together. That is why I'm in the state I'm in."

I was in tears too. "I don't care about karma," I cried wildly. "I just want to be with my children. I want my baby back and I want a normal life without all these upheavals and stupid lessons."

"Do you want me too?" Peter asked, his blue eyes penetrating my very soul.

I looked at him and my heart went out to him, this man I had gone through so much to be with. "Of course I do. You know I want to be with you," I said miserably.

"Then pack your things and come with me now," he ordered.

A picture of Sheena holding Christopher flashed into my mind. "Peter, I'm not going back to Sheena. I don't want to have anything to do with her or her teaching or guidance. I'll come back only if I can be with you alone."

"You don't have to see Sheena," Peter answered reassuringly. "We'll go off on our own and find work somewhere. Just come with me, that's all that matters."

I gave in. My sister-in-law was aghast but there was nothing she could say or do now to persuade me not to go. Peter's determination was more compelling than anything, so I packed my suitcase and left with him. I had been there exactly six weeks.

I knew that going back to my children in that way and then leaving them again was the worst thing I could have done to all of us. It upset the children, who had been learning to come to terms with life without me and now had had their connection with me reawakened. I was in turmoil again and Andrew now firmly believed I was bewitched by Peter and Sheena. He became even more convinced that he should keep the children as far away from my influence as possible, and applied for a court injunction against my having any contact with them until they were of age.

There was a lesson for me to learn from this experience, and when I went into the silence I was told very clearly that I had indeed held up the spiritual work but that in time it would all unfold. It was like the story of Lot's wife in the Bible. By turning to look back she disobeyed God's instructions and was turned into a pillar of salt. I wasn't about to turn into a pillar of salt, but my voice told me that my going back had prolonged the time it would take to unite me with my family in love and harmony. The lessons were obedience and patience. But it was no use blaming myself and wallowing in guilt and self-pity. I just had to admit that I had made a very big mistake, accept the consequences and learn the lessons so that I would never have to repeat such a heart-rending experience again.

PETER KEPT HIS WORD and found us jobs in a school in Hampshire. It was nowhere near Sheena, and she did not come to see us. I worked in the kitchen and Peter helped in the grounds as an odd-job man. After a couple of months we heard from Sheena that she could not cope with Christopher any more and she wanted us to have him back. We had to tell the headmistress of the school that we had a six-month old baby and fortunately she agreed to let us have him with us. How I managed I shall never know. But I got myself organised to cope with the baby and the job. On fine days I put Christopher in his pram, where he sat cheerfully watching the children while I worked in the kitchen. If it was wet, I put him in his playpen on the double bed in our caravan, where he played with his toys and stood up to look out of the window. When he was tired, he just curled up like a small animal and went to sleep. Considering all he had been through, he was an exceptionally good baby. If he had not been so co-operative, I would never have managed. It was heavy work in the kitchen and I got very tired but after a few weeks the strain eased. It was worth anything to have my baby back.

Shortly afterward I realised I was pregnant again. This meant a second illegitimate child. Although by this time I was free to marry him, Peter said that a legal ceremony was unnecessary since we had made our commitment to God. Marriages were made in heaven, not on earth, he said, and we shouldn't get married for reasons of security or to be socially acceptable. Again I swallowed my pride and accepted the situation. Again I felt I had no choice.

Peter started looking for a better job and found one catering for several thousand people at the Air University in Hamble, Hampshire. So we towed our caravan to a site nearby and it was there that Jonathan was born. Although Peter was with me and we had a midwife to help us, this birth was not as easy and harmonious as the previous one. Quite close to the time the baby was due, Peter went off to Scotland to look for a cottage for Sheena, which unsettled me. I was concerned that Sheena was beginning to draw Peter off again and I became emotionally strung up. Peter insisted that Sheena meant no harm to me or our family but that she needed his help. I couldn't refuse to let him go, but I was uneasy.

When Jonathan was about six weeks old, Sheena invited us to visit her in Scotland. She had a cottage on the island of Mull off the west coast. Peter asked me to take the two children. I really did not want to go but Peter was so insistent I couldn't refuse him. He so hoped Sheena and I would clear up the bad feelings between us and become friends that he half convinced me it could happen. It was so important to him. I think he felt torn between the two of us. He loved me and knew he was to be with me, and yet he loved Sheena too. She had given him so much and he wanted to help her in return.

The children and I went by train to Scotland. When we arrived in Oban there was no one to meet us, so I put the baby in the pram, piled our cases on top and, with Christopher perched on top of all that, I wheeled them down to the quay. The ferry crossing to Mull was uneventful, but there was still no one to meet us on the other side. I discovered a bus going across the island so we clambered aboard and settled down to a long, bumpy ride. When we were about half-way, there was a great commotion and hooting behind us. The bus stopped and Sheena's nephew, Douglas, got on board. He had come to fetch us. I declined his offer at that stage, as both children were asleep on my lap, and we bumped the rest of the way on the bus. Douglas drove us up the two-mile track to the cottage.

Kintra, the nearest village, was very out of the way, and I had no real idea of where we were.

Sheena welcomed us warmly and was especially delighted to see the children. Since several people were staying there, the atmosphere was pleasant and Sheena was very friendly to me. The weather was warm and sunny, the children were happy and after a few days I began to relax and enjoy myself. Mull is a very beautiful island, particularly when the weather is clear. This was the first holiday I had had in a long time.

Then, just as I was beginning to feel ready to go home again, I received a letter from Peter saying he had left his job at the Air University, since he couldn't stand working for an institution that didn't put people first. He said he wanted to practice living by the spirit, allowing God to guide his next steps. My heart sank. I was going to be left with Sheena again. Peter said he was going to tow the caravan up to Scotland and then see what would happen next. I was furious with him for putting me in this position, but again I felt helpless. Until he got another job, I was stuck with Sheena.

The atmosphere began to change in the little cottage. One by one the other guests left, until Sheena and I were on our own. Things went from bad to worse as we started to get on each other's nerves. The more she found fault with everything I did, the more I withdrew, and deep inside my resentment festered. She criticised the way I was bringing up the children and she didn't like having me around here, because she felt I was 'negative'. I suppose in a way she was right, as I was back in my worst frame of mind. At times I hated her. My moods swung up and down and, try as I might, I couldn't bring myself to like her or even be pleasant.

The cottage was quite primitive. It had no running water, so every drop had to be carried in a bucket from a tap at the top of the brae. We had a couple of oil lamps and a cooking stove that burned peat. All this was tolerable in the summer, when the evenings were long and light and the weather fine, but as the days began to draw in and it got dark earlier and earlier, my spirits dropped further. I was longing to hear from Peter that he had found a job and we would be together again. Instead he wrote to say he was going to look for work in Glasgow and that he would leave our caravan at Oban. Because it was a seasonal site, summer only, I had to stay where I was until something turned up.

Finally the strain between Sheena and me increased so much that she moved to another little cottage a mile away. It was a relief in a way, but I became very lonely. I kept hoping Peter would find something for us but he was having great difficulty getting a job. He had almost run out of money but he said he would pay the rent on the cottage and would send me money whenever he could.

I was miserable. I dreaded the winter, and the bad weather had already set in. The nights were getting longer and it had begun to be stormy and cold. Then out of the blue, late one afternoon, Sheena appeared at the door. Christopher ran to her, his arms outstretched for a hug and she swept him up, holding him close to her. In a tight, cold voice she said to me, "Eileen, you're in no fit state to look after this child. I'm taking him with me for his own good." I moved to protest but she pushed me aside and stepped outside into the howling gale striding off up the hill towards her cottage. Frantically I started after her, then ran back as Jonathan set up a howl. I was beside myself with rage. I began dressing Jonathan in his outdoor clothes, then I realised I wouldn't be able to carry both children back over the bog. Angry and frustrated, I resolved to tackle Sheena as soon as Jonathan was in bed.

As soon as Jonathan was asleep that night, I trudged up the hill through the bog. It was pitch dark and the ground was uneven and treacherous. When I got there, I flew at Sheena. She retaliated with equal venom and anger and we attacked one another like a couple of squalling cats. I have never been so angry in my life. Christopher was fast asleep and when I heard the wind howling outside I knew it would be an impossible ordeal to carry him through the bog in wild weather, so I told Sheena I would be back for him in the morning and stormed out.

Next morning I walked up the hill again to fetch him. The house was empty. They were gone. Sheena had caught the early bus to Oban and left the island.

I DESCENDED INTO A DARK HOLE. How could Peter leave me in such a dreadful situation? Twice he had made me take Christopher to see Sheena and twice she had stolen him from me. I was stuck in that wretched little cottage with not even enough money to leave the island and barely enough to buy the essentials to keep alive. Because my heart was so filled with bitterness and resentment, I was cut off from my inner voice. I didn't want to hear it. I felt that both God and Peter had deserted me and I was helpless and angry.

Depression and gloom set in. The wind howled, the rain poured down, rattling on the tin roof. It sounded as if all hell had let loose and thousands of tiny hands were trying to rip it right off. The candles would flicker and blow out. My food supply was diminishing. I reached an all-time low and again I thought about suicide. Then Jonathan would smile at me and wave his little arms, reaching up to me for love, and I knew that for his sake I could never bring myself to do it. If it hadn't been for him, nothing would have prevented me from drowning myself in the sea.

I was sent help in an unexpected form. One evening a man appeared at my door. His dark shape standing in the doorway frightened me until he put his hand in his pocket and handed me a newspaper parcel. Inside was some bread and butter. He mumbled something and disappeared but the next night he returned with something else for me in his pocket. This went on for some time. He was very simple and we did not have much to say to each other but I realised that he was doing this out of the goodness of his heart, so I accepted what he had to offer with gratitude. He also brought me a little peat from time to time, and eventually when I asked him to come in he sat by the fire in the kitchen and played his mouth organ.

As time went on we did talk a little but most of our communication was silent. Just having him there in the evenings helped me to stay sane. He was the only neighbour who ever came to see me. There weren't many and they kept very much to themselves. Anyway, I was too miserable to try to make friends.

My friend, Ian, continued to bring me bits of food and peat. At first I didn't know where they came from, but eventually I gathered that he lived with his parents and helped his father on the croft. As far as I could make out, he was bringing me food from the table. One night I could tell from the look on his face that he had something very special. He put his hand into his pocket and his face fell. As he turned out his pocket to reveal a mess of broken eggs, he was almost in tears. I washed it out and dried it in front of the fire, reassuring him that it did not matter.

Although he was a grown man, he was still a child in many ways. He was responsive and helpful, not in words but in action. How he knew I was in need I shall never understand, but he certainly kept me alive, rather like the ravens in the Bible who helped Elijah. This very simple soul was a gift to me from God. But for him I'm not sure where my food and peat would have come from. More important, he was someone for me to care about and appreciate when my bitterness and resentment threatened to overwhelm me.

After four or five months I began to come out of my depression enough to think about taking my life into my own hands. I decided to try to find a way off the island. Ian brought me newspapers and I answered several advertisements for companion-housekeepers. Whenever I mentioned I had a small baby, however, I was turned down. Since I did not want to be a housekeeper to a lonely farmer either, my efforts to leave Mull came to nothing. I got depressed again. I wrote to Peter but he was no help. He didn't sympathise with my bitterness about Sheena and Christopher, and maintained that she must have a good reason for doing what she did. My letters to him became harder and more bitter. I felt I was at the end of my tether.

Peter wasn't having an easy time either. He was working as a Kleen Eze brush salesman in Glasgow, struggling to make ends meet. It was a soul-destroying job. Whenever he could, he sent me a few pounds to pay for the baby's milk, stamps, candles and paraffin for the lamp. I longed for him to come and rescue me but he didn't even have the money for his own train fare.

Dorothy came to stay for a while in the cottage up the hill. She told me she wanted time and solitude to reflect on her life and discover what she should do next. Because she had come to that bare, cold cottage of her own free will, her experience there was enriching, in contrast to mine which was filled with pain. She said she was trying to live according to God's will, prepared to change course at any moment, and that Peter was doing the same.

"Yes – at my expense," I grumbled harshly.

The only other person who came to the cottage was the postman, when the sea was calm enough for the steamer to make the crossing to Mull. At that time of year contact with the mainland was sporadic because of the weather. I so eagerly looked forward to Peter's letters, hoping they would contain news of a reprieve from my prison. When they didn't, I would descend into gloom again, until I saw Jonathan kicking his legs and gurgling at me and my heart softened. It was as if he was reassuring me that there was a silver lining to those very dark clouds hanging over me.

The closer it got to Christmas, the longer and darker the nights became. Several times in the middle of a terrible storm, I would hear a tapping on the window. It was my friend come to see if I was all right. I'd wave and then he'd disappear again into the dark. It was as if I had a strange but wonderful angel of light looking after me. There was someone who cared enough to make sure I was safe. I was very moved.

For six months I had lived in that cottage on my own with my baby. During the long evenings I had plenty of time to reflect, sitting quietly on my own. Gradually my fury began to die down and I stopped feeling so sorry for myself. I found that if I took the time to still myself, I could hear again the still, small voice within. It had never disappeared; I had simply shut it out. I began to feel the love of God gently surrounding me. A number of times I pushed it away, wanting to have nothing to do with it. But it continued to come to me whenever I stopped to listen. I was desperately lonely and there was such love in that voice that my closed, angry heart began to soften. To begin with it was just a few words of love and comfort. I listened and more came, gently telling me to start to count my blessings. At first I couldn't see any blessings. Then, as I looked around, I realised how blessed I was to have a roof over my head, a baby who was always so good and happy, and a simple friend who cared for me. I gave thanks for it all: the food, the fuel, the company. From then on everything became a blessing for me, no matter how small: a tiny patch of blue sky, a seagull on the window ledge, the postman delivering a letter from Peter. My whole outlook changed.

Until the change, my reflections had been very gloomy and depressing but as soon as I accepted my situation, I began to hear the still, small voice within me again and to appreciate what I did have, instead of resenting what was lacking. The light began to get brighter. The relief was tremendous. I swallowed my pride and wrote to Peter that I was once more listening to God's voice. He was overjoyed. As my letters to him became more loving and less bitter, he could tell a change had come about.

Drawing every drop of water from the tap at the top of the hill became a joy instead of a burden; the smelly oil lamp was 'light' and I gave thanks for it and tended it with great love and care. The simple things of life took on new meaning as I gave thanks for it all. I began to look for the best in everything and it was amazing to see what happened as I went through a complete change of consciousness. As Christmas drew near, I was preparing to spend it on my own with Jonathan, without any resentment or bitterness. I had discovered a profound inner peace that nothing could disturb. And I knew deep within me that the worst was over.

Christmas day came. It was cold, bleak and blowy, with rain lashing at the windows and rattling the tin roof. There was a tap at the door. Imagine my surprise when I opened it to find Peter standing there, beaming, with a chicken for Christmas dinner under his arm. My cup of joy was overflowing, to be with him again on that very special day. He had kept it as a surprise and we had the most marvellous reunion. I knew then that we would not be parted again. I also realised that I had learned a vitally important lesson: to put God first before anything. For so long I had put Peter first. He had been my god, especially after I had run away from Sheena. I had depended utterly on him, and he had become more important to me than anything, even God. My time on Mull taught me a lesson I was to learn over and over in my life: when you set foot on the spiritual path, God must come before everything, no matter what the cost.

My inner voice underlined the experience: "To achieve absolute freedom, you must live fully those words 'Let go, let God'. When you do, all strain and resistance goes and you are no longer clinging on to anything of the self. You find the true meaning of absolute freedom. Strain comes when you are trying to cling on to something which you feel is being taken from you. You stick in your heels like a mule that refuses to budge, and then you wonder why you are so tense and every muscle aches. Everything you have is a gift from Me. Accept My good and perfect gifts, enjoy them to the full and then release them and accept the next lot of gifts. When you do this with everything, with the family, with Peter, your home, every material possession, then every spiritual gift, you will find true freedom and release from all strain. You will learn to live gloriously in the moment, taking no thought for the future because you have begun to understand the greatest secret in life, that we are One."

ON NEW YEAR'S DAY Peter and I left the island of Mull. We rented a room on the top floor of a tenement house in Glasgow, sharing a bathroom and kitchen with a number of other tenants, including Dorothy. It was not the most ideal home in the world but Peter and I were together and that was all that mattered to me. Both my guidance and Dorothy's made it clear that it was important for the three of us to stay close together for our spiritual work and that together we would be led 'to the land of milk and honey'.

Peter and I decided it was time we were legally married. Oddly enough my earlier shame at having two children out of wedlock had disappeared. The formal ceremony seemed almost unnecessary, as we could not have felt more married than we did then. Perhaps since I no longer desired it for reasons of security or social acceptability, God allowed it to happen. We were married quietly by a justice of the Peace, and then, miraculously, Sheena returned Christopher to us. My happiness was complete.

Peter was job-hunting again. When he went to the Labour Exchange, he was told there were no jobs available except one as hotel manager for a large hotel company. The official at the Labour Exchange was not very encouraging but Peter insisted on an interview anyway. I went with him to meet the general manager, Mrs Bruce.

"What experience do you have of hotel management?" she asked immediately.

"I have never run an hotel before," Peter replied honestly, "but I've had plenty of catering experience in the RAF. I was command catering officer on the Burma Front during the war, with 250 officers under me, so I'm certain I could manage an hotel."

"That may well be," Mrs Bruce countered, "but we're in this to make money. How do we know that you can run a business?"

"Well, I have learned through years of experience how to run an organisation according to spiritual principles of love, order, discipline and perfection," Peter responded, "and if a business is all right on the higher, spiritual level, it will be all right on the material level, including finances."

Inwardly, I gasped. How did Peter dare to mention spiritual principles in a job interview!

To my surprise Mrs Bruce said, "Yes, I can believe that, but my directors won't."

"Mrs Bruce, just give me an hotel to manage and I'll prove it to them."

I was sure by then she thought Peter was crazy, but she decided to give him the job! Then she showed us a photograph of the hotel Peter was to manage. It was like a huge castle of light, standing on a hill overlooking a green valley. Turrets and spires reached upwards and we knew beyond doubt that this was our place. When I turned within to God, I was told that this was our 'land of milk and honey' and that it would play an important part in our future work. Its name was Cluny Hill.

~ 4 ~

This is an important place, far more important than you can conceive. I, the Lord your God, ask you to build, build onto my chosen place. Whatever is done here should be done perfectly and with tone. Never at any time minimise the atmosphere here. It has radiations which cannot be seen but which nevertheless are there. Those who come here will be affected by them, even though they may not be conscious of it. This hotel is a demonstration of how a unit can be perfectly run through love, to prove that any business can be run under My guidance.

THE MOVE TO CLUNY HILL marked a new beginning. The initial 'training' was over; the real work had begun. Gone were my doubts about God's voice, my resistance to following God's inner direction. I was learning to turn within for comfort, reassurance and advice. The God within became my father, my teacher, my friend.

We arrived at Cluny Hill Hotel on a crisp, early spring day in March 1957. The air was clear and I was filled with a sense of great peace as I looked out over the rolling green golf course opposite the hotel. Cluny Hill itself was a local landmark, a cone-shaped hill rising out of the coastal plain to be seen for miles around, surrounded by green parklands and thickly wooded with beech and birch trees it was a popular place for walks, particularly up the spiral path to the top where a tower stood as a tribute to Lord Nelson, providing a view across the Moray Firth to the Black Isle north of Inverness, and Dornoch, even further north. And a large boulder at the foot of Cluny Hill reminded peaceful walkers of the time when witches were tumbled in barrels from the summit.

Cluny Hill Hotel itself was majestic, built up against the southern side of the hill overlooking the medieval town of Forres, which is mentioned in the opening lines of Shakespeare's *Macbeth*. Originally built as a health spa at the end of the last century, the hotel drew the English and Scottish gentry to 'take the waters'. The graceful reception rooms and dining room, with high ceilings and large windows, faced the huge expanse of green that was the golf course, edged by pine and larch trees. The bedrooms and suites, capable of accommodating about 100 guests, all had a view either of the golf course or of the beautiful woods that surrounded the hotel on three sides against the hill. The tennis courts had obviously seen better days when we first got there, and I could almost hear Peter's mental note to put that right at once. They were beautifully situated at the edge of the wood, with a classic Victorian-style pavilion behind, reminiscent of the days of garden parties and ladies in flowing crinolines.

We were appalled by the state of the staff quarters. The rooms we were given were cold, dark and gloomy and desperately in need of a coat of paint. There was nowhere for the staff to relax after hours, and one had to walk along a dingy, dimly lit, uncarpeted corridor to reach the staff bedrooms.

Fortunately we arrived before the start of the season, so we had time to settle in and establish our standards. We spent the little money we had on paint and brightened up our two interleading rooms, so our small corner at least was filled with light. The hotel had run down in the past years and was badly in need of loving attention. We were ready to give it. Our hearts had overflowed with love for the place from the moment we set foot on it.

We were fortunate to be able to employ Dorothy as Peter's secretary and the hotel's receptionist, and we felt strengthened by our spiritual bond. Almost immediately I was told in my guidance of the importance of Cluny Hill Hotel. We were repeatedly encouraged to put all our love and positive vibrations into it. The move to Cluny Hill also created a distance between us and Sheena, which I did not regret. Part of the agreement with Mrs Bruce, the general manager, was that we would have no one other than staff and guests staying at the hotel. So it was a parting of the ways.

I was being taught to take everything, no matter how insignificant, to God. My inner teacher told me: "My beloved child, I need you very close to Me, closer than you have ever been. Keep in constant communion with Me; let Me tell you what to do over the smallest things. In the time to come it will be vital and your immediate turning to Me will mean the difference between life and death, not just for you, but for hundreds of souls."

Every day, early in the morning before the children stirred and in the evenings after they were asleep, I spent time in meditation. I sat quietly on my own, waiting upon God. I had my pen and notebook ready and wrote down exactly what came to me. I was just like a child, and God's voice was that of a very kind, loving father, talking to me and guiding me. Although my initial resistance to accepting God within me was gone, I still experienced Him as separate from me.

Dorothy also spent regular times in the silence, receiving her own inner direction and writing it down as I did. Peter, however, no matter how long he sat or how hard he listened, had never been able to hear a voice. His guidance usually came in the form of a strong intuitive flash, which he would then check with me. No matter how trivial a detail might be, he always came to me for confirmation. He never had any doubts about my guidance, nor did he rebel as I did from time to time. His faith in God was absolute and whatever he was told through me he carried out with obedience. He was totally dedicated to God and the fulfilment of his part of the divine plan. Therefore he committed himself to building Cluny Hill into the most perfect expression possible of God's will. His own personal comfort, security or pleasure did not come into it.

Sometimes it seemed absurd to me to ask for guidance from God when the answer was obviously a matter of common sense. But I was told: "Never at any time be ashamed or think it is silly to come to Me with even the tiniest problem. That is what I am here for, to give you the perfect answer to every question. Then you can take action."

I had to learn to contain my natural impulse to step in when I saw something needed attention. When I did act before asking for guidance, I'd receive a rap on the knuckles: "My beloved child, if you go into the kitchen and see a few things need doing, it is not necessary to do them without My explicit guidance. You overstepped the mark this morning, with the result that you felt quite ill at lunchtime. I know you do not find this an easy lesson, but it is a vital one. It does not matter one iota what you have done in the past. Now you are to learn to do exactly what I ask you and nothing more."

I found it irritating to stop what I was doing to go within and ask whether an action was right. I had so much to do with two little boys under three and another on the way that often there seemed to be no time to stop. But God continued to encourage me: "I speak to you of the urgency of constant communion. You are slowly improving, although there are still times when you find it difficult to stop and ask. Yet that is what I mean by constant communion, when we can talk to each other the whole time on any subject whatsoever. Keep practising until it becomes the most natural thing in the world."

On one occasion I was at the end of my tether. I lost my temper with the children, snapped at Peter and finally went off to collect myself. God said to me: "You are allowing things to get on top of you. Bring every single problem to Me as soon as it crops up. My child, our close communion is so important, let nothing come between us to stop that flow. Remember, the enemy is delighted if he can get you into a flap because that is what cuts us off from each other."

I wasn't completely sure who this 'enemy' was, but it seemed to be any kind of negativity in people's minds or on the ethers that could undermine one's outlook and have a depressing or separating effect. Of course nothing creative can emerge from this frame of mind. So every time I was depressed, lost my temper or felt sorry for myself, I received a gentle reminder to look on the bright side of things and to draw closer to God.

Peter's faithful commitment to come to me for guidance at any moment of the day for the slightest detail was often maddening. I'd be ironing clothes or feeding the children and he would appear in our room.

"Can you get guidance on what I should do about these people who want a private bathroom?"

"Oh Peter," I said in exasperation, "can't you see I'm tied up right now? Can't it wait?"

"I need an answer right now," was his response. "You get guidance. I'll feed Jonathan."

So I went into meditation and received, "Make it clear that a private bathroom will be £10 extra and simply apologise for not making it clear in your first letter." Then Peter dashed off to send the letter immediately.

Peter refused to take my advice on anything unless it had come in guidance. It had to be written down and then he would act on it immediately, no matter what the guidance said.

I received: "My child, do not resent it when Peter turns to you for the answer to every problem. You know deep in your heart how important it is to bring everything to Me, but you fail to do so all the time. You are fortunate to have someone like Peter who will not take no for an answer. Dorothy is too. No one likes to have their mistakes spotlighted. But I have put you with Peter so that he can help you over this, so do not harden your heart against him."

In this way Cluny Hill was run entirely on God's guidance. Since we knew nothing about running a hotel, the details Peter asked me about were sometimes of major importance, but often quite mundane: "Keep Wilkie on those few extra days and get the paths cleared."

"Yes, My son, put the Pearsons and that other couple into the suite, and give the Duke of Bedford your best single room with private bathroom."

"My son, with regard to the evening suit, get the best quality. I want nothing second best for you."

"Appreciation goes a long way. Always remember to appreciate the staff for their efforts."

I received guidance on which staff to hire, how much to pay them and which rooms they should have. After the first season, our head chef moved on to become a hotel manager, so we advertised for his replacement. When a young boy with blue eyes and long lashes arrived for the interview, Peter said, "I'm sorry, it's a head chef I want." He seemed far too young to take on a job with that much responsibility.

"I was chef here three years ago," the lad, Charles Campbell, replied. "I'm very keen and I am a good chef."

"But you haven't had the experience of being head chef in a four-star hotel," Peter countered. He didn't add that he himself hadn't had the experience of managing one either. However, he spoke to the general assistant, who confirmed that Charles had worked at Cluny Hill for two years and that he was indeed a good chef. Peter was still reluctant to take him on, as he was determined to raise the hotel's standard from three to four stars, and the quality of the food was crucial. So he asked me to get guidance on Charles. I was told, "No one comes here by chance. I have laid my hand on Charles and he will never let you down. You will not regret taking him on." So Peter gave him the job.

Over the years we developed a close relationship with Charles, but he was also a thorn in our flesh. He was an alcoholic and gave us some tense moments. Nevertheless, there was a great love between us and underneath all his drunkenness and bad behaviour was a deeply spiritual person. He was extremely sensitive to people's 'vibrations' and Peter came to rely on his quiet, hesitant suggestions that a person was not in the right job or was not working with the right spirit for what we were trying to build at Cluny Hill. He understood the deeper reasons for our working together and supported Peter and me totally.

Charles' dark side sometimes came to the fore, however. One evening one of the kitchen staff came to Peter in consternation. "I'm sorry to bother you, sir," the lad said, "but Chef is a bit under the weather. I don't think he can serve the meal in his condition."

That was putting it mildly! When Peter went into the kitchen, he found Charles lying dead drunk on the floor. He dashed back up to see me. "Quick, Eileen, get some guidance for me. Find out what we can do to revive him."

I went into the silence, pen in hand, and to my astonishment I received: "Tell Peter to give him another whisky."

Neither of us would have thought of that as a solution to sober up a drunk chef, but as usual Peter followed instructions and poured Charles a stiff drink. It did the trick! He stood up and tackled the meal, producing a masterpiece and on time too. God's frequent comment, "My ways are not man's ways but My ways are perfect," was proved true in that situation.

One weekend the police arrived to say they had found the hotel van full of stolen food and they had caught the culprit. It was Charles. My inner voice said to me: "Do not prosecute Chef if it can possibly be avoided. Give him all the help you can. He is well worth fighting for. He will never let you down again."

The police were surprised when we declined to prosecute Charles. We waited for him to come back. When he didn't, I was concerned and disappointed but my guidance told me: "What Peter has done for Chef he will never forget to his dying day. I cannot promise you he will come back, because the choice lies in his hands. Humans are free to choose at every turn. On no account are you to get depressed, nor is Peter to accept this as a setback. Know that, with all his faults, Charles has a great deal of good in him, and that he is part of a much bigger plan that I have."

A month later Charles showed up. I received: "The return of Charles is a tremendous triumph. Be truly grateful. He is in his perfect place, praise be."

Charles had come back to get his things, dreading to have to face Peter and fully expecting to have to give himself up to the police. He assumed we had laid charges against him for the theft. His discovery that we had not done so effected a complete change in his behaviour. He became utterly dedicated to Peter and me and what we were doing at Cluny Hill, and even his drinking slowed down for a while.

I had a particular love for Charles and he was devoted to me. One reason was, I think, because I was never afraid of him and could handle him when he was drunk and out of control. Once when he threatened me with a large carving knife because he was annoyed with Peter for some reason, I told him, "Get on with it then and kill me, if that's what you want to do. But I'm warning you, it will make an awful mess!" Something snapped in him and he let me lead him away, as gentle as a lamb, to his room.

In some hotels the employees were treated very badly and we had many a battle to get money out of the hotel company for improvements to the staff quarters. All our staff knew we cared about them, whether they were part of our spiritual vision for Cluny Hill or not, and their response showed in what they put into their work. We were told in guidance: "My children, I want you to realise how tremendously important it is to do whatever you do in this place with love. Study the staff you have here: you will see that, whatever their job, they are learning to do it with love. If you asked them why, they could not tell you, but the reason is that I can have here only those who work with love in their hearts. The atmosphere is so important. You will find that those who remain here do so because they love the place. Charles drinks because he is unhappy, but he will not let you down. My son, in a very quiet way help him all you can. Be ever grateful for those I have placed here. Treat them as friends, not employees. Remember you are all one family in My sight."

AFTER OUR FIRST SUMMER the hotel closed for the winter season. As we had nowhere else to go, Peter, Dorothy and I were allowed to stay at the hotel, with the children. By the time the staff returned the following spring, we had painted all their rooms and each one had a vase of fresh flowers in it. Paying attention to staff and their needs, as well as spending money on their rooms, was unusual, and if it were not for uncompromising guidance, we might have been more hesitant about approaching the general manager on the subject. However, I frequently received messages encouraging Peter to speak up: "Miss M should have a comfortable room, because the staff have no sitting room. This can be brought up with Mrs Bruce. You may have to stick your neck out but make it quite clear that the happiness of your staff means a great deal to you."

Peter had to be very firm and positive with his requests for improvements to the building and the gardens too. Peter told Mrs Bruce quite openly that he was working first and foremost for God and that God wanted him to do the very best for the hotel. Once, to prove a point, he even showed her the guidance I had received. That set her back a moment. Then she laughed and said, "Well! I can't compete with that, now can I?"

Mrs Bruce liked Peter's energy and enthusiasm but had natural reservations about the way he went about getting what he wanted. She also had reservations about the way he talked about God. I was told in guidance: "Mrs Bruce is annoyed at your rocklike faith in My word. She has great faith herself but cannot see how I can guide every little detail. She knows you do not make decisions without My authority, so it is better not to talk about it." It must have been very disconcerting indeed for the general manager of a large hotel chain to be told that God had ordered a pot of paint for 'his chosen place'.

We were cautioned not to talk too freely to anyone about how we were running the hotel and our lives. "Say very little. Simply let people feel it, sense it, but do not talk about it. It is easy after a few drinks to become enthusiastic with someone who is particularly interested. but that is when much damage can be done."

Most of the staff knew that there was something different about our style of management, particularly since Peter frequently disappeared 'to check with Mrs Caddy', but by and large we did our best to demonstrate our beliefs rather than preach about them. Peter's enthusiasm did get the better of him on a couple of occasions and word got out into a newspaper under the headline: 'Hotel Run by God'. The directors of the company were most unhappy about this and came to see us, probably intending to get rid of us, but Peter was so enthusiastic and positive about all the improvements he was making that they took no action.

This event did make us more cautious, which led to a confrontation with Sheena. One of the conditions upon which we were allowed to remain in the hotel during the winters was that no one but ourselves and Dorothy stayed there. One wintry, snowy day not long before our first Christmas at Cluny Hill, Sheena appeared looking miserable and down-at-heel. Something in her had changed drastically. She seemed a shadow of her former self, almost as if her strong spiritual presence had gone, leaving behind nothing but a shell. When Peter told her that she could not stay with us, she became bitter and angry. She refused to accept the guidance I sought, which confirmed she was to go. Finally Peter was forced to turn her out. It broke his heart to see her toiling down the snowy drive, knowing he could no longer help her. Her role in our lives was over.

A few days later Peter went into town and bought Sheena a pair of shoes, as he had noticed hers were almost worn out. When he took them to her at the boarding house where she had rented a room, she accepted the gift with ill grace, accusing him of abandoning her and bringing the shoes out of pity or guilt, not love. He was quiet when he came home. "She's like a lost soul," he said sadly, "and there's nothing I can do to help her find herself again. I wonder if she remembers the time when she told me I would one day have to turn my back on her because my faith in God would be so strong. I didn't believe her then and I had no idea it would be like this."

Peter later came to understand that the reason for Sheena's downfall was that she had turned her back on the light and chosen to go her own way. She believed that the world would be saved by love alone and she could no longer accept the aspect of God which was the clear light of truth, an essential complement to love.

Our first winter at Cluny Hill was tough. There was no heating in the building and all the water was turned off except for one tap in the porter's pantry along the passage from our rooms. We turned the pantry into our kitchen and dining room, but having a bath became a real event. Every drop of water had to be boiled on the gas cooker in the porter's pantry, carried to our rooms in a bucket and poured into a zinc bathtub on the floor in front of an electric heater. We did not bath very often! Fortunately by the following winter when our third son, David, was born, the management allowed us to have water and an immersion heater in the bathrooms adjoining our rooms.

In the weeks before David's birth I had a difficult time. I had a constant throbbing headache and felt quite ill, which made me apprehensive about my guidance to have the baby at Cluny Hill, particularly since our doctor was strongly opposed to it. When I asked God about it, the reply was: "My beloved child, would I, your heavenly father, who has guided you through so many rough passages, allow anything to happen to you now? It is absolutely right for you to be in this place. On no account are you to go to hospital. I want you and Peter working together and if you go that will not be possible. Stay here with My blessings." So against our doctors wishes we stayed and David was born in Room 8 on a freezing cold night in January 1958. The birth itself was easy, with no complications, just as God had assured me it would be.

Sometime later I received: "My beloved child, it was I who joined you and Peter together to be made a perfect whole for My glory. It was I who ordained you to have those three children, Christopher, Jonathan and David, out of this spiritual union. Nothing has happened by chance. I have much for you and Peter to do and because of this work I do not require you to have any more babies." Just after this, I had to have my appendix out, so I persuaded the doctor to let me be sterilised at the same time. David was my eighth, and last, child. I was over 40 years old.

My job at the hotel was very much in the background. I had the three children to look after, which was quite a handful, but I also arranged all the flowers in the building. While I did them I radiated love to the flowers because God said: "When you arrange the flowers with love in your heart, love will bring beauty to them. I can use you in many ways." We were repeatedly encouraged to do everything with love, so that it would radiate out into the hotel and be felt by everyone there.

It was a challenge for me to stay calmly loving and unruffled with three little boys leaping and shouting about me. I seemed to have less stamina for them this time around than I had the last. Perhaps being 40 instead of 25 made a difference. My guidance stated: "You must learn to come to Me for help with the children. You need tremendous patience and left on your own you do not have it. Patience does not mean you let them walk all over you and do as they please; it meant that if you tell them to do something, you insist that they do it. But try not to lose your temper. A child loses respect for someone who is constantly losing their temper. Count to ten before you do or say anything angrily. And if you have made a mistake in asking a child to do something, don't feel you have to follow it through. Face your mistake. Children are very sensitive; they know when you are being unreasonable.

"Be firm with the children, but be loving as well. If they need love, give it to them without hesitation. Next time Jonathan has one of his tantrums, just hold him in your arms. Only love will cure him. Being firm and hard, or cold and silent will not help at all. My child, you will always find that love is the cure for all ills."

I was also tense about raising the children in the hotel, trying to keep them out of sight or at least well behaved in public, as well as doing my best to create a secure, loving family atmosphere. I was encouraged in my guidance to relax my vigilance a little. "Be not afraid to let the children mingle with the guests. They will open many hearts, so give them the freedom to go where they wish. You will find the freer they are, the less trouble they will be to the guests. Just be sensitive and see they do not worry people. Never allow the children to become a burden. They are a gift from Me to be enjoyed at all times."

Once we had a crowd of people arriving before dinner, around the boys' bathtime. I put the boys into the bath and left them there for a few minutes while I went to do something. When I came back, they were gone. Then I heard roars of laughter from the kitchen as the naked trio streaked down the passage and out into the main hall amongst all the new arrivals. The children were always up to something. Only my sense of humour and God's encouraging words saved me from total despair!

In the evenings Peter went down to the bar to mingle with the guests, while I settled the children in bed and then joined him for dinner. Dinner was often the only time we had together in the whole day to talk, but even then Peter was frequently called away and it was rare to eat our meal together undisturbed. Our rhythms were quite different the rest of the day.

I went to bed early so that I could be up with the boys in the morning, and Peter was always the last to bed at night, having checked over the whole building first. In the morning I unlocked the store room for the kitchen staff, which meant that Peter could sleep in a little later. So it wasn't easy to find time to spend alone together, to keep in touch. In my guidance I was reminded of the reason we were brought together: "Try to remember how vitally important it is for the two of you to be completely united working for Me. I need you both united in My divine love. It is easy to take each other for granted and that has a deadening effect on everyone. I have given you to each other to love and cherish, to work as one unit for Me. Through you My miracles can be brought about."

On the whole we managed to keep in touch but when all three children caught whooping cough, I became worn out and felt isolated from everyone else. At the same time Peter had been extra busy and we hardly saw each other. When we did, I had a dozen questions about what was happening outside my isolation unit and Peter became very impatient with me. He seemed to be too busy to stop and talk to me. Then I received this guidance, which I shared with Peter.

"I have often spoken about the importance of unity and how the enemy will do his best to drive a wedge in as often as he possibly can. This resentment you are feeling is all part of his scheme to disunite you, and so is Peter's gruffness. Peter has much on his mind, but that need not stop him from being civil when you ask him a question. Peter, My son, allow My child to be part of all that is going on. In this way she knows when prayers are needed. Remember, I have placed you side by side; you complement one another and one cannot do without the other."

I did not at all mind being in the background; in fact I preferred it. I would have stayed more in Peter's shadow had I not been told from within to go out and be with people. "You find it an effort to go out of your way to meet people. Know that opening up your heart and radiating love to all who come here is vitally important. By being close to Me and quietly remaining at Peter's right hand, you can help him tremendously. You are the perfect combination I have created for My work. Whereas Peter radiates light, you radiate love. The two must work hand in hand."

IN OUR SECOND YEAR at Cluny Hill Lena Lamont joined us as staff maid. She had been part of Sheena's group and received guidance similar to mine. Lena was a quiet, sincere person of whom I grew very fond. She and I worked closely together for years and helped each other with our children, as she had three of her own too. My guidance stressed the value of having such a diverse group of people working together. "You each have different gifts and have something to learn from each other. You can learn to apply the lessons in the way that Peter does and he has much to discover regarding sensitivity from you." Never could a more diverse group of people have been drawn together – Lena and I were both rather retiring and lacking in confidence, Dorothy had a lively mind and liked to discuss and question things, and Peter was always on the go, with his energy focused on doing.

During the winters Dorothy, Peter and I worked in the gardens, clearing and replanting them, spending our savings on shrubs and plants when money was not forthcoming from the management. In the winter of 1960 I received: "You have wondered why you have to do this job of clearing the whole place so thoroughly. You are putting radiations into the ground. There are also radiations deep within the earth and your work releases them." By the end of 1961 the changes were being noticed: "This magnetic centre is becoming more and more powerful. When people make remarks about the soil bringing out exceptional colour in the plants, you realise it is the radiations at work. When you hear about the peace and stillness people feel, it is these radiations."

Gradually we were introduced to the theme of radiating love. "It does not matter what you are doing, allow yourselves to radiate love. You do not need peace and quiet to do it. Start doing it when you are outside waiting or doing mundane jobs about the place. Every contact you have, be it with staff or guest, can benefit from it if you keep close to Me. Consider the position each one of you has been given: Dorothy is in contact with the guests in reception: Lena is with the staff, filling each room with the right vibrations; you are mixing with both staff and guests; and Peter is circulating everywhere, upstairs and downstairs, in and out of the garden. You are being used by Me, even if you are not aware of it. Do everything with love and it will show results."

The four of us started to meet as a small group to send out love radiances to people or groups around the world. One of our strongest telepathic contacts was with Naomi, the older woman Peter had met years before in the Philippines. Ever since their fortuitous meeting, where in the space of just a few hours they discovered their very close spiritual connection, Peter and Naomi had corresponded with one another. She now lived in the United States and Peter wrote her detailed letters about everything we were doing, particularly our telepathic contacts with her and others. She was able to confirm our experience with her own. Contacting Naomi – and others through her – in meditation made me feel like a radio ham, with Naomi as the central transmitter.

In December 1960 I wrote in my notebook:

> *This evening I was being used to send out love radiances. I felt rather like a radio station sending out hundreds of waves all over the world. Some of the waves seemed to be cut short as if they had hit a barrier and could not penetrate it, whereas others were being received and greatly used. Although I did not know who I was being used to radiate to – there were no names, no pictures – I had this feeling of power leaving my being to be sent to those in need. I knew Naomi was included in this transmission because I could feel her reception which was, as always, wonderful and clear.*

It was becoming obvious that we were part of a bigger picture. "Start sending radiances to the group known as the Arizona group. As the love flows, it will unite you with this group. Get a globe and start marking the centres on it. You are part of a tremendous network and each member is closely linked." Our correspondence with Naomi confirmed that there were other people in the world who were having similar experiences to ours and who were also sending out telepathic messages. For some reason we were connected but the purpose was unknown. "Just send out love and the rest will come about," I received in guidance. So we did just that.

Radiating love also became very much part of my personal life. Throughout the years we lived at Cluny Hill, I sent love to my other five children and their father, affirming that one day we would be reconciled. "Tomorrow is Suzanne's birthday," I was reminded in my meditation. "Hold her in your thoughts and in your heart. Pour out love radiances so strongly that she cannot help but be affected by them. She is to know that you never forget her. Love will open her heart, so send her love and it will not fail to work wonders."

For years every letter or gift I sent to any of the children was returned unopened and all contact with them was absolutely forbidden by the court until they were 18 years old. But my guidance continued to encourage me: "I have promised you that you will be reunited with your children. Do not allow yourself to be depressed. Your reunion with your children will be perfect and in My perfect timing. There is more involved with the question of access to the children than you can conceive. I want you to rejoice and see My hand tracing a perfect pattern through everything." These words and many more like them helped to comfort me and keep me going, but I did miss the children terribly.

I was told this was all part of learning to open my heart and radiate love to whoever needed it. But it was easier for me to do this on the inner, in meditation, than to come out in public and show myself. I was told: "My child, you find it a tremendous effort to give yourself to people all the time, especially after the long winter in seclusion. Do it gradually until it comes easily to you. See the good in all you meet and never take them at face value. Let Me guide you to those who are in need. Be very sensitive; open your heart. Know that you are doing this for Me and be willing to accept a few hurts. Feel all the needs around you and answer those needs. Sometimes it may be a word here or a small act there, or it may just be silently radiating love to someone. Work very closely with Me."

Meanwhile, Peter was thriving in his efforts to make Cluny Hill into the showpiece of the district. The building was clean and neat as a new pin and our bookings were increasing steadily each year, with many guests returning year after year. Peter went to great lengths to organise outdoor activities, including pony-trekking, and dinghy-sailing and water-skiing on Findhorn Bay. Nothing was too much trouble. The tennis courts were well looked after; once a week we had Scottish country dancing in the ballroom and the bar and ballroom became a popular venue for local people as well as residents of the hotel. The gardens were lovely – the sweeping hill in front of the main door leading to a secluded rock garden with goldfish flashing in the pool and surrounded by rhododendron and a colourful herbaceous border. The extensive vegetable gardens provided fresh vegetables and the food served was always of the highest standard, something Peter was very particular about. After five years Peter achieved his goal: the hotel's rating was raised from three to four stars. He had done well and loved every minute of it.

EARLY IN 1962 WE RECEIVED a shock that changed the course of our lives. The management informed us that we were to be transferred to the Trossachs Hotel in Perthshire. We were filled with disbelief. After all we had poured into Cluny Hill, how could God allow it to be snatched from under our noses? It was a severe test of faith. In guidance I received: "When plans have to change because of man's free will, know that I will never desert you. I will guide your next move so that the very best will result from it. All you have put into Cluny Hill has been absolutely necessary, as you will see in the future. Simply know that nothing is lost and great good can come out of this. Accept what I say, My child, and cheer up."

Peter did everything in his power to persuade Mrs Bruce to have the decision reversed but the move was inevitable. She obviously could do nothing to prevent it. I was told: "Mrs Bruce cannot change the plans about moving you from here. There is much involved that she was unable to disclose to you. Accept the offer of the Trossachs on the understanding that this is to be a year's trial. Do what I ask in faith. Trust Me." Reluctantly we resigned ourselves to move and make the best of it. Fortunately we were taking most of the staff who had been closest to us, including Dorothy, Lena and Charles. So at least we were not alone on foreign ground.

The Trossachs Hotel was beautifully situated in a glen beside a loch, with rugged mountains rising high on either side. The valley was lush, green and very moist, with soft, mossy undergrowth in the pine and beech woods that skirted the loch and continued up the sides of the mountains. Because of its location in the valley the hotel caught the rain and was surrounded by fine mist almost every day. The soft light through the mist gave an ethereal quality to the place. It was very beautiful.

In contrast with our arrival at Cluny Hill five years previously we were now given the red carpet treatment. The best suite was set aside for our family, one that Queen Victoria had occupied when she stayed at the Trossachs at the end of the century. Obviously the directors wanted to make us comfortable and happy there and we guessed that they were hoping we would pull the hotel's standards up, as we had done at Cluny Hill. The staff house was clean and pleasant and far more comfortable than the staff quarters at Cluny Hill, with a spacious living room fitted with radio and television. On the loch in front of the hotel a boathouse with facilities for water-skiing and sailing was already established. There were ponies nearby for pony-trekking into the hills, and a tennis court as well.

Everything, in fact, that Peter had struggled to acquire for Cluny Hill was already laid on at the Trossachs. It should have been perfect.

To begin with Peter and I dismissed the rumour that the Trossachs was 'the graveyard of managers'. We felt we could overcome anything. And it seemed such a marvellous place, even though Charles grumbled in his thick Scottish brogue, "The evil is in the very bricks of this place and you won't be able to remove it."

"That's nonsense, Charles," I argued with him. "With God's help and with our love we will raise the vibrations here and make it as popular as Cluny Hill. After all, the facilities are good and we have a solid core of staff who know the ropes. We should have no trouble bringing some stability to the place."

Charles remained unconvinced and mumbled something about 'dark forces'. I paid him no more attention.

For a while I seemed to be right. Then gradually things started to go awry – small things at first, but disturbing. In spite of the above-standard living quarters, the staff began to grumble. One could put it down to the remoteness of the hotel: we were eight miles from town and it wasn't so easy for them to escape from work, which understandably might lower their morale. But I also began to notice that the drinking was gradually increasing, and then a couple of people who had previously been extremely reliable left without notice or explanation. On top of that, one of the young girls took an overdose of sleeping pills and had to be rushed to hospital.

None of these events in isolation could point to anything suspicious but, as they increased, I began to wonder what we had been led into. My guidance encouraged us to continue to pour light into the place and to give of our best, but it was not all that easy. When our head porter, who had been with us for the five years at Cluny Hill, suddenly took to the bottle, I went to see him. He had no idea why he had started drinking, as in all the years at Cluny Hill he had never once been found drunk. I told him it had to stop. He was sober for a while but then he got drunk again and I had to take him home to his wife and ask him not to come back. The same thing happened with the housekeeper and she had to go too. It was as if these people were using alcohol to escape from something. Maybe Charles was right.

One evening when I was dancing with Peter in the ballroom, one of the waiters hurried over to us and called me to the telephone. On the line was Charles' girlfriend, quite breathless. "Mrs Caddy, please could you come quickly! It's Charles!"

"Where are you?" I asked anxiously.

"I'm phoning from the boathouse. Please hurry!"

I jumped into the car and tore down to the boathouse, forgetting to ask anyone to come with me. There I found Charles floundering around in the water at the end of a rope, with a frightened Madge clinging to the other end. He couldn't swim and was so drunk he couldn't pull himself out of the water. He just hung there, cursing and bellowing. I held on to the rope and together Madge and I eventually managed to pull him to safety. Then I discovered he was wearing a wetsuit with several pounds of weights tied around his waist. He had been determined to drown himself.

"Charles, what do you think you're doing?" I asked as we led him, stumbling back to the staff house.

Angrily he muttered, "Nothing will get rid of the evil that is in the very stones of this place – not all the light in the world."

MY GUIDANCE HAD consistently encouraged us to pour more and more light into the Trossachs, but it didn't seem to be doing much good. The assistant manager, who at the beginning had been most charming and helpful, had become surly and uncooperative and Peter swore he was purposely working against us. When I went to talk to him, he told me that his wife was having an affair, which explained his jumpy nerves and erratic behaviour. The next we heard was that his wife had gone, leaving him with two children. I sat and listened to him pour his heart out and helped him with the children as much as I could, but there wasn't a lot I could do to cheer him up. He, too, blamed the Trossachs. "This never would have happened if we hadn't come to this godforsaken place," he said bitterly.

All these events could be brushed aside as a spate of individual problems had it not been for Peter's frame of mind. I have never met anyone with a greater ability to turn adversity into opportunity and if it were possible Peter would have done it. But he was just not happy there. He did his best, putting in long hours trying to lift the hotel out of its doldrums; however, his enthusiasm was gone and his energy seemed to drain away. At Cluny Hill his love for the place had shown in everything he did and his energy had been boundless. But he couldn't put an equal amount of love into the Trossachs – it just wasn't there. Instead of tackling projects with his familiar verve, he did them out of responsibility and duty. He was dispirited and apathetic. This alarmed me more than anything else that had happened at the hotel.

I received pages of guidance about the Trossachs: "In this place much love needs to be radiated out, because love is a shield to protect you from the powers of darkness. The Trossachs is My final test for you. Can you withstand the powers of darkness or will you succumb to them? Never regret having been sent here. There have been many lessons for all of you that you would not have learned had you stayed at Cluny Hill where you were so fully protected. You have learned the hard way to turn to Me for everything, but most important is that you have learned this very important lesson."

I never really had much idea what was meant by 'the powers of darkness' but there did seem to be something about the place that was oppressive. It felt dark and gloomy. Even the weather got us down. What we first experienced as misty, ethereal beauty very soon became relentless, depressing rain. The sun shone only rarely and then only in sporadic breaks in the clouds. The rest of the time the skies were grey, the hotel itself was dark and heavy and our spirits sank lower as the season went on. Our increasing problems with the staff were compounded by this feeling of darkness all around, undermining what we were trying to do, pulling us all down. It was intangible and yet it was real. I think everyone in the hotel felt it, including the guests.

We were relieved when the season ended. We could hardly wait to get back to Cluny Hill. Peter wrote to the general manager saying he had given the Trossachs his best try but knew his heart was not truly in it, so we would like to return to Cluny Hill as soon as possible. He also mentioned that a friend of ours, Naomi, was coming to visit us from America and asked permission for her to stay in the hotel with us. We had no real sense of what we were going to do that winter and whenever I asked for guidance on our plans, it was ambiguous and vague. "The only way is to live from day to day. Planning ahead for you is quite useless. You have to take one step at a time under My direct guidance, knowing that all will work out perfectly if you learn to live this way all the time. Take no thought for the morrow, what ye shall eat or what ye shall drink, nor what ye shall put on. You will see what I mean in the days to come." It was all quite baffling.

The day before the general manager came to do the end of season stocktake, I received: "My child, I want you to keep very, very positive about everything tomorrow. If you are in constant touch with Me, you can change quickly in midstream without it throwing you out. You must be ready to do this. Be willing to change your plans at a moment's notice."

When Mrs Bruce arrived, she called Peter and me into the office. She handed us our books and the balance of our wages and told us that we were to leave. We had four hours to pack our things. We were stunned. There was no explanation as to why we were being dismissed and Mrs Bruce was under no obligation to give one. The stocktakers found nothing amiss in the books, the stocktake was accurate down to the last teaspoon, and as far as we could make out, they found nothing wrong with the way we had run the hotel. When I asked Mrs Bruce, she vaguely mentioned that they were rearranging the staff. It was a severe blow to us all. We had been so certain we were going back to Cluny Hill.

Within four hours we were gone. We packed the car with our belongings and Dorothy's and picked the boys up from school. We had no idea where to go or what to do. In a state of numbed shock, we spent two nights at a hotel in Lossiemouth, a fishing village a few miles up the coast from Findhorn, at the company's expense. That was Mrs Bruce's parting gift to us, which was decent of her.

What had gone wrong? We were convinced that we belonged at Cluny Hill and God had even told me that we would return there. The day after we left the Trossachs I received: "Stay at perfect peace, right in the centre of the hurricane, as you did yesterday. I know it was a great shock to you, but I tried to prepare you very gently. I want you to know that only the best can result from this. You may not see it at the moment but you will. Your faith will be strengthened in a new way; you will be drawn together. As you take one step at a time, you will find that things work out perfectly."

~ 5 ~

Think of this as a great new adventure. You are going to a new country where there are new people with new customs. They speak a different language and live in a different way and all your old ways won't fit into this new adventure. Start looking at things in a completely new light. It will not be easy because it is strange. You may feel awkward, you may feel lost. It will take time to understand what people are talking about. It will take even more time to learn to speak their language. You are like a very small child. In the spirit of adventure enter into the new. In the right spirit it can be such a joyous adventure. You will have no regrets. Perfect love casts out all fear. Put your faith and trust in Me and step ahead with confidence.

ALL WE OWNED WAS a caravan which we had parked on a site near the beach at Findhorn. We had saved very little money, since most of it had gone into improving Cluny Hill and its garden. We certainly didn't have enough to buy a house. Our caravan was in good repair thanks to the work Peter had done on it the previous winter. When we had been told in guidance to repair it, we had had no idea we would need it for ourselves so soon!

So we moved into the caravan. Dorothy found a room to rent in the village nearby and the boys were delighted to be living so near the beach. My heart was filled with gratitude that this small, temporary step had opened up for us. Life wasn't so bad after all. It was rather like having a family holiday and for a few weeks we relaxed and enjoyed ourselves. The pressing need was, however, to find a place to park the caravan for the winter, as ours was a seasonal site open only during summer. My guidance told me, "This situation will show you who are your friends." It certainly did. Peter and Dorothy signed on to draw unemployment benefit and we began to contact people we had known from our Cluny Hill days. When Peter was manager of the hotel, we were frequently invited to cocktail parties and dinners, but when we returned to the area without a job and with nowhere to live these people were not interested in us. It was bad enough having to suffer the humiliation of Peter standing in the dole queue, but when a rumour circulated that we had been sacked for stealing money from the hotel and I was shunned in the High Street in Forres by people I had known quite well, I was mortified. To this day I have never found out why we were dismissed, but I suspect it had something to do with our unorthodox way of working and Peter's refusal to tow the line. My guidance reassured me: "If you had remained at the Trossachs, it would have meant battling with the dark forces all the time. On no account are you to feel you have failed. Accept this experience as a clear example of the grip the powers of darkness now have in the world."

That was my first experience of these powers of darkness. There was no doubt in my mind that something of a negative nature had been at work and now I knew that we were being prepared to 'fight a battle for the light'. I did not know how or why. I was also reassured that we would return to Cluny Hill one day, although God gave no clue when that might be. "I want Peter to know that he is the guardian of Cluny Hill. Therefore one day he will go back there and great will be that day. Have no fixed time in mind but accept this as My promise, so that no matter what you are to do you can hold that goal in mind. Always keep very positive about your return to Cluny Hill. But it will not be under this company."

Finally, after a month's search for another site for the caravan, we found a space in a hollow at the Findhorn Bay Caravan Park, a mile down the road from the village of Findhorn. I was reminded of the many times we had passed it on the way to the beach and commented, "Who would want to live in a dump like that?" The area we were offered really was like a dump, with rubble and litter all over the place. There was an old garage standing in one corner, its windows broken and weeds and brambles all around it. The one advantage of the site, however, was that it was well away from most of the other caravans and the hollow felt secluded and private.

So on 17 November 1962 we towed our caravan to the hollow, where it has been ever since.

I was resigned to spending the winter in our poky little caravan. I wasn't happy about it but I accepted it as a temporary step. I pinned my hopes on what God had planned for the future and set about making us reasonably comfortable in the meantime. It was a cold, bleak winter that year. The water froze in the pipes and we had to carry what we needed from the public toilets several hundred yards away. But the children loved the cold, snowy weather and pulled each other on sledges to the village school every day. David was 4, Jonathan 6 and Christopher 7.

Our living space was unbearably cramped. The three boys shared a small room at one end, with a single bed and a double bunk. All their clothes and a few toys were stored in boxes under the beds. At the other end of the caravan was the living room, dining room and bedroom all in one. Our double bed folded up into the wall during the day and each night before we could let the bed down we had to pile two armchairs on top of the settee, move it to one side, stack the four dining chairs next to it and fold up the table. The bathroom led off this room, so any time anyone wanted to use it they had to walk through our bedroom. We had no privacy at all. The narrow passage between the boys' bedroom and the main room was my kitchen. I had a two burner gas cooker with a tiny oven next to a very small sink. It was a squeeze for anyone to pass by me when I was cooking. This was the full extent of our living quarters.

Not long after we moved to the new site, I was given this guidance: "Learn to count your blessings and give me constant thanks for them. Then you will see how mightily blessed you are. I tell you very clearly that unity is absolutely vital between all of you. It will have to be fought for and held. The atmosphere in this caravan is so important to the work. Accept that I have placed you here in this confined space so you can all learn to work together in perfect harmony. If you can find unity on the big issues, you can find it on the smaller ones too. It means sensitivity and understanding on everyone's part You are all as different as chalk and cheese, but remember that it is not by chance you have been brought together under these circumstances. It is all in My plan. Therefore you have something to accomplish. If you can do it under these conditions and find unity, other groups can do it too. Never despair, I am with you always."

All my life I had longed for security and never really found it. That longing made me afraid of new places, new people. Even as a child I was afraid to step off a boat or a train to see a new place, a fear that has plagued me all my life. Every now and then, just when I thought I'd found my security in God, something happened and I'd be stepping off a high diving board into the unknown again. Every time that awful fear gripped me. I couldn't expect Peter to understand because he didn't even know the meaning of fear. My guidance said: "You cannot go back and you cannot remain static. You have to go forward, straight into the new unknown. It is something you can do only on your own. My child, as you turn to Me more and more, that fear will go. Unless you take the plunge once and for all, it will be like opening and shutting a door, letting a wonderful stream of light in and then shutting it quickly because the light is too bright. Cast your fears on Me and know that the future is glorious for you. My peace be upon you, and My blessing."

What was this 'new unknown'? What more did I have to go through before I could live in peace with my children and husband? We were told over and over how important it was to build harmony amongst us, to raise the vibrations within us and around us. Every aspect of our lives was concerned with raising vibrations. Initially I had no idea what was meant by 'vibrations', but I gradually began to feel them building up like a high energy. When I was angry with the boys or irritated with Dorothy or Peter, I became aware of how it shattered the peaceful, loving atmosphere which we had built up. I was told that it was up to me; that as I thought, so I would bring about. It was so important to think positive, loving thoughts and it was also very difficult!

I despaired when the boys marched through the kitchen with their friends, their boots caked with mud, scattering coats and hats as they went, just after I had spent all morning tidying their things and scrubbing the kitchen floor. Very often I was irritable and impatient with them and then blamed myself for losing my temper. Or when Peter came in for a bath after a day in the compost heap, the smell was so strong that I'd snap at him while he was waiting for the water to heat. I simply couldn't get away from the smells, the dirt, the disorder. I cannot stand living in chaos and it took all my time and patience to achieve anything like the standard I wanted under the circumstances.

In my time of stillness with God, I was told: "Start the day by finding Me right there in the very centre of your being, knowing and feeling My peace and serenity for the rest of the day. So often you are woken up suddenly by one of the boys and your immediate reaction is to feel resentful and to bite his head off. All those little things that annoy and irritate you are for a purpose. You are being tested dozens of times a day, so strive as you have never striven before to be different. Keep on longing for it by seeking My help."

The problem was how to meditate with so much going on in such a confined space. In desperation I turned within. "Why don't you go down to the public toilets?" I was told. "You will find perfect peace there."

I was aghast. What a thought! To sit in a public toilet to listen for the voice of God? I couldn't imagine anything more undignified! Nevertheless, when I thought about it, God was absolutely right. Late at night or very early in the morning I was unlikely to be disturbed. So that is what I did, no matter what the weather. Even when it was cold or snowy, I wrapped myself in my winter coat and sat in the toilet for hours with my notebook and pencil, recording the most beautiful visions and messages. It was a perfect solution, however unorthodox. I could no longer doubt that God was within and that it was possible to meditate anywhere.

OUR DAYS WERE FULL, particularly when spring approached and we started planting a small garden and building an annex to the caravan for Dorothy to live in. Our guidance stressed that Dorothy needed to be right there with us, building up the vibrations in the caravan and the garden. We were told to do everything in the right spirit. "Time is not what matters but unity, co-operation and positive thinking. Know that every time you put the spade into the soil, you are putting in radiations. Love that vegetable garden, use all My gifts and be grateful for them. Let it be a joyous time for you all as you create a place of harmony and beauty. You can be sure that something is wrong if there is no harmony amongst you. It would be far better to stop and do nothing than to do something which causes discord. The work on the annex must be guided in every way. It has been given to you for a purpose: to teach you to seek My guidance over every step and to learn to work together in perfect harmony. It is not just a job to be completed to give Dorothy somewhere to live. It is here to teach you some very valuable lessons. You have plenty of time. I want you all to be very aware of the vibrations around this place. They emanate from each of you, so you are each responsible for the right vibrations."

We were all such different personalities with varying interests and points of view. Dorothy and Peter sometimes talked about things that were beyond me, esoteric subjects they had studied and I had not. I often felt like an ignorant fool next to Dorothy and all the feelings of inadequacy I had experienced as a child in my relationship with my sister came back to me. Like my sister, Dorothy had the advantage of brains and education. She had been to university, was intelligent and well-read and could discuss things with Peter that I couldn't. She never lorded it over me, however, nor did she ever imply that she was in any way superior to me. It was all in my own mind. But if she neglected to wash up the dishes, I grumbled to myself about her and then I would receive this kind of inner advice. "Unity does not fall into your laps; you have to strive for it. Every now and then there is a blockage because relationships are strained or there is intolerance or criticism within. It does not always come out into the open, which is worse, because something that is suppressed cannot have the light of truth shone on it and it goes on festering."

Dorothy and Peter frequently had a clash of wills. Peter's way was to go steaming ahead with a project as soon as he knew it was right to do it, with little thought for what we might want to contribute. Sometimes he and Dorothy were at loggerheads over how things should be done. Invariably Peter just went ahead and this made Dorothy furious. Peter was so action-oriented that he could never see the point of talking about doing something. He would just do it.

The only time I was comfortable voicing what I felt was when it came in the form of guidance from within. Peter had absolute faith in my inner voice and would follow it to the letter as long as it was written down. His confidence helped me to trust my guidance, especially when it seemed strange and challenging. This was the strength of our relationship. God had brought us together to do special work, and we had the deepest sense of spiritual purpose in our union. Our concentration was pin-pointed on what we were doing, and there was so much to do, we never stopped to question it.

I looked up to Peter and his approval meant everything to me. He knew all about spiritual laws and principles, and I knew very little, just what I was learning through my guidance. So while Peter affirmed my connection with God totally, his attitude also, unknowingly, reinforced my secret belief that I was worth nothing just as myself. Instead of being myself and expressing my own views and feelings, I did my best to become the kind of person I thought Peter wanted me to be.

For example, in the evenings while Peter sat reading or watching the television I mended his and the boys' clothes or knitted jumpers for them. Sometimes I got so tired of mending and patching and longed to indulge a passion of mine – knitting dolls' clothes. I love making little things. But I couldn't bring myself to do something purely creative for fear of Peter's disapproval. Peter would probably never have noticed, far less commented on what I was doing, but foolishly I denied myself the pleasure of a creative hobby for the sake of avoiding a possible rebuke.

I received guidance encouraging me to value myself and my own contribution, but it took many years for it to sink in: "I have told you many times that I need you to bring through a work that no one else can do. You are indispensable to Me. You have been comforted by this thought but you have never fully grasped the immensity of it. You have the greatest gift that anyone could possibly ask for. You know that God speaks to you and guides and directs your entire life. Never compare yourself, your situation or your life with any other soul. This only causes discontent and criticism. When you spend all your time counting your blessings, seeing the very best in everything and the beauty all around you, you will waste no time in comparisons."

A reprimand from God was even worse than one from Peter. I squirmed with shame, especially when I had to share it with the others. "I know how you feel, My child, when I have to speak severely to you and pull you up, but you can be grateful that I do this, because then you can do something about it. It is uncomfortable to have a blind spot floodlit with My light, but it is because of My great and tender love for you that I do illuminate all these sores so that they can come into the light and be healed."

I felt very annoyed. I was being treated like a small and difficult child.

Why was I the one to receive the ticking off? Why not the others? I felt very vulnerable to criticism and these resentful thoughts would weigh me down. Then God would suggest: "Keep a light touch with whatever you do, like the touch of a butterfly or a summer breeze. What a difference it would make not only to you but to those around you. Try to see the funny side instead of allowing things to get you down."

My spirits rose and fell like mercury. I was constantly encouraged from within to stabilise my emotions, to gain a sense of perspective by doing something for others and counting my blessings. I must have been a difficult student in those days! "All this conflict within you is the old skin you are shedding like a snake. Sometimes it gets stuck and you need to wriggle even harder to move it, but know you will shed it and move into the new, and great will be the rejoicing. Never despair; I am with you always."

There were so many uncertainties: would Peter find a job? How would we manage to live on so little money? What was to happen in the future? Nothing was secure. Each week I put the £8 from National Assistance, £1 10 shillings from child allowance, plus Dorothy's contribution into a jar on the mantelpiece to pay for gas, electricity and fuel for the stove, with the rest for food. There was never any left over. I was told by God: "I will always meet your needs but not your wants. You know there is enough money for those needs but it does mean you have to be very closely guided by Me over all your purchasing. It is not necessary to save for a rainy day. There will always be enough, rest assured of this." We lived on an extremely tight budget, but it was true: our needs were always met, often in miraculous ways.

My security was challenged yet further: Sheena appeared again. Somehow she heard we were living at Findhorn, which was not far from the school where she was teaching music, and one day she unexpectedly turned up at the caravan. She was grey in feature, hair and clothes, hardly recognisable as the Sheena we had once known. She came to see if we were still getting God's guidance and in a pathetic way she wanted to link up with us again as in the old days. But clearly it was not right. I asked for guidance while she was there: "My beloved child, the past is past and finished. I tell you now Sheena has no part in your lives. What she does she will have to do on her own without you. She has her own life to live. Let her live it. She does not fit into the plan I have for you. She knows this but refuses to accept it, like someone drowning clutching at straws. She should go and stay out of your lives."

Sheena was very angry and said my guidance was false, but she did leave. I was no longer afraid that she would draw Peter away from me. She didn't seem to have the same power over him any more. However, her attachment to Christopher was as strong as ever. The old fear gripped my heart and I became obsessed that Sheena might pick Christopher up from school and disappear with him. She had taken him before and now that she had so little else in her life it seemed even more likely. Each morning as the boys set off to walk the mile to school, I wondered whether I would see Christopher cheerfully bursting through the door that afternoon.

My fear utterly swamped me, so I took the situation to God in my meditation. "Dear God," I prayed, "what am I to do? I am so afraid of this woman, I can hardly think of anything else."

"My child, what you need to do is phone Sheena and ask her if you can drive over to see her with the boys."

"Oh, no, I couldn't, I just couldn't!" The thought filled me with terror. "Can I ask Peter to come with me? Or Dorothy?"

"No, this is something you have to do alone. Drive over there yourself and take all three boys with you."

It took me a few days to pluck up the courage but I eventually phoned her. I was shaking from head to foot as I stood in the phone box. I managed to ask her if I could bring the boys to visit her. She was very rude and offhand but she said I could and I arranged to go the following afternoon after school. The first hurdle was over and I felt strangely relieved, but I still had to confront her in person.

When the boys came home from school the next day, I packed them into the car. My knees felt weak and my head ached but I was determined to go through with it. We drove the twelve miles to her house and by the time we reached her door I had managed to calm myself. I rang the doorbell and Sheena answered it. She gave me a stony look but then turned to the boys and welcomed them. As I stood there looking at her, all I saw was a lonely, unhappy old woman. For the first time in all the years I had known her I felt compassion for her – and some sadness. Something inside me broke away. I was no longer terrified of her, no longer afraid that she could affect me in any way. I was free.

Sheena was extremely unpleasant to me that afternoon, ignoring me part of the time and then making cutting remarks about me, Peter and the children. For the first time ever I simply took what she was saying without any reaction. I didn't feel hurt or upset; I just saw her unhappiness and felt sad for her. An enormous weight had lifted from my shoulders and from my heart. I kept thanking God for what had happened and I realised how blessed I was to have a husband I truly loved, three wonderful boys and a home, even if it was just a little caravan. And I had God. Sheena had nothing and was filled with bitterness and resentment – she who had had it all before.

This experience of having the courage to face my greatest fear was one of the most important lessons I have ever learned. I had turned Sheena into a monster in my mind and had been incapable of seeing her as she truly was. I had always given her more power over me than she really had, and my fear and insecurity had clouded the fact that she too was a human being with feelings and failings, just like me. Once I was over that hurdle, nothing Sheena did afterwards ever concerned me.

A few days later I was standing outside our caravan talking to someone and Sheena came around the corner. I turned to God within me and asked how I should behave. "Behave as I would," God said to me, and in that moment I literally felt my heart open, and love – the purest love – flowed towards her. It was a miracle and I thanked God for it. It was proof that I had overcome my fear.

Sheena never fully cleared her resentment of us, probably because she could not accept that what we were doing at Findhorn did not include her. My guidance was so clear that her place was not with us that there was little more we could do than offer our friendship. Finally she left her job in the school and moved away, and we lost touch with her. Several years later we heard that she had died in Edinburgh of a cerebral haemorrhage.

MY INNER LIFE in the meantime was growing and flowering into an experience of extraordinary joy. Every evening I spent a couple of hours in meditation, experiencing visions, light, colours and a level of purity that transported me to another world. It was so rich and beautiful that it was hard sometimes to come back to the world of domesticity and children. Of course, I had my doubts. Was I living in a place of illusion? Perhaps everything I was experiencing on these inner planes was simply my imagination. God's response to such thoughts was that I should have faith. "Before you open yourself, ask for cleansing and purifying. When you are in that state, only the truth can filter through, because I would not allow anything false to come through. That is your greatest protection. Have complete faith in what is happening at this time, because so much of it is in the higher realms which you are unable to see with your human eyes. But you feel it and know it with your higher faculties which are far more reliable."

Every evening Peter, Dorothy and I spent an hour or two in meditation on our 'inner work'. We were connected with Naomi, who was doing similar work in the United States, and she gave us a list of magnetic centres in various countries to which we radiated love and light, making telepathic connections and linking us all in a worldwide network of light. It was done in absolute faith, as our only confirmation that these centres existed was an inner knowing. Sometimes I received a vision of the members of these groups. One was a group of businessmen in Turkey. I saw them quite clearly dressed in formal suits around a central figure. I had a vision of a group in Holland that was in some way connected with the Dutch Royal Family, another group in Siberia and another in South America. I also connected with Aborigines in Australia and Bushmen in the Kalahari Desert in Southern Africa. Dorothy was also given pieces of information to help identify and visualise the groups of people to whom we were radiating, and we all reached out in absolute faith, sending love or light as was appropriate.

We were told: "The work you are doing in the evenings should be taken in your hearts until you feel you know the vibrations of each centre. With some of the magnetic centres you feel very little. Spend time with these during the day or night, until you begin really to experience them and get to know them. Each of them needs to feel part of the whole. This is a network of light; therefore each should be linked with the others. If you sense that there are some that are standing on their own, it is because they are not sure how and with whom to link up. Learn to feel the intertwining and intermingling of the vibrations of each centre until not one is left on its own. The strength comes through the linking up and uniting of the centres."

As Peter read out the names of the centres each night, we tuned in to each one to radiate our love through the heart or light through the centre of the forehead, depending on what we felt the particular centre needed. God likened it to sailing a boat, having to tack first one way, then another. When I sent love out, I felt a very gentle ray flowing from my heart to the person or group. When it was light, it was like a powerful beam going out from my forehead and I would feel it reach its target. The two were distinctly different experiences.

This work, done in faith, with no concrete response from any of the magnetic centres, required a special kind of understanding: "To understand is to stretch your imagination, to try to live the other person's life. You must be careful, because it is so easy to trample and crush if you are not very sensitive. I have asked you to do this with each of the magnetic centres. To understand them is a formidable task. Each one is different and has to be handled differently."

Our own unity as a group was essential to carry out this work and so we had to become more sensitive to and understanding of one another before we could hope to do the same on inner levels with people we did not know. Sometimes I would despair of ever achieving this depth of understanding, as often I couldn't put it into practice even with my own children. Always I was reassured: "What you are learning daily with the children and each other can and will fan out into a vast work. It has to start right here with where you are. Unless it starts at the source, it will be useless."

I contacted a group of priests in Brazil who were being used as transmitters for radiations to South Africa. We never knew whether their work was conscious or not. In fact it seemed to me that some centres were as old as time and fully aware of their mission but others were young and as yet had no idea of what they were to be used for. In one vision I saw a pattern of light woven by what seemed to be threads of light connecting the magnetic centres. It was a definite pattern – but it wasn't finished. Much of this work I didn't really understand, but I wrote down whatever I received and shared it with Peter and Dorothy.

I was constantly being told that in this spiritual life there are no 'on times' and 'off times', that the periods I spent on higher levels, communing with God, receiving wonderful messages and visions or radiating out to groups were not to be separated from the rest of my life – my 'own' life –

where I was a mother and wife. It was all one life. It was difficult always to feel this oneness and I often created little compartments in my life. I demanded my own time, which caused conflict and confusion in me. "I want you to learn to let yourself dissolve completely into Me, so there is no division of the time you give to Me and the time you have to yourself. It should all be one and the same."

Very often, when I passed into a heightened state of consciousness, I did not want to come down to the ordinary things of life – looking after the family, cooking, cleaning and washing. I was reminded gently and lovingly that I could not live with these peak experiences all the time. They were given to recharge me, so that I could return to the ordinary ways of life and live those experiences in joy, love and service to my fellow humans.

Our inner work gave purpose to our daily lives. Everything we did had a greater purpose. We worked in the garden not just to feed ourselves; we were putting radiations into the ground. Our interactions had to be harmonious to raise the vibrations and our thoughts added to their strength. We were building a magnetic centre. We were told that one day others would join us and were reminded constantly that the work we were doing was far greater than any of us could imagine. "It is necessary to keep pouring the radiations into the very soil, building up power all the time. The greater the power, the quicker the right people will be drawn here. Each of you has a special part to play in putting radiations into this place. Yesterday you felt it for the first time as you put the compost on the ground. You became pin-pointed in what you were doing and felt the radiations flowing through you. You felt what you were doing was really beneficial to the plants and soil."

I didn't understand exactly what we were building a magnetic centre for and it seemed absurd to think that our little group, living in a caravan park far away on the Moray Firth, could have such importance, let alone draw others to live with us. Nevertheless, I carried on listening and recording, no matter how uncomfortable the messages were, no matter how difficult it was for me to make the time to meditate. This communion with God became my life blood and I felt if ever I stopped listening and receiving I would die. I sensed an urgency within me; there was so much work to be done and I had to keep open to receive the next installment of the unfolding tale.

I could sit and meditate for a long time and nothing would come, but as soon as my pen touched the paper it was like switching on an electric current. The words flowed. I was told: "I work through each of you in different ways. This is the specific way I work through you as My channel. You know when you need guidance from Me, you can receive it instantaneously. Like a flash of lightning it is there. You can find the answer immediately; therefore you hold great responsibilities in your hands. Never take this gift for granted. The time will come in the future when you will no longer have to sit down and record everything I have to say to you. You will learn to have your antennae out all the time, listening for every minute instruction as I send it forth. As Peter now has to be guided in action, so will all of you do the same. You will listen, you will hear, you will act without a moment's hesitation."

My years with Sheena had taught me the discipline of sitting regularly in meditation, and the joy of communing with God now made it easy. I longed for my times of silence, and the nourishment I received from them made it worth the effort of going out in snowy, windy weather. Nevertheless there were some nights when I was reluctant to leave our snug little caravan. The early mornings were even more difficult. I was told that these were the times when I grew the most, spiritually. I found that hard to believe when every thought, every movement, was an effort, and sometimes I was so tired it took all my energy even to grasp my pen. It was as if everything was trying to prevent my being there or even writing a word. Those extra few minutes in bed in the morning were so tempting but I knew that if I missed my time with God for the sake of a longer sleep, the rest of the day would be filled with unnecessary difficulties. I had to discipline my thoughts too, so that I didn't allow irritation or negative thinking to ruin the atmosphere. Like water, I was told, if thoughts are harnessed, they become power.

ONCE WE REALISED that we would be living in the caravan for sometime we decided to make a small fenced-in patio to give us a little privacy. Because we had so little money, we relied on lucky finds to build it. Someone told Peter that there were some burst bags of cement on a nearby rubbish tip, so he picked them up, and Dorothy and I collected some stones for the hard core. We bought a do-it-yourself wattle fence, dug holes for the stakes and concreted them in. That little patio was such a joy to us in the years ahead and we had some wonderful meetings there.

Our tiny garden of a few lettuces and radishes gradually grew to provide all our vegetables. Although Peter was in charge of the garden, Dorothy and I did a lot of work there too and particularly enjoyed scrounging for composting materials. She and I often went to the beach to gather seaweed for the compost heap. We followed the high tide line and if we found a dead swan, a seagull or even a salmon, we brought that home in the car too, holding our noses all the way. We also took buckets and shovels along to a nearby field to gather up horse manure. It's amazing how compost-conscious you become when you have a garden to nourish.

Dorothy also spent time tuning in to the plants and one evening she told us that she had had a powerful inner contact with what felt like the spirit of the pea plant. It had told her that the nature spirits – or 'devas', as she called them – were working in co-operation with us to develop the garden. As her communication with the devas of other plants and trees developed, we realised that the forces of nature were responding to our spiritual work and that something very significant was to come out of all our work with plants.

Dorothy's communication with the devas enriched our gardening experience. I was told from within: "Dorothy's wonderful contact with the angels of various plants will make a tremendous difference to your work in the garden. You are working with nature, with the nature spirits and elementals who create the living plant life, and gradually you are finding harmony with these. What is happening is something completely new. This is the way the new world is to be created. The radiations and everything else Peter has put into the soil to nourish it are making this a very special place to be used tremendously in the days ahead. And you, My child, are learning to make My word live. By this means all things can be manifested in form."

It was exciting to grow vegetables under the direct guidance of the angels in charge of them and the garden flourished, producing bigger and better crops each season. Dorothy's contact with the devas meant that she and Peter had to work in closer co-operation with each other, and a new unity began to emerge in our group. Our sense of common purpose was strengthened even more. Naturally the disagreements didn't disappear altogether and once in a while I'd hear a heated argument outside my window about whether it was better for the plants to have classical music played outside (which Peter enjoyed) or to have just the songs of the birds (which Dorothy preferred)! More often than not, Peter's will prevailed, his being the stronger of the two.

DURING THE FIRST THREE YEARS in the caravan we lived in seclusion like hermits. Very few people came to visit us and apart from Peter and Dorothy's weekly trip to the labour exchange to collect their National Assistance money, we rarely went into town. My intense work in meditation made me increasingly sensitive and vulnerable. After a brief trip into Forres, which was only a small town and not all that busy, I returned home weak and shaken. I felt like a snail without a shell and was reluctant to leave our quiet haven again.

I was told in my guidance to avoid going into the hurly burly of town as much as possible and to remain close to the caravan. "When you go out from here your vibrations are greatly lowered and then they have to be heightened again to enable you to continue your inner work. It is important to keep your vibrations raised. If you need a break, take a walk and enjoy the wonders of nature around you." I was, however, given an effective method of protecting myself by seeking the sense of stillness and peace in the very centre of my being. "When you are in that state, the wrong vibrations ricochet off you instead of penetrating your whole being and causing damage." I found that it also helped if I put on a shell of protective light. This I did by imagining myself surrounded by light. Three times I encircled myself, feeling the light going round my whole being. In that centre of peace and stillness I managed to venture forth for a short while without being utterly devastated.

We were told that our aim was to raise our vibrations, and to help us to do this we were given instructions on what to eat. "You are building light-bodies; therefore absorb the light which you get from the food in the garden. This food is tended by the nature spirits, devas and angels who help provide the life force. It is not the amount of salad you eat; it is being in the right state when you eat it. Always give thanks for what you are given. This is vital food and it is precious. Your aim is to cut out all body-building food and eat the food that has the highest life force." We were told to refine our eating gradually, doing nothing drastic, but to follow the diet I was given from within. It had nothing to do with any known diet, so we could not turn to books for direction. We learned to live on vegetables from the garden, honey and fruit, phasing out first red meat, then white meat and poultry, then fish and finally cutting down on eggs. We found our sensitivity grew and we became more in touch with the spiritual realms and the nature forces in the gardens.

I ate only one meal a day of raw foods and drank pints and pints of pure, clear water, with no tea or coffee or stimulants of any kind. I was told that, as our bodies became finer and less dense, our skin would absorb substances from the ethers and the sun and air. "Bathing in the sea is good for the body. It tones it up. The more fresh air and sunshine you get the better, but on no account is this to become a fetish. Do all in moderation and enjoy it."

To be honest I got bored eating raw food all the time. It was a real struggle. Peter and Dorothy ate mountains of salads and lots of garlic, which is cleansing for the body. At first I refused to eat raw garlic until the smell forced me to in self-defence. But I didn't try to make the children eat only raw food. They had a cooked lunch with meat at school every day and in the evenings I cooked them a light meal with eggs, cheese or vegetables. We never tried to impose our way of life on them and allowed them to join in or not as they wished. Occasionally one of them would sit quietly with us while we were meditating, but most often they would be outside playing with their friends.

IN MY NIGHTLY MEDITATIONS I was introduced to a theme that was to be the cornerstone of my thinking. All along I had been told to banish negative thoughts and replace them with positive ones in order to raise the vibrations. Towards the middle of 1963 I began to receive specific instructions on the art of positive thinking. I was to learn that one can create anything through one's thinking and that there were specific techniques, such as repeating affirmations, for achieving this.

Peter's first spiritual teacher had given him a course of lectures in positive thinking which had provided him with the basis for his extraordinarily optimistic outlook on life, his pin-pointed concentration on the task at hand to the exclusion of all else and his determination to persevere until that task was complete. I sometimes felt Peter's positivity was almost inhuman, for he had no experience or concept of what it felt like to be afraid or to have doubts. His commitment to his unfolding spiritual work was unshakable. He had been told through my guidance and by others that he had been prepared through many past lifetimes for this work, and he believed it. He would allow nothing to get in the way. The reason he was shattered when I had left him to return to my children was that he believed my action was holding up God's spiritual plan which involved the two of us and desperately needed to be fulfilled. His commitment, drive and strength of will made him a difficult person to live with at times. I had none of his training or conviction; mine had to grow and unfold gradually within me over the years.

I was given this insight into Peter: "Consider the qualities of rock. It is firm, immovable, can withstand all the elements without being affected in any way. Peter is a rock. He has rocklike qualities which are absolutely· essential for the tremendous work he has to do. He must know where he is going and must sweep aside everything that stands in the way. It is a hardness and a ruthlessness which you find hard to understand because it is so opposite to the way you work. But that does not mean it is not right. I have given each of you different qualities to develop which should never at any time be compared. Suppose Peter were uncertain of himself, pulling himself up and wondering if he was wrong, or supposing seeds of doubt kept popping into his mind? He would be of no use to Me. I need him absolutely rock-like and immovable for this work he has to do.

"He is a great leader, and you will all need to accept this. He needs the full backing of all of you, although he will not waver in his task, whether you support him or not. He will bulldoze his way through to the goal and to victory. When you get annoyed or irritated by the way he handles things, try to realise how very, very difficult his task is and, instead of making it more difficult by resisting him, try going with it, try to understand and see what a difference that makes. Being a leader is a difficult and unpleasant task, but a true leader is not one who succumbs to the first bit of opposition. Doubts and fears have no place in his life. In the future you will see why I have chosen Peter to lead not just a handful, but many, many souls who will be drawn here when the times comes."

I began to study the lectures on positive thinking. I read them each evening, saying the affirmations aloud over and over again. I felt very silly sitting by myself repeating 'I am power, I am truth, I am love' and hoped no one would walk past and hear me! Besides, I didn't believe what I was saying. I still felt more of a miserable sinner than a powerful being of light. However, with encouragement I persisted and gradually my attitude began to change, imperceptibly at first and then quite noticeably. In a letter to Naomi, Peter commented:

> *Eileen is now a completely changed person. In fact at times she is rather like me in her positivity and cannot understand why she has been so long in learning that we are what we think we are and that it is only fear, doubt and negativity that limit us. Eileen can now see that, while God has been planning a perfect life for her, she has been cancelling it out by working in the opposite direction with her fears and negative thinking. Miracles are happening. She cut her thumb badly and affirmed, "I can heal," and a little later the cut was completely heated with just a tiny mark to remind her of it. God says this is just a small manifestation of what is to come in the future. At the moment she is just bubbling over and wants everyone to share in these discoveries she has made.*

Of course, these changes did not happen overnight, and I slipped back many times. But I had made a breakthrough. I had grasped the importance of attitude of mind. One day when I went into town to do some essential shopping, instead of the usual ordeal I found everything falling into place perfectly. Never had I done shopping so quickly and effortlessly. I found everything I needed without the least trouble. As I returned home, a great surge of joy and thanksgiving went through me when I realised that God's truths were coming about. I was putting all I was learning into practice, and it worked! In the stillness I received: "This is the most important thing you have ever learned in your whole life, and because of it your life has changed. You have been born again into the new, and the old is no more."

Peter was a great example to me once I got beyond my resistance and resentment. Having lived with him for so long, and so closely, I tended to take his good qualities for granted. But now I began to see why he focused his concentration on certain things to the exclusion of all else. To be able to manifest something in form takes pin-pointed concentration and tremendous positivity so that none of the power is dissipated. God told me: "You can learn so much to help you to live positively if you study Peter's way of life. You may have lived with it for years, but you have lived with many truths and they have meant little to you. At this time part of you is being awakened that has been dormant. You will find a new and deeper understanding of Peter and his way of life is developing."

I found that as my attitude improved and I became more secure in my relationship with God and in my own role in the group, I could appreciate the qualities of the others more. The repeated guidance on unity and teamwork was beginning to become a reality for me. I could feel us as parts of a body, each with its own job to do and yet all equally important to the functioning of the whole. We all began to put more emphasis on what we held in common rather than our differences. We still found that our main uniting factor was on the spiritual level. It was harder to bring our personalities into harmony but gradually it became a little easier to rise above the difficulties that arose from living together so closely. We never engaged in long discussions about our personal problems, however. As the years progressed, living together became more like the teamwork we had been encouraged to develop for so long.

Our daily lives and interactions as a group provided the practical classroom. Just thinking positively was not enough. We had to learn to act positively too. We watched a television programme on a group of mountaineers climbing in the Himalayas and I was staggered at the effort it took them to gain just a few inches of ground. The very thought of it made me feel exhausted and I despaired of ever achieving that kind of tenacity. I was told: "The reason for your despair is that you fail to live in the moment. You look ahead and think how impossible it all is. Just take one step at a time and enjoy it. Feel the exhilaration, the triumph."

The next day I was struggling to dig a trench in the stony earth of the garden when I hit a large boulder. Normally I would have given up, but this time I changed my tactics and scraped away at the edges, steadily loosening the boulder until finally I was able to move it. I was delighted when this small event was used in my guidance as an example of the importance of dogged persistence. "By doing that, anything standing in the way will be pushed aside. All this stood out so clearly as you worked, so you were not only doing a job but also learning an important lesson as well."

The purpose of learning to think positively and to control our thoughts was to learn how to create form by our thinking. "It is necessary to learn to ask for what you need. You are not to expect everything to fall into your laps but, as you ask, your needs will be fully met. Think of that which you need as a fact now, and keep on doing this until you see it brought about. You can bring about anything. You have seen this happen in several ways. You are truly grateful for all these gifts because you know they are from Me. They come through people because this is the way I work. People are My hands and feet to bring about My perfect gifts."

My first real experience of this 'art of manifestation' came when we needed £76 to pay for repairs to our car. We wanted to keep the car and yet on our small income that amount was way out of reach. I hated having a bill hanging over my head, so I was determined to do something about it rather than be forced to sell the car. When I was meditating on this, I was told to write to my solicitor in London and ask if I could have some of my money that had been tied up in my former marriage settlement. I held the amount in my mind, wrote the letter and waited for a reply. His first letter said that it was impossible to touch the money, but he asked whether I had ever received an income tax rebate on it. I had not, so I wrote and said so. Shortly afterwards a second letter came with a cheque for £76 – exactly the amount we owed. I was dumbfounded at first, but then sent it off to the garage with great joy and thanksgiving in my heart. Our need had been most perfectly met.

Not every example of creation by thought was as effortless as this, however. Naomi wanted to come and live with us and we were searching for a caravan for her. We found one that was perfect. When I went to God to ask what to do about it, I was told to write to Peter's father and ask him for a loan of £200. I thought this would be an awful cheek, particularly as he thoroughly disapproved of what we were doing but, as God had told me to do it, I went ahead. The letter I received back shattered me. He was furious that I had dared even to suggest such a thing and gave me a long, angry lecture about how Peter should get a proper job and how irresponsible we were not to bring the children up with the proper values. In response to my tears, God said: "There are lessons you have to learn. Have patience, persistence and perseverance and all will be well."

Then I was told to write to my sister and her husband with the same request. My sister's reply was even worse than my father-in-law's. This really threw me off balance. God said to me: 'Don't worry about the money for the caravan. I will open up another door for you. Know that I want you to have that caravan and see it as yours one day. This is teaching you to have unshakable faith, to follow My guidance, no matter how strange it is. Humans have been given the gift of free will, my child, and I can stretch forth My hand but I cannot force any soul to take it. I show you the way, but you of your own free will have to take it and follow it."

A few weeks later Dorothy's brother, Don, visited us. He was a shy person and I had met him only once before. When I received in guidance that I should ask Don for the £200, I absolutely shrank from it. I barely knew him and felt it would be most presumptuous. How could I ask a guest, a virtual stranger, for that much money? But God was unwavering. "You are wondering how to approach Don about this money. Ask him for a loan. Let there be no strain or stress. Just bide your time and approach the subject fearlessly and positively. You have need of the caravan and the money to purchase it. If I am with you, who could be against you? You have come up against two blank walls but it doesn't mean it will happen again. You are learning to be persistent. Never give up. Try another route and another until you have found the right one. It is My will; therefore your desire is not for yourself."

All evening, as we sat and chatted in the caravan, my stomach churned and the words went round and round in my mind. Eventually I found the courage to ask him. He sat and listened to the whole story but said neither yes nor no. When he left the next day, he still did not mention it and I did not ask again. Then I let go of the idea and more or less forgot about it.

Some weeks later I took the mail out to the field nearby where Peter and Dorothy were harvesting potatoes. There was a letter for Dorothy from her brother. In it was a cheque for £200. I burst into tears. My heart was filled with deep, deep gratitude to God and to Don, who was God's instrument in bringing about the promise. It had been extremely difficult for me, but I had held fast and it had worked. It was a most profound lesson and one for which I was eternally grateful.

Naomi eventually came from the United States to join us in spring 1964. It was a big step for her and not an easy one, as she was in her seventies and used to a very different life, surrounded by comfort and people to look after her. We did our best to make her comfortable. Her coming completed the 'four-square foundation' which marked the next stage in our growth from a family into a group. In a vision I saw God's hands laying four large stones in a square that was a solid, unshakable foundation for a temple. I was told we were those four and that we were ready to embark on the greater work. "The temple is now being built. The rock-like foundation has been laid. The four-square foundation – Peter, Dorothy, Naomi and yourself – has been established. The building has begun. Stone by stone it will grow, and it will grow fast. My child, I am well pleased with the work that is being done. Be prepared for great changes ahead, greater than you could ever imagine."

Our inner work with the magnetic centres intensified and with Naomi's great sensitivity we were able to reach and identify the centres more clearly. At the same time I was receiving stronger indications through my guidance that the world situation was deteriorating rapidly. "Wake up to the turbulent state of the world. Humankind is drawing further away from the source of all good into the darkness. You can feel the unrest, the disquiet, everywhere. Humans have brought this upon themselves by their self-will. They have made the choice of power, greed, hatred, jealousy and envy and must take the consequences. There is no hope of averting the landslide but exactly how it is to be brought about can be sped up or slowed down by the behaviour of the human race. The situation will become worse. Darkness will gather speed and envelop many of the countries of the world because people have turned their faces away from Me.

"You feel this is all very depressing, my child. Stand back and view it all from a distance and do not become involved with these shattering events. Be prepared for anything but be uninvolved. Think of the story of Noah. Your circumstances are very similar. He went ahead and did what I asked him and never allowed his mind or the opinions of others to mar the plan. My child, this place is a fortress created by radiations from above and below and within. It is the most powerful fortress that can be built."

The increasing urgency of these messages and similar ones received by both Dorothy and Naomi made me concerned about our proximity to the sea. From the sound of it we should expect tidal waves and gale-force winds, and the Findhorn peninsula is very exposed. What was the point of building a magnetic centre in such a vulnerable place? God's response was: "Do you imagine I would put you in a place where, when there is the first upheaval, you would be swamped? You will be safe, absolutely safe. I will never forsake you. Hold in your heart the same feeling you had during the war when you had bombs falling all around you. Your faith is a hundredfold greater now. Now you see why it is vital to make contact with the magnetic centres. All over the globe there are places where the light shines forth day and night, becoming stronger all the time. So lift up your heart; let it be as strong as a lion and yet as gentle as a dove."

For three years we had been virtually cut off from contact with the outside world and we had learned some priceless lessons. But our time of seclusion was coming to an end.

~ 6 ~

A whole new world is opening up for you. Be not afraid. This centre is becoming a beacon of light which will draw souls to it. Turn no one away. Judge no one, but see My hand in everything. Expand your thinking. You can do your part by holding the visions I give to you. This place is My fortress. It will flower and flourish because My blessings are poured upon it, because I am guiding and directing all that is done here. The young and old, all nations, all colours, all creeds, shall gather together in perfect peace and harmony in this place. See the work expanding beyond anything you have ever imagined, sweeping across the world like a mighty flame. My blessings are upon you and the work that you do.

IN SPITE OF OUR lack of money and the cramped conditions, those first years at Findhorn had been, on the whole, good ones. By the end of the third year I had begun to enjoy our life. The children were content, had settled into school and made friends easily in the village and caravan park. Our garden was flourishing and producing almost all our fresh food, which made balancing our tiny budget easier. We were a happy family unit with Dorothy living in the annex and Naomi and Lena and her children in their caravans close by. Our meditations were rich and fulfiling and much of the disharmony we had experienced had been smoothed out.

No sooner had I accepted this way of life and become comfortable with my daily routines than I received the following guidance: "Your time of seclusion is over. I have told you that you will be coming into contact with more and more souls. This place will become a sanctuary to those who are seeking the light. The magnetic power grows stronger every day and as it increases more souls of like mind will be drawn to it. Refuse to help no one when they come. Meet the need, but remember the pattern will not be the same for each of them, so be very guided with each soul that comes along. Some may come not knowing what has attracted them. They need very gentle handling. Feed My sheep and tend them, radiating My divine love and light to them. You each have a distinct and specific work to do with each soul who is drawn here."

I absorbed this information with fear and disbelief. I still could not see why people would be attracted to us, living where we did. I saw nothing particularly special about what we were doing. My inner life and my practical day-to-day life were still quite separate in my mind and I found it hard to imagine anyone wanting to come and help dig our garden and join in with our subsistence style of living. In fact, if we had been offered an alternative, I would have taken it gladly. Peter had been to dozens of job interviews and each time had been unsuccessful. He even applied for a post as store manager at the local RAF base but when they read his previous record in the RAF they refused to accept him for the job, as it would be 'below his station'. A number of times he was almost accepted for hotel management jobs, until his prospective employers spoke to Allied Hotels, who owned Cluny Hill, after which he was always turned down. My guidance continued to confirm that this was in the plan but the employment officer was mystified. Peter accepted it all quite happily and continued to work in the garden. After a while I too accepted things as they were and began to enjoy our simple outdoor life.

Now this new dimension had to be included in the scheme of things. Peter's response to my guidance on the expansion of our work was enthusiastic. Immediately he started to make plans to extend the area of the garden, seeing the possibilities for future growth and development. Since I didn't like the idea at all, I responded to his enthusiasm like a wet rag. I had no desire to emerge from our secluded life. I liked it the way it was. Besides, it took all our time until late at night to take care of what we had. We had no more time or energy for anything bigger. I went over in my mind how impossible it all was. We could barely fit six of us into the caravan at one time for a meal, and cooking was a feat in itself. How could I possibly manage to feed and accommodate more? And where would the money come from anyway?

I worked myself into a state of resentment. I was still feeling very sensitive from the long hours of meditation and my special diet, and the thought of coping with a lot of people, particularly if they were questioning us about what we were doing, made me feel once again like a snail without a shell. I had never felt comfortable with too many people anyway and had had to struggle to keep up appearances when we lived at Cluny Hill. I didn't want to tell others about the strange and wonderful experiences I was having in my inner world. These experiences were precious to me and I just couldn't bear to have strangers make a mockery of them. They would think I was crazy. For all I knew, they might be right.

God was very gentle with me. "My beloved child, let not your heart be troubled. Relax in My love and truth. First seek that inner peace and stillness; when you have found it, you can begin to stretch and stretch. Never limit Me. I have so much to reveal to you and I have given it to you bit by bit so that it will not overwhelm you. It is only your thoughts that limit Me. Read and re-read what I say to you each day. When I talk about faith belief or trust, dwell on those words. Affirm that you have absolute faith and trust in Me, until you know that you have. Listen to Me, converse with Me, discuss your problems with Me. All this draws you closer to Me."

True enough, once I began to accept that there were changes ahead for which I would be prepared in good time, my inner turmoil diminished and I was able to relax and become involved in the new lessons that were being given to me. I worked with the souls God placed on my heart, sending out love to them in very much the same way as we did to the magnetic centres. Some of these people I knew personally; others only through corresponding with them. I sent out love to Andrew and my children too. Because I was allowed no contact with them for years, I often became despondent but I was encouraged from within to continue to send the children gifts and letters and to radiate love to Andrew and each child in my meditations. In this way I held on to my faith in God's Promise that one day we would be reunited.

Sometimes I had the name of someone else placed on my heart and I would radiate love or healing to them. I often wondered what good it did, sitting there and sending them the love and the light radiances as I was directed. But I was told: "It is very important to do it constantly and not to let up. It does not matter if you see no visible signs. This is where faith is needed. The final choice always rests with that soul. All you can do is what is asked of you, but if that soul chooses to take the other path do not be concerned. Release them into My hands and be at peace. This is divine love."

Once in meditation I asked for my spiritual name. I had read a book about how people find their spiritual names and I was curious about mine. The word 'Elixir' flashed into my head. I asked God if this was it, and I heard: "What a long time I have had to wait for the penny to drop. Yes, indeed, that is your spiritual name." Then I recalled sitting and meditating in Sheena's fiat in London about ten years previously. I had felt as if a hot brand was placed on my forehead and the word that was branded there was 'Elixir'. At the time it was just another of so many strange experiences and I simply recorded it and thought no more about it. Now I was told the meaning of the name. "Your true name, Elixir, is described as eternal life, Which means that you are and you radiate forth eternal light. Bring this truth to mankind; bring belief to the unbeliever; bring hope to the hopeless; bring healing to those who faint along the way; bring comfort to those who sorrow and are broken-hearted; bring love to the unloved and despised. Stretch out and expand. There is no limit to the expansion, no limit to the vastness of your work. With the expansion I, the Lord your God, give you the help, the understanding and illumination. Therefore now do you indeed serve me to the very best of your ability, Elixir My beloved child."

I WAS IMPATIENT TO SEE the results of the work we had done on the inner levels and often doubted that there would be any, but I was cautioned to have faith. In good time the greater picture would be revealed to us and we would see growth and expansion beyond our wildest imaginings.

In August 1965 Peter's parents wrote to say they were moving house and they asked Peter to come to Devon to help them move. Peter saw this as a good opportunity to take Dorothy and Naomi to Glastonbury in the south of England and to contact people in spiritual circles in Britain. We had been told in guidance that it was time for the magnetic centres to begin to link up, and Peter was anxious to make those connections as soon as possible. He wrote a number of letters but was puzzled that he had no replies by the time they were ready to leave. They set off, leaving me on my own with the children for the first time. They were away for a week and Peter rang me at the call box on the caravan park every night, keeping me up to date with his extraordinary coincidental meetings with a number of people who were central to the New Age spiritual movement just beginning in Britain. Among these was a remarkable woman named Liebie Pugh, who was the focal point of a spiritual group known as the Universal Link.

This journey, with all its fortuitous meetings and instances of being guided to be in the right place at the right time, launched Peter into a series of trips away. In Glastonbury he had met Tudor Pole, founder of the Chalice Well Trust, set up to safeguard and preserve the ancient Holy Well in Glastonbury. Peter shared with him our experiences of connecting in meditation with Glastonbury as one of the magnetic centres we had been given. Tudor Pole received this with openness and confirmed that our work had not been unfounded. Peter returned from Glastonbury absolutely delighted with everything and bringing with him our first visitors, Dr Daniel Fry and his wife. They stayed with Naomi in her caravan, which was a tight squeeze but nobody seemed to mind. I cooked a special meal for everyone on my two-burner gas stove and we managed somehow to seat eight people in our living room. No one even noticed the crush because we were having such a stimulating discussion. My fears had been brushed aside in the excitement!

The obvious next step for Peter was to visit Iona, the island off the west coast of Scotland which has long had a spiritual connection with Glastonbury. So a month later he was off to Iona where he met John Walters who owned the St Columba Hotel. John was preparing to buy the other hotel on the island, the Argyll, and Peter offered to help him run it and plant a large vegetable garden there. Peter met some other interesting people, walked around the island visiting points of spiritual interest and returned home bursting with enthusiasm and excitement for the next phase opening up for us. In a vision of Iona I saw a great angel of light with wings outspread hovering over the whole island as if guarding and protecting it from the forces of darkness. It reminded me of a mother bird just about to alight onto its nest of eggs that were ready to hatch.

On the strength of Peter's feeling of connectedness with John and the island and the possibility of helping with the hotels, we decided to go to Iona together. We went in October. It was the first time I had left Findhorn for three years. It was a big step, but the gentle peace of the island drew me, allowing me to feel confident and comfortable about making the long journey. We had to cross the island of Mull to reach Iona and, as we approached it on the ferry, memories of my time there, first with Sheena and then alone in the cottage, flooded back to me. In spite of the pain I had gone through, the island seemed to welcome me, offering a reconciliation and an invitation to enjoy its beauty. My former distress dissolved and I felt a great love for the wild, rocky place that had brought me back to Peter and, more importantly, to God.

My first view of Iona, as we turned the corner into the tiny village of Fionnphort after the ride across Mull, was breathtaking. The beautiful green island, bathed in the soft autumn sunlight so characteristic of this part of the world, radiated tranquillity. The old abbey nestled against the soft, rolling hills behind it, reminding all who came here of the monk St Columba. He had come to Iona from Ireland many centuries before and kept the light of Christianity burning through the dark times of Britain's spiritual past.

We stepped onto the tiny ferry boat that braved the choppy waves to Iona. It was a pilgrimage so many before us had made and I felt connected with all those souls who had held the light burning in their hearts and had come to Iona to nourish their faith in God. Robert Louis Stevenson, Mendelssohn and Shelley had all spent time here. Mendelssohn had composed Fingal's Cave after visiting the island of Staffa not far away, and Stevenson had based the location of his book Kidnapped on a tiny island adjacent to Iona called Erraid.

We were warmly welcomed by John Walters and stayed with him in the St Columba Hotel. I felt as if I had come home.

During our visit I received a beautiful vision: I saw a great comet hanging over Iona. Its tail seemed to reach down and touch the very centre of the island. A great light filled the whole island, just as if a mains switch had been turned on. I was told in guidance: "This has been a very important and valuable pilgrimage. The linking together of these three centres of light – Iona, Glastonbury and Findhorn – is very important. Because you have come here in the right spirit, because you have absorbed the right radiations and in your turn have poured in radiations, you have become one with this place. Lift up your heart in deep gratitude for the beauty and glory and the wonderful experience of being here in this place of such spiritual power."

We were on Iona for only a few days but we had made a deep inner connection both with the island and with John and others whom we met. Again it was a confirmation that the work we had done in meditation for the network of light was indeed a reality on the physical level as well, and for this experience I was deeply grateful. It became apparent that the Argyll Hotel was not the place for Peter and me, as our work was at Findhorn, but the link we had made was far more important. I returned to Findhorn refreshed and nourished, with a deeper commitment to continue the work we had been doing and to expand myself to include whatever God had in store for us next.

MY GUIDANCE GAVE ME a great deal of information on how to handle the souls I was told would be drawn to us in their multitudes. I was as yet unable to cope with the idea of very many more than five or six so 'multitudes' sounded rather exaggerated and I dismissed it as God's way of getting me to stretch my thinking. God told me that my training had been rigorous not only for my own benefit but so that I would be able to help others on the spiritual path as well.

One of my greatest concerns about these people who were supposed to be coming to us was how we would know whether they were genuinely interested in our spiritual life or just looking for a free place to stay. I had been told to turn no one away, to give out love unstintingly so that not a soul would leave feeling empty. We were to open our hearts and our home to all who were drawn to be with us, no matter who they were or how strange they seemed. What if they took advantage of us and our openness and then went off without making any contribution? It seemed a huge risk to accept just anyone who turned up without knowing anything about them and their intentions. We might be inundated by 'freewheelers' or even worse.

In the mid-sixties the hippy movement was just beginning. We had not met any of these young people who had rebelled against the materialistic society they lived in and our only impressions of them came from newspaper reports and other people's opinions, none of which were very favourable. From what we had heard these people were 'dropping out' of work, university and society in general and wandering aimlessly about, living in a very unorthodox manner and looking for an alternative way of life. They seemed more interested in singing songs, playing guitars and lounging about than getting down to any hard work. With 'flower power' the rage and our involvement with gardening, the nature kingdoms and the beginnings of a small community, I was afraid these people might be attracted to us without any commitment to the spiritual life we were leading or to the hard work that was needed to survive. Peter's parents had already accused us of being hippies and that had incensed me. The last thing I wanted was to become identified with an irresponsible way of life. I had no idea at the time what was behind the hippy movement or what they were really searching for; to me they just looked scruffy and unkempt with their long hair and peculiar clothes.

I was reassured countless times in guidance that the right souls would be drawn to us because of the magnetic power of the place and the radiations of light that emanated from it. "You need never be concerned about the ones who come here, no matter how unlikely they may appear on the surface. Never judge a soul from the outside shell. Like attracts like. Seek for that spark of light within each soul and you will find a uniting force. Whoever comes to this place seeking will always leave in a different state. They cannot help but absorb the powerful radiations here. If they are in harmony, they will go uplifted and return again and again; if they are not, they will be uncomfortable and will leave with no desire ever to return. It is what is within that really matters and only I can reveal to you what is within each soul. Keep close to me and you will not go wrong."

So again I had to proceed in faith, putting aside my fears and doubts. I had to accept that people would be drawn here by a resonance with the light in their own hearts. I was also told that one reason we had been placed in such an out of the way spot was to ensure that only those who really wanted to find us would bother. For the merely curious it was too in-accessible; those to whom it was important would make the effort. "When you accept that this truly is a centre of magnetic power that draws souls from all over, you will see that the call will come to them and nothing will stop them. Distance, expense, time will mean nothing to them. That is why you must be ready at any hour to receive anyone, even to accommodate them."

I had a lot to learn about how to help these souls on their spiritual path by sharing my experiences of being guided by God every step of the way. It had been a painful process much of the time, learning to let go of my own control over my life to let God in, and it seemed to have taken such a long time. "When a soul comes here, it comes for the truth. It may not like what it gets; it may wriggle and squirm; but deep down, when the going gets rough, it will be everlastingly grateful for these words of truth. Simply accept that they have been drawn by the light. If they choose to stay here, there will be many lessons for them, but they will learn them far quicker than you have. You have been pioneers and have made the way easier for those who follow behind. The pruning will be very quick. It is not the pruning that is painful; it is the resistance to it that causes the pain.

"A piece of metal has to be tried and tested before it is used for something important, to see whether it can stand up to the strain it will have to endure. Many lives could depend on it. So it is with each of my instruments. I have often had to pull you up over your faults and failings and you often resented it. But always it has been for your own good. My greatest desire is to have a trustworthy instrument – my hands and feet – who never hesitate to do my work, no matter what."

I had to learn to pour out love without limitation and to know when a soul was ready to be given truth or 'light'. "Some will be ready to receive the light straight away; others will have to be prepared before the light of truth is shone upon them. The light can be very painful, especially if resisted, as you well know yourself. But every soul will be hungry, so feed each one with the right food."

The uniqueness of each individual was stressed over and over in my guidance. The image of a jigsaw puzzle was used: we were in the process of putting together a gigantic puzzle, with all the thousands of pieces mixed up. "It might look just a jumble of lines and colours to begin with, making no sense at all, but gradually, as the pieces come together, a picture begins to emerge and each piece has its place in relation to all the others."

The people who were being drawn to us were like the pieces of that jigsaw puzzle. Each person had a special gift or talent to give to the whole and it was up to us to draw the very best out of them. "Never must any soul be pigeon-holed. Each will have come along a different path and must be allowed to express its gifts freely. Their goals will be the same, so see the group as a perfect body with each part doing its work perfectly, moving in harmony with the others. Each part is necessary to complete the perfect whole and must be free to perform its function in its own specific way. This means elasticity of heart and mind to bring about the wholeness that is vital."

We had to be open to the many spiritual paths people had come along. There is no one path to God, no right way exclusive of any other. We had already seen this in our own small group where our spiritual backgrounds had been so different. I was warned: "Great sensitivity is needed, for each soul will come on a different beam and should be fed on the food of that specific beam or ray. The four-square foundation must be solid, open and willing to see the different paths without necessarily walking on every one. You will find that each soul has a unique approach and may receive messages in entirely different ways. Never be critical or imagine there is only one path. Each soul needs to trust implicitly what comes through it as a channel, and disbelief or criticism from another will cause chaos and confusion in the group. Learn to trust one another implicitly, for without trust there is no love."

Learning about love and the difference between compassion and sympathy was an ever-expanding process for me. I had grown up believing it was better to keep quiet than to say something that might upset people or hurt their feelings. Only with my children did I feel I had the right to pull them up when they had gone astray, which to me was a loving act. But I shrank from doing that with anyone else. It upset me to see people in trouble but usually all I dared do was sympathise with them and try to help smooth things over. God told me: "True love is not soft and indulgent. True love is very firm and loving, holding out a strong hand, ever ready to help. Love does not pander to the lower self, offering sympathy, because to do so would simply weaken and destroy. My divine love sees nothing but the very best in every soul."

I had experienced the power of the divine love I had radiated out in my meditations and wanted to be able to translate it into my daily encounters with people. That was more difficult. I also found it frustrating and depressing when, having been told from within what a soul needed in order to reconnect with its spiritual path, I sent the love and the light as directed and then saw no apparent effect. I was reassured and slightly amused to discover that God commiserated with me on that score! "Be not disappointed when things do not work out as you thought they would. There are many factors involved in people's lives and the greatest of these is free will. The final choice rests in each person's own hands and can upset the most carefully laid plans. Try to imagine what it is like for Me. I can see the perfect way and gently and lovingly I reveal it to a soul. Quite suddenly that soul decides it knows better and turns its back on my plan. I have to sit back and watch that soul make a mess of the situation; I can do nothing until it decides to do My will of its own free will. The final choice lies in the hands of that soul. All you can do, My child, is to know with all your heart, mind and soul that you have done all you can and have left no stone unturned. Should that soul choose another path, you must have no regrets. You will be handling many souls, My beloved child, and, though each one will be different, these are all basic principles which have to be learnt."

In my mind I struggled with a paradox. On the one hand I had seen how my own negativity, fears and emotional insecurity had interfered with my spiritual growth, with my connection with God. Peter supported and accepted my higher self, in evidence when I expressed myself clearly, lovingly and confidently, but he tolerated no negativity of any kind, particularly if it was accompanied by an emotional outburst. My guidance seemed to support his attitude. On the other hand, these feelings were a part of most people's experience and my guidance about love stressed the need for total acceptance and love for the whole person – a divine love which never criticised the other's failings. How was I to reconcile these two apparently opposing truths? What I couldn't understand was where compassion came in. How could I empathise so deeply with someone, understanding their pain because I had experienced it myself, and at the same time not encourage them to wallow in it? How could I be totally loving, in the way God was teaching me without giving support to a person's lower self?

PETER'S TRIPS AWAY CONTINUED and each time he returned even more excited than before, more often than not bringing someone with him. Early in 1966 he introduced me to a soft-spoken Scotsman from Edinburgh, R. Ogilvie Crombie or ROC as we came to know him. As we sat around the table in our caravan, ROC, a white-haired man in his late sixties, told us in his quiet, unimposing manner about his most extraordinary encounters with the nature spirits in the Botanical Gardens in Edinburgh. His story was like a fairy tale. As he described to us his first meeting with a little fawn called Kurmos, I was transported back into my childhood when elves and fairies had captured my imagination and I had almost believed they were real. I had grown up with the stories of 'the little people' that were so alive in Ireland but had come to believe that they were just a curious part of the Irish folklore, with no basis in reality. But there was something about ROC that was so genuine that one simply could not disbelieve him. He was a cultured man who had spent most of his life studying science, metaphysics and philosophy. His flat in Edinburgh was filled with thousands of books of every description. The quiet power and authority behind his manner carried such conviction that I felt I was in the presence of an exceptionally wise man who understood the nature of reality in a far wider sense than I did.

In spite of my respect for ROC, I didn't feel very close to him. Peter spent a lot of time with him and looked to him constantly for advice. They made a journey together visiting the spiritual 'power points' in Britain and returned with more stories of ROC's encounters with nature spirits and with Pan. They shared with me that ROC had run into several places which were dominated by the 'dark forces' and that a major part of his spiritual work was to transmute these into forces of light. I was mystified by this. I had experienced some sort of dark presence at the Trossachs and I had been told about the battle between light and dark in my guidance but my job had always been to turn my thoughts around to the positive and build up the light, giving no support to anything negative. I couldn't understand why ROC couldn't just work with the Christ energy in the way I had been taught to do. Why go out looking for dark forces? They sounded like energies outside ourselves and I had been taught to turn within for everything. If everything was within each of us, how could ROC work with things which were not?

I was very much at odds within myself about this, particularly since Peter thought so highly of him. I turned to God for some resolution to the disparity of our approaches: "ROC's role is to spotlight the evil, the darkness, and vanquish it. Peter and he are a very powerful force and must work closer and closer together. You know I have asked you to rise to realms where all is one, where all is unity and harmony with no duality.

This is the state of consciousness you are to aim for. You have your role and ROC has his. You are at opposite poles in the work you are doing, and in spite of this you have a deep love and respect for him, even though you cannot go along with him. This is an example of where there needs to be unity in diversity."

Peter tried to explain it to me further: "The forces of dark and light are an essential polarity in the world. The forces of darkness are our testers and at this time they are becoming stronger because of all the negativity in the world today. That is why it is important for us to be positive at all times and never allow a chink of negativity into our consciousness. ROC's real work is to balance these forces of darkness with light."

It took me years really to understand what Peter and ROC were talking about but in the meantime I found I could trust that ROC's work was important for our group. This was underlined for me when one day, as Peter and I were driving through the countryside, I saw a cluster of pine trees standing straight and strong, while every now and then I caught a glimpse of one lone tree which had been blown over and lay uprooted on its side. Suddenly I saw this as a clear symbol that unity was essential to withstand the storms of change. It helped me to accept the diversity among us and to be more willing to work toward perfect unity and harmony in our group, no matter what our differences might be.

I still had times when I felt rebellious and resented being used by God and by Peter. I wanted to feel I had a choice about what I did with my life and I questioned many of the directions I received in guidance. God gave me a gentle prod: "My beloved child, let your understanding be of the spirit. You cannot hope to understand things of the spirit with your mortal mind. It just does not make sense. It is like trying to decipher a code which cannot be broken. Let go and as you allow your consciousness to rise so will you understand My truths in the clarity of crystal, gleaming and shimmering in their glory. They will become you, the real you. Surrender your all to Me and learn to live twenty-four hours a day by the spirit, in truth."

Sure enough, when I did get into the state of feeling at one with God every moment of the day, I was filled with overwhelming joy and freedom. I felt so joyous I wanted to dance and sing, and I was encouraged to make this a constant experience. I did wonder how free will fitted into the scheme of things. How should we use it? Why did we even have it at all? It seemed that whenever I used my free will it was counterproductive to the overall plan. But I did feel an extraordinary freedom when I was in touch with my inner spirit-with God – for long periods of time. There was a key there somewhere.

WE HAD TWO SIGNIFICANT gatherings in the spring of 1966. The first was at Easter, the second at Whitsun. We had five guests for Easter – ROC, Iris and Ellie, Anthony Brooke and Monica Parrish, all of whom Peter had met on his travels south. Anthony and Monica had formed the Universal Foundation and had strong links with Liebie Pugh, as had Iris and Ellie. Our time together was exceptional and we experienced our spiritual connection even more deeply than before. We had been drawn together for a purpose and each of us felt it.

On Easter morning we had a profoundly moving meditation together and came out into the spring sunshine feeling elated, our hearts overflowing with love and joy. As I looked up, I saw a tiny lark soaring high into the clear blue morning sky, singing its ecstatic song for all to hear and rejoice with it. My heart lifted and connected with this little bird; it became for me a symbol of risen thinking. That day I was given in guidance: "This Easter time has been a turning point in all your lives. You have become one in My love and truth, to work together in a specific way you as yet do not fully realise. Keep close together, even when you are apart. Distance means nothing when you are united in My love. Rise, rise, rise! This is the time of resurrection. This is the time of tremendous expansion of consciousness, of great joy."

Never before had we experienced such oneness and love for each other and here began a new expansion of our group. Iris and Ellie returned frequently and helped start the process of sorting, typing and editing my guidance to make a booklet. The following year we printed the messages on an old copying machine and began to send them to all who asked under the title God Spoke to Me. I was told to keep it simple. "It is the very simplicity of those messages which will help many souls far more than you have dreamed. Let them open people's hearts so they long to give, but do not charge for them. All your needs will be fully met. My supply is limitless. Simply remember it is My word that is being sent forth to fulfil a deep need in a world in great travail."

TOP LEFT   *Aged 8 in Ireland, –'I loved my doll, Nanouche'.*

TOP RIGHT   *On board ship aged 13: I was responsible for my brothers Paddy and Rex and younger sister Torrie on the long journey from school in Ireland home to Egypt for the summer holidays.*

BELOW   *A much publicised society wedding in Kensington, London to the returning hero, Squadron Leader Andrew Combe, 1939.*

TOP   *Christmas 1963 – My first family of five children. For many years I looked at this photograph on my mantelpiece every day to help me visualise each one as I sent my love out to them.*

BELOW   *With David (3), Jonathan (4), Christopher (5) and Peter on the steps of Cluny Hill – 1960.*

Aerial view of Cluny Hill Hotel.

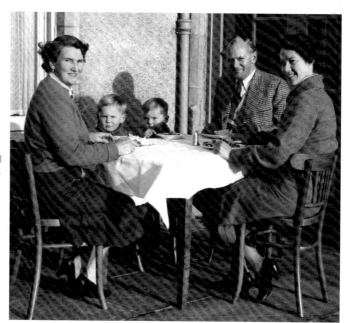

Lunching outside the Cluny Hill Hotel with Peter and Dorothy Maclean.

Our caravan and Lagonda car.

TOP
An early view of our caravan on its present site with Dorothy, Peter and myself on our newly built patio, with the beginnings of the garden on the sand dunes behind us.

CENTRE
Cedarwood bungalows around the central garden.

BELOW
Construction of the community kitchen and dining room.

PEACE
BE UNTO ALL WHO ENTER THIS MY
SANCTUARY
MAY MY PEACE DESCEND UPON YOU.
MAY MY LOVE INFIL YOU.
MAY MY LIGHT GUIDE YOUR EVERY STEP.
CAST ALL THE OLD ASIDE AND BECOME NEW IN MY SPIRIT.

TOP   *With David Spangler, Myrtle Glines and Peter.*

CENTRE   *With my best friend Joannie.*

BELOW   *The sign on the door to the Sanctuary.*

*And my Findhorn family grew and grew…
(with the Universal Hall in the background)*

With all my eight children, together for the first time ever, to celebrate my 80th birthday in 1997.

In front of 'Cornerstone', the ecological house at the Park built for me by my son David.

With co-author Liza Hollingshead.

With 19th grandchild Caitlin.

A recent picture, coming out of the Sanctuary.

photo by Adriana Sjan Bijman

Six weeks after Easter, at Whitsun, another group of people gathered. ROC was with us again and also four unexpected guests who arrived out of the blue, bringing the numbers up to 17. How I managed to feed them all, I don't know! We met on our small patio and talked and meditated together. Most of our visitors that weekend had been drawn to us because they had some connection with the many prophecies of the imminent destruction of the world, and some were members of the UFO society who believed that we had a common mission in the world. No one expected the rush of power that came into the group that weekend. We all experienced our consciousness being lifted and tremendous love and light – the power of the holy spirit – being poured into us. We felt as if an expansion had taken place, as if a new dimension had opened up. I received a series of messages in guidance that raised our discussions onto a level far beyond the possibility of the impending doom of the world.

I was told: "Rise out of the mire of despondency, behold My light within you, above you, around you and ever before you and *know* that wherever there is light, there is no darkness. Let there be joy and laughter, giving and receiving, a pouring forth of the holy spirit. This is a day of destiny. Lift up your hearts in deep thanksgiving. The tide has turned!"

We were all awestruck by the power of the guidance which came through me and its implications for our respective beliefs about the destiny of the world. "A tremendous power has been released and nothing can stop its onrush. You have all been brought together at this time so My holy spirit can fill you. There is no going back. Your lives have become new. All that is happening now is uniting the work you are doing for Me until there is no division. What you have experienced is in preparation for something far greater than any of you has ever contemplated. Glory, glory, glory, My heaven *is* here on earth!"

In some unfathomable way the tide had turned. Instead of working to prepare for the possible end of the world we knew, we now pledged ourselves to work as one to establish the new kingdom of heaven on earth. It was a momentous change in attitude for every one of us. We were told that from then on each soul would have to make the choice to step one way or the other. "You will find that many souls who have been sitting on the fence will now choose the way of the light. Pigeonhole no one, as some may seem most unlikely. Simply send forth this powerful energy which will do its own work."

I had a vivid dream the night before everyone left. I was standing on the edge of a big pool of pure, clear water. Someone was showing me how to throw a stone right into the middle of the pool so that the ripples would go out evenly all round. The bigger the stone, the more powerful the ripples. In guidance I was told: "Everything stems from the centre of your being like the stone thrown out to the middle of the pond. The ripples go out from the centre, touching everyone and everything in its area. Your area is expanding daily to the four corners of the earth. As the power that goes forth from this centre of light through each of you increases, the area grows until it encircles the whole earth."

When all our visitors had gone, I experienced the strangest welling up of emotion. Although my tears flowed, they were not ones of sadness or regret at saying goodbye to our friends; they came from a much deeper place in me that I did not understand. "It is the opening up of your heart centre which makes you feel everything so deeply and makes the tears flow so easily. It is a feeling of elation and deep, deep thanksgiving. Everything looks different and more beautiful, as if you went to sleep in the winter with everything lying dormant and now have awakened into spring. All is made new, but only because of your own free will have you chosen to open your eyes to see the new." I felt limitlessly expansive. This love could go on for ever, and I *knew* the meaning of limitless love, limitless truth, limitless wisdom. I *was* it.

IN THE SAME YEAR, 1966, I discovered my deep connection with Liebie Pugh. Peter had met her at her home at Lytham St Anne's in the north of England on his first trip south to make contacts in the new spiritual movement. My first meeting with her, however, was in meditation.

Anthony Brooke, who was very close to Liebie, was staying with us for a few days and we talked a lot about her and her extraordinary impact on the people who had been drawn to her. Anthony felt she embodied a unique quality of love; he himself had been deeply moved by his contact with her. Later, in our meditation together, I became aware of Liebie's presence there with us. Then I saw before me a being of great stature and light and I recognised the face of the master Jesus, the Christ. I heard a voice say distinctly, "Master," and Liebie and the Master were one and the same. There was a smell of fresh lambs wool from her robe in my nostrils.

I felt confused. What did this mean? As if in answer the voice said, "Talk to Anthony."

After lunch I took him aside and told him of my experience. I immediately saw that it sparked some kind of recognition in him. As I talked, Anthony was holding both my hands and suddenly I began to shake all over with a strange mixture of fear and exaltation. Finally the shaking subsided and a great peace and oneness came over me as I asked to be used for the highest. I felt utterly at one with Liebie and the Christ and I heard the words, "I am the Way, the Truth and the Life."

I wrote to Liebie, telling her all this, and we began a wonderful correspondence which continued till she died. On one occasion I wrote:

> *I share this with you because you are probably the only one who could fully understand it. This morning as we were radiating love and tight as a group, I became obsessed by you: your name kept ringing in my ears. Then I seemed to become a tiny red corpuscle which entered your bloodstream via the throat and began to course through your whole body. It was as if I had to pour life force into your being. I was so tiny and yet I was life itself. I don't even pretend to understand the meaning of this. I don't think I am 'going round the bend', although so many strange things seem to be happening to me; I no longer have any fear. Some time ago an experience like this would really have frightened me but this time I just went with it and found such joy in it, praise be.*

Not long afterwards, as I sat meditating in the public toilet, I felt the most terrible pains in my body, worse than anything I have ever experienced before. Wolves were ripping my insides out, eating me alive. Then I became aware of Liebie Pugh – and the pain was hers. I couldn't make out what it was all about and I ran home sobbing to tell Peter.

"Peter, I don't understand what has just happened to me. I felt this pain, this agony, inside me and yet I knew that somehow it was Liebie's pain, not my own. What does it mean?"

Peter listened carefully, but he was as mystified as I was. "I really can't explain it, Eileen, but don't worry about it. You've had so many extraordinary inner experiences; it will be explained all in good time. Just try and forget about it."

I tried to forget but it was impossible. Liebie was on my mind day and night. What was the pain? Then a letter came from Kathleen, a close friend of Liebie. "You know, of course, that Liebie has cancer," she informed us. Now I understood the pain! I had picked it up even though I had never met her or known about her illness. I felt as close to her as if we were one person. Never had I identified with anyone as closely as this, not even with Peter or my children.

The experiences continued. I wrote to Liebie:

> *This evening I was meditating. My thoughts were with you and I seemed to become one with you, suffering great pain. I was given a vision of your body disintegrating; it was a slow and very painful process. My heart ached; my whole body was wracked with pain. I wept and called out to God, asking him why it had to be done this way. He said it was all in his plan, and not to resist what I was being shown. As your body disintegrated, I saw in its place the Christ in a wonderful, radiant light and it was made clear to me that this was how it was to come about. Do you understand? I don't, but it was absolutely clear that this is the truth, so I accept it and pass it on to you. Let me share some of this pain, dearest Liebie.*
>
> *In your love and service, Elixir*

Soon after, I received her reply.

> *My Elixir*
>
> *To know that you are actually registering a bit of the extreme degree of the pain gives me this comforting little assurance. It is stiff — recently it has been extra so — and I wanted to tell you that your sharing it has helped. I still hope it is rare and short, I always feel I am such a coward about it (you will understand) and your writing and sharing about it as you did helps me. It is easing a bit now.*
>
> *This is the way it must be from now on — the Risen Consciousness. When I find myself in the new dimension, all is Love and Light. I hold you in that dimension in the now, and always.*
>
> *Your Liebie*

This letter brought me indescribable joy and I treasured it. Then, one day as I was sitting waiting to take the boys out, trying to create a sense of peace with the three of them jumping all over me, God told me to re-read Liebie's letter. I took it out of my handbag and, as I started reading, my eyes seemed to be opened anew. I saw the words 'My Elixir' and I understood fully my experience of being the red corpuscle. I was her elixir. I was a fountain of healing helping to lift her into a higher state of being. I felt full of awe.

The next day in meditation I was given the words: "You are Mary, the mother of Jesus the Christ." I was shocked. That sounded blasphemous to me. How could I possibly be Mary? That morning, as I was on my knees making the boys' beds, I asked God how it could possibly be true.

"Can you accept it as a 'ray', the Mother ray, the Love ray? There are many, many souls on the Mary ray."

Of course I could accept it, put this way! The idea of many people being on a ray of expression similar to that of Mary, the mother of Jesus, made sense to me. It meant that I – and all those other people – had an affinity with those qualities we associate with Mary. Then, coincidentally, I read a book, The Michael Power of Glastonbury, in which the author describes her experience of becoming Mary and being told to 'take this to all the Marys in the world'. The essence of quality of Mary could be given to others on the same ray of expression. The pieces of the jigsaw started to fall into place for me. I began to understand my deep compassion for Liebie in her pain.

And so I finally came to meet Liebie at her home at St Anne's. We spoke very little; there was no need for words. I sat holding her gloved hand, wanting more than anything to pour into her the strength and love she needed. I felt as a mother does towards a beloved child in need. My heart was filled with an indescribable love for her. Several times while I was with her she stood up by the fire and seemed to grow as great in stature that her presence filled the entire room. It was a very strange experience and one I have never forgotten.

My relationship with Liebie was unique, exalting and painful. Her letters were an inspiration to me, encouraging me to 'make the word live', so that not one word lay idle. She helped me see how everything fitted together perfectly. I wanted to shout from the rooftops, "I'm not mad! I'm not mad!" as she confirmed that the inner experience I was having with her was real. I wrote to her:

> *I do not understand the meaning of the terrible pain I have shared with you, but I accept it as part of God's plan and revelation. A part of me seems to understand so much, whereas the other part of me seems like a helpless little child, completely lost, trying to find its way. This is, I suppose, the difference between being in the third dimension and being in the fourth dimension where all is so clear and in the light, where truth is Truth. My love to you, dearest Liebie, and again thank you, thank you for your help, your understanding and your love.*

By the end of 1966 Liebie's health was failing but her spirits were high. I was given a vision of her lying in agony and heard the words: "My child, put your hands underneath and lift." I did this, but she was too heavy, so I cried out to God for help. As I continued, I found strength had been given to me and I could lift her. As I did so, she turned into purest light and I knew that this was the true meaning of 'risen thinking'. I also knew that was what I could do to help her, lifting her and my thoughts into the light at all times. Every day I meditated on lifting her, sending her loving thoughts and paying no more attention to the pain in her body.

In December Peter was called to St Anne's for an important meeting of the Universal Link, people connected with Liebie and her work. I remained at Findhorn, meditating as often as I could during the day and night. On the day of the meeting I meditated alone all day with Liebie's photograph on the table in front of me, joining them on the inner realms. At noon the photo suddenly fell off the table and I knew that part of her was gone. I felt her spirit moving away from her body, becoming lighter and freer every moment. At 11:30 that evening she left her body. I was filled with the deepest joy as I felt Liebie released from the earth plane into the plane of light where she belonged. There was no regret or sadness, only perfect joy. Liebie's task was complete.

I was given powerful words by God about the significance of this change: "Today is a day of days. There will be a tremendous release of power, so be ready to receive it and absorb it. Remember when things look their worst that this is a great time of rejoicing. There will be a time when faith and belief in each one of you is fully tested. You may not yet have fully realised that the power from St Anne's has been implanted here. You will expand very rapidly. This will become a centre of fully dedicated souls, so be prepared."

AT THIS TIME I WAS ALSO TOLD that Peter and I had a very close link with Joan Hartnell Beavis, who had been Liebie's supporter and protector, taking care of her every need in the most dedicated and loving way. When I went to St Anne's for the vigil for Liebie, I felt this connection with Joanie and a strong bond of love began to grow between us. Not long afterwards she made arrangements to move to Findhorn.

Joanie became my greatest friend and staunchest supporter through the years, an open, accepting listener to all the tales I told her, no matter how bizarre or traumatic. She has been a true friend in every way – perhaps the only real friend I have ever had. Once, after I had been in hospital for an unpleasant operation, I returned home feeling weak, as if the life force had drained out of me. Joanie put me to bed in her spare room and tended me with devotion day and night. As I lay there in my weakened state, all I could think of was how I would love a piece of steak! I couldn't ask that much of her; for years she had been a committed vegetarian. The craving persisted for days, until finally I plucked up courage. "Darling, I don't know how to ask you, but I have a craving for meat. Could you possibly get me some?"

Without a moment's hesitation Joanie drove into town and stood in line in the butcher's to buy steak for me. She did this every other day until I was better, with all the love in the world and without a thought for her own distaste at the idea of going into a butcher's shop, let alone cooking the meat herself. To cap it all, when my doctor came to see me, he thoroughly approved of my new diet and, as I was unable to sleep, encouraged me to have a 'dram' of whisky at night . . . the best Scottish medicine! So this, too, Joanie bought for me and my energy returned rapidly. Peter always loved to tell this story and watch people's reactions. He felt it was a good illustration of how there are no hard and fast rules about anything, least of all spirituality.

It was Joanie who gave me my first washing machine. I protested violently as I felt I had nothing to give her in return. I was told in guidance to be grateful for the gifts I received. "I have told you all your needs would be met from My limitless supply and now you behold this coming about.

The reason for the gift is to simplify the work for you so that you have more time for My work, which is what really matters in life." I was deeply grateful and thought it was a novel way of looking at the value of modern conveniences!

The following year was filled with building, receiving people and sharing our life with them, and we were busy and fulfilled. As the year came to an end, we looked back at the growth that had taken place in ourselves, our gardens and our budding community – for that is what it was by now – and saw how miraculous it all was. From nothing had sprung a small garden of Eden and from three we had increased to twelve, all in little more than five years. Our connections with others on the same spiritual 'wavelength' were solid and deep and we could see that everything God had promised was gradually coming about.

On Christmas Eve 1967 I was told from within to ask Joanie and Peter to take me up to the top of Cluny Hill to a special place we had found years before. I was told: "I need the three of you as *one* at that specific time." There had been a great many predictions from all sorts of sources that the world was going to end at about this time, that Judgment Day was at hand. I paid no attention to these prophecies of doom and gloom, as I was committed to raising my consciousness towards the light. So on Christmas Eve at midnight we followed the clear instructions God had given me: "Stand with Peter behind you and Joanie and you hand in hand. Peter is to put his left hand on your shoulder and his right one on Joanie's. Stand like that, letting the power flow through you, welding you into one. Then, when I tell you, stand in a circle with Peter on your left and Joanie on your right. From the time you get out of the car until you get back into it again Peter is to be on your left and Joanie on your right. The force of power that will flow through you will be tremendous, but it will be perfectly controlled. You are doing this not just for yourselves but for the multitudes, and the outcome will have far-reaching results. Be prepared for anything."

As we stood together holding hands, I felt my body fill with light. I began to tremble violently and then collapsed, unconscious. Peter and Joanie supported me and even they, who both claimed to have no sensitivity at all, were rooted to the spot. Finally, as I came to, I experienced an absolute oneness with Peter, with Joanie and with the entire universe. I felt I was plugged into the cosmic power source and that we three had provided some sort of anchor or earthing point. We were all moved beyond words and had no idea what it all meant, nor what had actually happened.

We returned home in a state of radiant exhilaration. Something truly momentous had occurred – for us and for the whole world – but we were incapable of defining what that might be. Immediately afterwards I received: "My beloved, lift up your heart in deep joy and gratitude for what took place at midnight. You three are now one for all eternity as you were in the beginning. You have completed the full cycle. Nothing will ever separate you, for you are now of one mind, one heart, one spirit in Me.

"This is the turning point for every soul. The die has been cast, and each soul has to make a choice: a turning towards the light or to the dark. The day many have been waiting for is over. The cosmic power released at that appointed moment, felt by you and many others, has begun to reverberate around the universe. Nothing will stop it. It will gather momentum and power and it will be sensed by many as time goes on. Some may be disappointed because there was no outer manifestation. Nothing has gone wrong. It is simply that man has misinterpreted what has been prophesied. It has often happened that way.

"This is the beginning of the universal happenings all over the world. This place will become world-renowned, for nothing will be able to stop the expansion of the work going on here. This release of cosmic power into the whole of the universe is far greater than you can ever imagine. Your feeling of an uplifted consciousness is the start of great changes that will be felt by each individual everywhere. Forge ahead from strength to strength with My hallmark deeply imprinted, and be at perfect peace."

~ 7 ~

In a vision I saw Peter holding a banner on high, embroidered with a single red rose. On his right hand stood Sir George Trevelyan and on his left was Anthony Brooke. Following them was a great multitude of people, carrying spades, picks, sickles, baskets of food, pots and pans and all the implements needed for reconstruction. I heard the words 'Pioneers of the new age'. Every now and again there was a great shout from them all, "Hallelujah' and as they shouted their praises a great wave of light went out from them. Above I saw on a higher level great and lesser beings of light watching over this great multitude, and I felt something tremendous was happening.

WE WERE LAUNCHED into an intense, exciting time of expansion. My inner life was focusing more and more on building the community and less on my personal struggles. Almost overnight, it seemed, word of what we were doing in our tiny corner of Scotland had spread and all sorts of people, young and old, began to arrive on our doorstep, drawn by the magnetic spiritual power which had been generated. There was so much to be done: we needed to find more accommodation; we needed a Sanctuary to replace Naomi's caravan, which was too small for us all now; and the gardens were expanding rapidly to provide fruit and vegetables to feed the increasing numbers of people. It was a busy, fulfiling time.

Initially the people who were drawn to us had heard about our work through their connections with spiritual circles in Britain. Many of those who got in touch with us had known Liebie Pugh and were part of the Universal Link, while others had met Peter on his trips south, particularly at a conference held by Sir George Trevelyan, one of the pioneers of the new spiritual movement in Britain who was to become our close friend and supporter. Sir George was so enthusiastic about what we were doing that he brought Lady Eve Balfour of the Soil Association up to see the outstanding results of our cooperation with nature in the garden. The report she wrote on her visit in turn caught the imagination of many people and prompted them to visit us. They did not come in droves to begin with, just a small trickle, but the word was to spread to the extent that by the end of 1970 we would have about fifty people of all ages living with us. Our little booklet, God Spoke to Me, reached many people who were moved by its simple, clear message and came to see for themselves what we were doing. Some of them stayed; others continued to visit and lend their energy, support and enthusiasm to the growing community.

One couple, Aileen and Ross Stewart, were to play a vital role in the future of the community. They had known Joanie for many years and Aileen was very interested in what had been happening at St Anne's and had visited Joanie there. Ross was a retired naval captain who understood a great deal more than he was prepared to let on, particularly to his naval friends. However, when they first visited us as Findhorn, he was most apprehensive about 'these spiritual types'. I think he had an image of people living up in the clouds, aloof from the mundane world and ready to launch into heavy preaching on moral and religious values at the first opportunity. He soon came to see that we were perfectly practical. Not long after Ross and Aileen arrived, their dog disappeared for a while and returned covered in black mud, smelling like the neighbouring pig farm she had obviously been visiting. I saw Ross looking sideways at me, wondering how this 'spiritual type' would react. Naturally I scooped the dog up in my arms and took her into our tiny bathroom, where I dunked her in the bath and gave her a scrub. I was no stranger to unpleasant smells after Peter and his compost!

That same evening Peter took Ross and Aileen down to the small hotel in Findhorn village where they were to stay.

"Will you have a drink, Peter?" Ross asked.

"I'll have a pink gin," was Peter's prompt reply.

That clinched it. From that moment Ross and Peter got on famously, exchanging stories about the navy and the air force before moving on to talk about the deeper things they each felt so strongly about.

"I was rather dubious about coming here," Ross confessed, "because some of Aileen's friends are so airy-fairy. But it's a relief to see that you are not above living in the normal world. I feel we have a great deal more in common than I first thought."

Ross wanted to hear more about what we were trying to achieve with our budding community. Peter was always ready to provide an explanation to anyone who showed an interest. "Our aim here, Ross," he began, "is to bring the kingdom of Heaven down on earth. Each of us has come along a different spiritual path and people of all religions or no religion are welcome. It's a totally new concept of living. We're pioneering a new way of life which will require a new type of person. We shall be given more and more scientific proof that the teachings of all the great masters and teachers down the centuries are not impossible moral injunctions but exact, precise and definite facts. Thus, science and religion, rid of all narrow dogma, will come together in total harmony."

Peter paused and took a sip of his drink. Ross stirred. "Some people would say you're just opting out of society and encouraging others to do the same," he commented.

"Ah, but we're a *working* group," Peter emphasised. "Everyone who comes here has to be willing to contribute their talents and to work hard. There's no room for those who want to drop out of society or sit back and do nothing. The fact that we are trying to build a strong group centred in God doesn't mean that all we do is meditate together. We have to translate that into practical terms, so that we are expressing God's love and unity every moment of the day."

Ross nodded in growing understanding and interest. "Well, it's certainly a huge task you've set yourselves," he said. "How do you even know where to begin?"

Peter smiled. "We just do what has to be done, step by step. If something seems impossible, we go ahead anyway in faith and trust. We usually don't have the necessary money or resources at the beginning but if we act as a unified group, depending totally on God's unlimited supply, we usually find that we achieve our aims."

Ross responded enthusiastically. "In all my experience of working with the men on board ship," he said, "I've known that the spirit of co-operation and unity was the most important factor in achieving our goals. When it is happening, God is present, although we don't always acknowledge it. How much more we could achieve if that common spiritual connection were consciously recognised. We'd become true soldiers of God!"

OUR TRUST IN THE ART of manifestation was central to this stage of building the community. We still had no income and any expansion was done in absolute faith. One morning as I was waiting for Joanie to take me into town, I stood beside her bungalow looking over the tangled mess of gorse and rubble and in my mind's eye I had a vision of seven cedarwood bungalows before me, surrounded by gardens, trees and flowers. When I shared this vision with Peter, his immediate response was, "But you couldn't possibly fit seven bungalows in that space!" I shrugged and left it at that. I had had so many strange visions and inner experiences which seemed to make no sense at the time. Besides, if Peter didn't think it would work, then probably it wouldn't.

That evening, however, I was given this guidance on how to manifest a vision into physical form: "I give you a clear vision – for example, of those seven bungalows – and with your inner eye you see them clearly placed there. Now hold that visions, fix that photo with fixing solution to make it permanent, and work on it from there. Actually see the seven bungalows placed in their rightful positions and do not concern yourself about who is to have them. That will all come. See that whole area a place of beauty and perfection and know that it is but the beginning of a great expansion here. All will be brought about, guided by Me."

Not long afterwards the two caravans that were situated on the edge of this area were moved, so Peter went to measure it out. "You were quite right," he told me. "There is room for six more bungalows to go behind Joanie's. But where will they come from?"

"I don't know," I said, "but my guidance has said to hold the vision for them and they will be there."

So we set about manifesting them. We marked out the plots and started to clear away the gorse bushes. The owner of the caravan park was quite happy with any attempts to improve the appearance of the place, and let us get on with it. Then someone offered to tip a lot of building rubble there which helped to fill in the hollows and provide a more solid base on which to build. When Aileen and Ross Stewart heard we were planning to put up some bungalows, they wanted to buy the first one. I received the vision of the bungalows on 28 January 1968 and by Easter Sunday, 14 April, three of them had been erected, complete with furnishings. Anthony Brooke and Monica Parrish bought the second for the Universal Foundation. The third was paid for by a dear friend of ours, who had wanted to buy a bungalow for our family. Since the need for guest accommodation was urgent, Peter decided that for the time being we would stay where we were so that the new bungalow could house some of our many visitors.

In the meantime the need for a Sanctuary was paramount. Naomi's little caravan, which had served us so well over the years, had become far too small for our ever-expanding numbers, and it was clear that the time was ripe for a special building for meditation and times of quiet for the group. I held the vision God had given me of a simple cedarwood building for this purpose. In spite of this, it was slow in coming.

Since most people who were drawn to us initially had been involved in spiritual circles already, many of them were very sensitive to other realms and received their own forms of guidance. Peter loved to hear guidance from sensitives and mediums and always took them to the spot earmarked for the Sanctuary the moment they arrived, encouraging them to share their visions with him. It didn't bother me, as my own guidance was so clear and explicit. Besides, it was pointless to disagree with Peter, as he didn't listen to what I or anyone else had to say unless it came in the form of guidance from a higher realm.

So whenever Peter told me that someone had received a vision of the Sanctuary with an inner and outer sanctum, or with a glass dome to let in the light, or even with a hole in the ground to let in the earth energies, I said nothing. I held the image of a simple building with no extensions or trappings inside or out and let everyone else get excited about their visions. I knew they wouldn't work out, but I was too meek and unsure of myself as a person to voice my opinion.

Finally, Peter came to me. "There's all this energy and enthusiasm for the Sanctuary, and it's obviously a need, as Naomi's is too small for all of us, so why isn't anything happening? Could you get some guidance on it, so we can find out what is blocking it?"

Without saying a word, I turned within and wrote down: "My beloved, as soon as there is absolute unity concerning the Sanctuary, it will be brought about. It is not enough to say a Sanctuary is needed. When I give you a clear vision, that must be held without deviating. Up to now there have been too many different ideas from various people and the perfect picture has become blurred. Let Me stress again the need for beauty and simplicity. You hold the vision of a simple cedarwood building and I have shown you where it is to go. It is not to have any extensions. The Sanctuary will be the focal point of the whole community and it must be perfect in every detail. The secret of manifesting is to have a very clear picture; to be completely united about it and know that nothing can stop it coming about because it is part of My perfect plan for this magnetic centre."

Instantly Peter dropped all the other ideas about painting it in colours having a certain spiritual significance, or adding rooms for healing, or putting a dome on the roof. He wrote to ROC telling him about the confusion as a result of listening to different sensitives and trying to incorporate their embellishments into the design. Peter acknowledged: "Again it has been brought home to us that it must be God and God alone who gives the direction and reveals the way. There is a great need for unity on the matter of the Sanctuary." Peter may not have paid any attention to my personal opinions but when it came to my guidance he was willing to drop all other ideas and follow it to the letter.

From then on things went smoothly. We ordered a prefabricated building of cedar and the money for it came in unexpected ways. Manifesting the Sanctuary was an important step for us and we learned many lessons. We were told to order the very best materials, carpeting and chairs, and when the time came to pay for them the money would be there. I was told: "All must be pleasing to the eye; all must be harmonious and blend in perfectly. The most expensive is not necessarily the best, however, so never be guided by prices when choosing something. Feel deep within and know it is absolutely right, then go ahead and get it. Count not the cost. Remember what I have said about beauty and simplicity and don't get carried away by anything exotic. When in doubt, be very still and allow Me to reveal the right things."

When it came to furnishing the Sanctuary, we used the colours given in guidance to ROC: gold, green and magenta. We chose a dark green carpet that would wear well and a friend who owned a furniture factory ordered it for us. When it arrived, we were informed that he had paid for it as well. It was a leap in faith to order fifty chairs to be covered in expensive washable velvet dralon, but we did it. They were beautiful. When I was told in guidance to order another twenty, I swallowed. The miracle happened when that very day we received a cheque from someone in Canada for the exact amount we needed! We chose heavy magenta and green curtains to keep in the warmth on the long, cold winter nights when the sun went down at four o'clock and didn't rise again until eight the next morning. And as each bill came in, somehow we had the means to pay for it through the donations of so many people who had visited us and wanted to support us in what we were doing, and also many who had never even seen us but had read *God Spoke to Me*, the little booklet we continued to send out on request.

I had specific guidance not to put any ornaments or artifacts into the Sanctuary, as it had to be a place of peace and harmony with no allusion to any one spiritual teaching. "Great care must be taken that the Sanctuary is not cluttered up by gifts from people who want to contribute something to it. You will have to decline their offers gracefully and lovingly. Let there be nothing that will distract or label you in any way, so all can enter and become part of the whole instantly. It will be the vibrations in the Sanctuary that will strike people more than anything else, so right from the start let it be a place where all who enter will feel perfect peace and love surrounding them, and stillness will fill their whole being with nothing to disturb or distract."

Then I was given these words to be inscribed in beautiful handwriting and placed on the doors of the Sanctuary:

> *Peace be unto all who enter this My Sanctuary,*
> *May My Peace descend upon you,*
> *May My Love infil you,*
> *May My Light guide your every step,*
> *Cast all the old aside and become New in My Spirit.*

On Easter Saturday 1969 the Sanctuary was completed. And on that very day a beautiful silk weaving representing the sunrise arrived by post from the Donovourd Weavers in Pitlochry. We placed it on the wall in the Sanctuary – its only adornment. On Easter Sunday we held our first meditation there and I was full of joy and thankfulness for this still place in the heart of the community.

IN ADDITION TO MANIFESTING buildings and furnishings we also began to attract more and more people. When Peter drove down to Hull earlier that year to order the first bungalows, he ran into Dennis, a young friend of ROC's, who had heard about what we were doing and was keen to come and see for himself. Coincidentally he had just given up his job, so he packed his rucksack and came back with Peter.

"All I want is fresh air and plenty of exercise,'" he told Peter.

"Well, you'll get plenty of both with us," Peter replied, grinning, as he sped back up the motorway. And he did. Dennis was responsible for laying all the foundations for the bungalows and the Sanctuary. He was an extremely dedicated worker, a perfectionist, and he put all the right vibrations of love and care into the foundations he was building. Others turned up to help, and the air rang with the sounds of shovelling, hammering and singing all spring, as every able-bodied person lent their energy to the buildings in progress.

A friend of Dennis, John Willoner, who was teaching in England, came up to visit him several times and joined in the work with enthusiasm. Finally he gave up his teaching job and brought his wife Janet to live with us. They were the first of a new wave of younger people drawn to us and added a new dimension to our group. They worked from dawn to dusk, doing anything at all that was needed with such enthusiasm and willingness it was a joy to have them around.

Not all the young ones fitted in as easily as Dennis, John and Janet, however, and we had some difficult experiences with a few who thought this was a hippy commune complete with long hair, dirt and drugs. They were swiftly disillusioned and sent on their way. Others just weren't ready for the sort of commitment to work that we, and most particularly Peter, expected of them and they moved on of their own accord.

Although there was a tremendous amount of work to be done and we all spent long hours on the job, there was also time for fun and laughter, and particularly for walks and hikes in the hills and swimming in the icy waters of the North Sea on our doorstep. Peter has always loved the outdoors and he gladly went off with the others to climb mountains and swim, although not as often as he'd have liked to. Our three boys loved these hikes and frequently went along too. They camped and walked, climbed mountains and cliffs, and went caving and canoeing in all weathers. John and Janet were particularly close to Christopher, Jonathan and David. Having been teachers they had a special affinity with the children, who were by now nearly teenagers. The fact that the boys had so many people with whom to do interesting things did, I think, make up for having two parents thoroughly engrossed in the work of building a community from scratch. Although I was always there for them and put my job as mother before other work, nevertheless I was doing many hours of meditation each night and would never, even if we'd lived an ordinary suburban life, have had the time or the inclination to go on the kind of outdoor camping trips John and Janet organised. And although Peter greatly enjoyed the outdoors, the responsibilities of the growing community took much of his time and attention, leaving little to spare for the three energetic lads.

Peter and I worked very closely together. We were frequently described as the perfect balance between light and love and we functioned as two halves of one whole. From time to time Peter had to wield the 'sword of truth' with force and clarity. He was uncompromising in his standards of perfection and positivity and expected nothing but the best from everyone who joined us. All who put themselves before the good of the whole or who expressed a single negative thought received a swift shaft of light from Peter. He liked the image of a gardener I was given in guidance: "You have witnessed the pruning of a rosebush with all its stalks cut right down until there is nothing left but a stump. As you beheld it, your heart ached and you wondered whether the pruning had been too severe or even if it was really necessary. Then in the right season you see healthy, strong shoots springing forth, growing in beauty and strength to bring forth the most glorious blossoms for all to enjoy. You realise that, if that severe pruning had not taken place, the bush would have grown up tall and straggly and the blooms would have been small and stunted. So it is with people."

I was told that this was one of Peter's roles – to prune those who were drawn here of all the old, the negative. He had been trained to do this by

Sheena, who had very effectively used the sword of truth on him. I did feel at times that Peter's expectations of people were too high. He felt they should have the same stamina and standards of perfection as his own. His eagle eye missed nothing and he had the uncanny knack of appearing round the corner just as someone was sitting down for a rest or a chat, giving the impression that they had done nothing else all day!

It fell to me to spend time with people, talking about their problems and helping them to work things out in a more gentle, loving way. I knew what it meant to be stripped of everything, to reach rock bottom, when all that was left was to cry out to God for help. I could empathise with those souls floundering in their search for God within themselves, battling with their stubborn, unyielding personalities; I had been through it all myself. At the same time I could encourage them to persevere, as my own experience had shown me that it was well worth the struggle. And although my relationship with God was very sound and very, very deep, the struggles had never ceased altogether.

Peter had never experienced such difficulties, as he had always been committed to putting God first in his life. Never having been through the pain of separation and loneliness, he could not understand why anyone should bother with emotional traumas, which only got in the way of doing God's work. He was right in a way, but whereas he failed to see that when you are immersed in emotional resistance it takes over, making it difficult to see the light at the end of the tunnel, I could understand it perfectly. So Peter's light and my love were a perfect complement to each other. There was no conflict; our goals were identical.

WE DID HAVE SOME unusual people turning up, and if I had not had so much guidance, repeated over and over, about being open to everyone who was drawn to us, no matter how they dressed or what they looked like, I am sure we would have turned many wonderful souls away. So, although some of the young people who found us were long-haired, scruffy and very often dirty too, we welcomed them and gave them a place to stay until Peter had discovered why they had come. It was always Peter's job to do this, and his interviews were short and penetrating. He looked for three qualities in a person: a sense of being guided to the community by a higher force; a practical skill that was needed; and a willingness to work hard. If any of these was missing, he let them stay for a night and then sent them off. If, however, someone turned up who was an obvious 'manifestation' for a particular job, Peter welcomed them with open arms and was prepared to overlook personality, dress and lack of spiritual background, for all these could change in time. He was quite dispassionate, even ruthless, with those he felt were just here for the ride. He would say: "This is a working community, not a place to drop out or come for a rest cure. If you're willing to serve, to work hard with a consciousness of perfection, then you can stay. We expect you to be in Sanctuary every morning, punctually, no lying in bed until all hours, and to give of yourself one hundred per cent. This place is built on God's work, and that must come first." And this applied to everyone, no matter who they were.

I remember well when Eddie joined us. One afternoon a short, dishevelled young American wandered in through the gate looking for the community. Apparently he walked around for some time until finally he ran into Pete Godfrey, a gnome-like middle-aged man who was in charge of building maintenance. Pete showed him around and then took him to Joanie's bungalow for tea. Tea at Joanie's had become a tradition and there were regularly five or six people there every afternoon at four o'clock.

Joanie was appalled when she saw Eddie. He was dirty, having slept out for several nights previously, and his straggly hair hung below his shoulders. He looked completely out of place sitting on her brocade armchair, drinking tea out of a fine bone china tea cup. The others who were there, all older members of the group, asked him some rather guarded questions, having had some unpleasant experiences with people who had taken advantage of our hospitality before, and finally Joanie offered Eddie a bed for one night only. Then she sent him off with Len, a younger man in charge of the work crews, to give him dinner and show him to the seven-berth caravan we had acquired specifically for our younger visitors. It was cramped but sufficient.

The next morning after Sanctuary, Peter met him in the office. He looked penetratingly at and through Eddie with his X-ray eye. He wasn't interested in the outside; he was looking to see what his inner condition was. What truly was his reason for coming to the community? Had he been directed here by God?

"What do you do?" he asked.

"I'm a writer and an actor," Eddie replied, somewhat daunted by Peter's searchlight gaze.

"Can you type?"

"Yes, I can – and I'm fast and accurate."

"Let's see how you get on with this, then," Peter said, handing him the notebook in which I had written my guidance of the previous night. He left him in the office with Dorothy but popped in all morning to check on him. Peter had no complaints about Eddie's work but had no hesitation in passing several comments about his hair, dirty boots and general appearance. Eddie came down to lunch, where I was serving the soup. I saw this miserable, down-in-the-mouth fellow standing there with his bowl, looking for all the world like a lost sheep. I smiled at him as I handed him his soup.

"Cheer up," I said. "Life isn't all that bad." Then I introduced myself. His face lit up.

"So you are the lady whose guidance I read?" he exclaimed. "Someone showed me a little book of yours and when I read it, I just knew I had to come here and find out more about you. There was one small piece which moved me so much. It changed my life! So much of what was in that little book is what I've been feeling myself for years and it was the first time I have ever heard of anyone else who thinks like me." Eddie's face shone, his earlier hangdog expression completely transformed. He had come to stay.

That was how Peter and I worked. In my guidance we were compared to a clock. "Your work must be done quietly in the background. Peter is the face of the clock and the hands that turn round, revealing the time. But you are those tiny cogs that turn quietly and steadily in the background enabling the face of the clock to do what it has to do. Both are essential; you must work in perfect unison to bring forth results."

So often when people came under the forceful beam of Peter's light, they were catapulted into a new awareness, while my love for them helped to soften the blows to their ego and to allow love to begin to flow from them. I kept very much to myself, in the background. My voice was my guidance which Peter read out in the Sanctuary every morning. If anyone wanted to see me, they had to seek me out. I preferred to hide away and didn't believe I had much value in the community apart from channelling guidance night after night and being a reference for Peter when he needed guidance or confirmation for a decision.

I was also extremely busy. As well as looking after the three boys and Peter, cleaning, washing, ironing and mending, I did all the cooking for the community with Joanie. We also did all the buying. She and I did everything together. Joanie is a perfectionist and painstakingly slow, and I like to get things over and done with, so we were constantly chivvying each other. But it was done with great love, and only she and I knew how deep that was. We cooked for everyone for two years in the kitchen in her bungalow, and they all ate in the living room and on her patio. We had seven standard meals which we repeated each week and we often joked that we hoped guests wouldn't stay longer than a week or they'd have the same thing all over again!

We cooked only vegetarian food – all with potatoes, as no British meal is complete without them. Everyone loved the food. I even received guidance not to let it become too much of an emphasis, as that would detract from the true reason for people being there. I was amused, as I thought we cooked only simple fare. But it was wholesome and I suppose that was what everyone appreciated.

As soon as Joanie realised I was making nightly pilgrimages to the public toilet for my meditations, she offered me the spare bedroom in her bungalow. I received confirmation in guidance to accept and from then on I adopted an even deeper meditation rhythm. I slept for a couple of hours each night, then waited upon God for five or six hours, listening, recording and reading as guided by my inner voice, until 5 a.m. when I went home to be ready for the family. I was always there when the children awoke to give them their breakfast and get them off to school. Then Peter and I went together to morning Sanctuary with the rest of the community and Peter read out what I had received the night before. It was always relevant, often sparking off something in someone else, giving them the direction they needed just at that moment in their lives.

My guidance for the community was similar to that for myself or Peter – simple, dear words of profound wisdom: "Love is something which is. It does not have to be talked about; it expresses itself in your life as naturally as breathing. It reflects itself in your whole being and attitude. It is the real you. It is Me in you. Love is absolutely free. It can never be boxed up, for that is not divine love; that is human possessive love which cannot withstand the stresses and strains in life. Divine love is limitless. It can withstand anything. The little self and its reactions are pushed out of the way when divine love flows freely in and through a soul. With pure love in your heart you can go anywhere, face anyone, for you have within you the strength of My divine love."

The quality of relationships was, as ever, vitally important and we were given clear directions on the subject of sex and promiscuity. "It is vitally important you set a standard about sex and do not condone loose living among the people who come here. You are pioneers of the new and therefore it is important you set your standards high and firm. Sex is a sacred act and should be treated as such. This is not being prudish or narrow-minded; it is setting a high spiritual standard. Live beyond question or suspicion yourselves, so that all who come here know exactly where they stand, no matter of what generation they are. You and Peter have a great responsibility to set the standard, with My help. Find this understanding and never let anything come between you."

This guidance applied to us personally too. When Joanie had first joined us, the love between her, Peter and myself was so powerful I was frightened by its intensity. I thought Peter had fallen in love with her, and I was shaken by my guidance that we three were God's foundation of love in our group. I was told, "This is all in My plan. The foundations of light have been laid. The foundations of wisdom have been laid. And now the foundations of love are being laid, which shall be the last and the greatest. I need three to anchor these tremendous powers. Triangles within triangles. Rise above all that is personal into My divine light."

At the same time I was having a difficult time dealing with physical sex because of the intensity of my inner life in meditation each night. After several hours in a heightened state of consciousness the last thing I felt like was making love physically, even though my love for Peter had not diminished in the least. Sometimes there was such a powerful force of a strong earthbound quality pouring through him that my body could hardly stand it. I felt as if I was being used to earth an electric current and long after Peter was asleep I lay trembling with the intensity of the contrast between heaven and earth, between the rarefied spiritual world I was being lifted into and the earthly world where all God's guidance was being carried out. When I turned within for help on how to handle this situation, I was told: "Peter needs to understand that he wields great force from which he must learn to step down when he is in close contact with you, otherwise you will be thrown completely off balance. You will have to help him, for he does not even realise the full strength of the power he holds in his hands and is apt to use it unthinkingly and with a lack of consideration. Deep love and understanding is necessary between the two of you to keep the balance. Also, you are going through the change of life which upsets the whole of your make-up."

God also told me: "My beloved, you can be completely at one with Me on all levels without ever touching or seeing Me with your physical being. This is divine love. You wonder if two human beings can find that love together and reach that complete oneness without sexual intercourse. I can assure you that they can, but it will call for deep understanding and dedication. This is something new for you. You can learn to rise above intercourse and still have this tremendous love flowing between you, for it is vital that the love does not stop flowing. Without love the work would become completely dead."

Peter never agreed with this, but there was so much else to do and think about that we didn't talk about it much. Peter so completely supported and relied upon my guidance, which was for the most part received during the night, when I was meditating in Joanie's spare room, he rarely complained and I assumed he didn't mind that I was not sleeping with him. The work we were doing together building this spiritual centre was so rich and purposeful, it seemed a small sacrifice to make for God.

Nevertheless, in the first months after Joanie joined us, I was concerned by Peter's love for her and consumed by fear that they might sleep together. I was confused and bewildered about it all, even though my guidance reassured me that the love between Peter and Joanie would never come to physical expression. Then the precious triangle would be forever broken. "Remember, this is no ordinary triangle. Simply let the love flow and tell Peter to allow nothing to spoil something that is quite unique and precious. See that My will is done without any diversions. Your own relationship with Joanie must be so strong and unshakable that it will be able to withstand anything. It is My love that is flowing between you with such force."

What bewildered me even more was the depth of feeling between Joanie and me. God told me that it was perfect and would continue to grow deeper, but I was still concerned. I had never experienced anything quite like it in all my life. I was told: "Be at peace. The time of testing for each one of you has had to take place so that there is nothing of the self left. Try to spend time in the evenings together, the three of you, just to find that peace and understanding that is so necessary for the unity of the whole group. Love unites. Love is the only answer. Let My divine love flow through you three. You, My beloved, must continue to live this strange life. It is essential for the work I am preparing for you. It is right for you to sleep in the room in Joanie's bungalow. I must be able to call you at any time during the night or early morning. You need the full support of Peter and Joanie in all that you do, for you three are to become one in My love and light."

The relationship between Peter, Joanie and myself was cemented by the powerful experience of Christmas 1967 on Cluny Hill. We indeed became one in God's love. Joanie's friendship became an anchor in my life and with her and Peter to keep me down to earth I was in no danger of floating off into higher realms, never to return!

WE WERE NO LONGER just a small group of people living in a few caravans. Our work with the nature kingdoms and the startling results of our co-operation with the devas had begun to attract attention and in 1969 we had over 600 visitors, including a team from BBC television. Some came for just a few days, others for several months, to help with the building, gardening and maintenance of the community. It was miraculous how often someone with just the skills we needed turned up at the perfect moment.

During that year, in addition to the Sanctuary, all seven bungalows of my vision were erected in place, the garden around them was landscaped with winding paths, a rockery with a lily pond and waterfall, and trees, shrubs and flowers were planted. It was a picture. In addition we erected the first of three more bungalows across the road, all of which were bought by people coming to live with us, and acquired three caravans including the seven-berth for our young visitors. The printing machine had its own building next to the office and we were sending out copies of God Spoke to Me as fast as they could be printed. We had a prefabricated building equipped for joinery, plumbing and electrical work. The road had been resurfaced and the original garden had been extended to include a beautifully designed herb garden.

One day in March, Peter, Joanie and I were talking about the problem of catering for our increasing number of guests using only Joanie's small kitchen and seating everyone in her bungalow in two sittings, and we realised that another arrangement would have to be made in the near future. The enormous amount of food we had to produce twice a day was beginning to overwhelm us. I was also finding it a strain doing all the cooking as well as looking after the children with my rigorous nightly routine of meditation from midnight to 5 a. m. I was tired and needed to sleep in the afternoon.

That very day a friend who was staying with us mentioned that she felt it was time we had a central kitchen and dining room and she wanted to help finance it. Immediately Peter, went into action. He found a suitable site on the other side of our drive, contacted the owner of the caravan park and went to see the planning officer – all in one day! He discovered that the Planning Committee was having its quarterly meeting the following day, so in true style Peter drew up plans that evening, submitted them to a sectional builder the following morning and had the plans in for approval by lunchtime that day. The estimated cost was higher than we had expected, but my guidance confirmed we were on the right track. "Fear not, My little flock, for it is My pleasure to give you the kingdom, and when a kingdom includes a community centre in it, a community centre of the very best will be forthcoming. Go ahead in absolute confidence and order it. Never limit Me in any way. I want only the best."

So we went ahead and by June that year we had a community centre with a carpeted dining room and a kitchen fully equipped to cater for 100, just in time to receive a bus party of 40 people.

The final manifestation for that year came in the form of a new home for Peter, myself and our three sons. It was obvious that we were overcrowded in our little caravan, but a bigger space for us came very low on the list of priorities. Besides, we had adapted to living on top of each other and gave it little thought. One day in November, however, Peter was ill and retreated to the boys' bedroom to rest. He was appalled at the lack of space they had – two bunks and a single bed in a tiny room with just enough space to walk in between the beds! I suppose he hadn't been in their room much and certainly never fully appreciated it until he spent a day in there himself.

"This room is far too small for these three boys," he called to me in the kitchen. "We'll have to do something about it – get another caravan added on or move to a bigger one. They can't live in such a cramped space. Can you get some guidance on it?" I smiled to myself. For how long had I been saying that very thing? My guidance confirmed that indeed it was time we moved, and into a bungalow of our own. "It will be given to you by the many, not the few, who see your need and will want to answer it in every way possible. You are, as a family, the heartbeat of the community, and a workman is worthy of his hire. So make your needs known and aim for perfection."

It was Joanie who got the ball rolling. Of her own accord she wrote a letter, had it copied and sent it out to all the people who had stayed with us over the years and to all those on our mailing list, many of whom we had never even met. It was the first time an appeal had gone our from our group and the response was overwhelming. In no time the £3,500 we needed for a bungalow had arrived, in small amounts as well as larger ones. It was so moving to realise how many people supported us and what we were doing by contributing in this way.

Once we received the green light to go ahead, Peter wasted no time. He tackled the task with drive and decided that we were to move in on New Year's Eve, so that we could start a new year and a new decade in a new home. At the time it seemed impossible, but that never deterred him. On Christmas Day, as I walked out of the Sanctuary and passed by our nearly completed bungalow, my heart was so filled with love, wonder and gratitude that I felt it would burst, for there, manifested in form, was the home God had promised the many would give us. I saw before me not just a house but a most wonderful gift from all those dear people. They were, I felt, God's hands and feet – channels that had made this possible by their love and contributions.

Right up to the last day of the year the place was alive with joiners, painters and people laying carpets. Pete Godfrey worked around the clock to have the central heating on in time. On New Year's Eve we moved into our new home. We all saw the new year in together there and gave thanks for it and asked God's blessing on it. The bungalow was full of wonderful people and I was overflowing with gratitude.

When we looked back over the year, we were astounded at what had taken place so quickly and without effort. At the beginning of the year we had known expansion would take place because God had told us it would, but never did we realise to what extent and at what speed! In my guidance on 28 December 1969, God said: "Because I have guided you step by step along the way, you have been able to undertake that which you would have thought was impossible. The vast expansion which is to take place here in the midst of your lives will simply unfold like a flower. Just take it all in your stride and then look back and see how the seemingly impossible was made possible." We were now fourteen adults and three children.

In 1970 the momentum of expansion continued. I received a vision of Pineridge with four craft studios and more bungalows built along the edge of the adjoining farm. I saw a children's playschool there as well. Early in the year a group of young crafts people – potters, weavers and artists – received inner direction to join us and very soon work was under way on the studio buildings. Many of the young people were talented musicians and dancers, and we spent many an evening in the new community centre enjoying classical concerts, dance performances and some very amusing skits, all put on by our own members. Our numbers had grown again – to forty-two adults and nine children in less than a year. There was never a dull moment. We had even more visitors than the year before and the printing machine was rarely quiet as the demand for information about the community increased.

It was also during these years that we received charitable status and became the Findhorn Trust, with Ross Stewart as Chairman of the board of Trustees and Joanie the Secretary. Our Trust deed stated our central purpose as:

> *The advancement of religion and religious studies and practices . . . by teaching, example and demonstration of the validity of the essential truths of all religions and spiritual teachings and. . . to help those who sincerely seek by the increase of their Knowledge and the development of their Being to achieve a greater understanding of the purpose and meaning of life and its relationship to God's universal plan.*

ALTHOUGH COMING TO the community at Findhorn was exciting and inspiring for people, it was also a challenge – not just in terms of the work, which was very demanding with long hours and no weekend breaks, but spiritually too. I was told: "People who come here will be tried and tested to the hilt, so they know without a shadow of doubt that this is the place for them. No one who wants to come here is to be encouraged or discouraged. They must know from deep within what is right for them without any outer help. They must be very flexible. If they are unable to be, then they are not ready to join you here."

Our main responsibility was to turn people within and encourage them to find their own sense of inner direction, their own still, small voice within. So often it seemed easier for me to get guidance for someone, but I was cautioned against this. "You are no help to a soul if you do all their spiritual work for them. They need to stand on their own two feet, take the time to turn within and tap the source of all wisdom themselves. Get confirmation for them if it is really necessary. In the days to come each soul will seek within and work from that centre. They will not need a mediator of any sort. This is but an interim period when confirmation through mediums and sensitives is necessary, but all that will go. When each soul seeks and finds that direct link with Me, the messages I give you daily and which you record so faithfully will no longer be needed. No longer will it be theory but a hundred per cent living and practising this way of life every moment of the day and night."

Perhaps the most significant guests we had that year, 1970, were David Spangler and Myrtle Glines. David was a young American who himself had been receiving guidance for some years and had done some lecturing on spiritual subjects in the United States. Myrtle, his partner, was considerably older than him and specialised in Personology, a personal and spiritual counselling technique. Years back someone had sent us a copy of a paper David had written entitled *The Christ Experience and the New Age*. It had made a deep impact on us because his ideas were so closely in line with our own. Normally I would not have read something like that, as my reading on esoterics was quite limited, but I was drawn to pick it up and, once I had started to read, I couldn't put it down. It took me into another dimension. Every word was like a letter of fire. When I heard it was written by a 19-year-old I could hardly believe it. Peter also read it and we knew that somehow we were to make contact with this man.

Nothing came of our desire to meet David Spangler until a few years later, when he wrote to say that he and Myrtle were coming to Britain on a lecture tour and would like to visit us at Findhorn.

When I first met David I was not at all impressed by him. Myrtle was having tea with me when David walked in. I looked at this young man and wondered how he could possibly have written such amazing material. He sat down and drank his tea and Peter joined us. I was astonished when Peter suddenly asked David to speak in the Sanctuary that evening. No one was allowed to speak in the Sanctuary; it was a place of silence. Peter, however, had been prompted from within to ask him to do so.

David stood beneath the Sunrise Panel and spoke. I can't remember what he said, but while he was speaking I had an extraordinary experience: he as a person seemed to disappear and in his place was a huge and very wonderful Being. I knew then that there was something exceptional about this young man and I felt very close to him. However, being aware of this special quality made me put him on a pedestal and I was quite in awe of him.

Finally I was sitting in Sanctuary one morning and I was told very firmly: "Unless you take David off that pedestal, you will never be able to communicate with him." Yes, I thought, after all he's only a 23-year-old who loves chocolate cake. I went immediately to his bungalow and told him: "David, I want to take you off that pedestal right away, because I really want to communicate with you." He roared with laughter and from that moment on we were the best of friends. The love and respect we have for one another has continued to grow and deepen with the years.

Peter was very close to David and spent far more time with him than I ever did. They discussed developments in the growing community and it was through David's presence that the educational side of life here began to blossom. Myrtle's contribution was helping with people's personal problems and I learned a great deal from her about how to handle people, for which I am eternally grateful.

David and Myrtle had originally intended to visit us for three days. Instead, they stayed three months and returned the following year for a further three years. After lecturing for so long David was happy to have found, at last, a small group of people who were actually living what he was talking about.

The impact of David and Myrtle on the community was immense. As part of David's role in helping us to become aware of the larger context of what we were doing, he began a series of lectures on the new age and its values. We used to meet in the Universal Foundation bungalow in the late afternoons or in the Sanctuary in the evenings. David said that a turning point in the consciousness of humanity had already happened and that we were embarked on an utterly new phase of our path towards God. The time of waiting for the second coming of the Christ was over. This time the Christ had not appeared in a physical body but had been born within the hearts and minds of humanity. It was now the time to realise this and bring it into expression. David's picture was far wider and more esoteric than mine, but the one complemented the other perfectly.

These sharings culminated in a direct revelation, through David, of Limitless Love and Truth, the very same being or quality that had been expressed through Liebie Pugh. At the time of her passing we had been told that the energies which had been anchored at St Anne's had been transferred to our group in Findhorn, and now I understood what that meant. The connections went deep, far deeper than any of us, least of all I, could ever have imagined. It was evident that a new cycle was just beginning for us all.

~ 8 ~

Have I not told you that you will be reunited with your children in the perfect time? See My wonders come about. Hold fast and know that all is very well; be very patient and never cease to radiate love and more love. Never be fainthearted. My promises will come about. You will be united with your children and glorious will be the uniting. Love will win.

THE NEW BEGINNING marked by the arrival of David Spangler coincided with the completion of a cycle in my personal life. When I had left Andrew for a new life sixteen years previously, losing contact with my first five children had been a dear price to pay. I realised that my turning back near the beginning had made that price even higher and, even though I was reassured over and over in my guidance that one day we would be reunited, my faith was sorely tested when one attempt after another to bring about a reconciliation failed. Love, love, love. At times I felt so powerless, having nothing but my unacknowledged love to give to these children I had borne. Did they ever feel it? Did they know that I still loved them dearly, that I was there for them whenever they chose to make contact with me?

I desperately wanted to see them again but I was not willing to drag up unpleasant incidents in my relationship with their father to prove to the courts that I was right and he wrong. My guidance confirmed that this was not the way. In 1958 Andrew had achieved a court ruling that the children were in his sole custody until they were 18 years old, until which time I was to have no contact whatsoever with them. My letters and parcels were returned unopened and the only news I had of them was through my brother and sister who kept in touch with them and sent me photographs from time to time.

When I wrote to Andrew he replied harshly that as far as he was concerned I was dead and did not exist. The children did not know I was trying to keep in touch with them and must have thought I had forgotten them completely. I kept on trying to make contact until I received a letter from a solicitor saying that if I continued they would take me to court. I felt so angry and bitter that my heart almost closed altogether.

When I turned to God for help, I was told: "Keep a constant flow of love going to the children. This is vital, for without love it will be impossible for them to break their bonds. Hold Andrew in great love. I have promised you that you will be reunited with your children at the right time, if you simply follow the guidance I give you concerning them. Trust Me and hold on in faith, with great patience. Let not your heart be troubled but see My finger tracing a clear, perfect pattern through all that has happened. Know that the best is coming about for each of them, Andrew as well. Keep your heart open, no matter how painful it is for you, and keep that love flowing towards all of them. They are in very great need of love, and love will win."

This I did, even though there were times when it was so painful I felt my heart was breaking. It was most difficult to overcome my bitterness and resentment towards Andrew, as I felt his moral judgement of me was unjustified, but by trying to see the best in him and raising my thoughts to the higher levels where my other spiritual work was being done, I felt my hardness gradually beginning to dissolve.

"See Andrew as My child," God told me, "made in My image and likeness. Know that I have need of him. Hold out My gifts and light to him." As I did this, I started to feel compassion for him. When I opened my heart to him, I could feel his pain and understand why he was doing this with the children. He was afraid that if I got in touch with them he would lose them to me. His commitment to Moral Rearmament would not allow him to feel any compassion for me, because from the MRA point of view what I had done was utterly wrong. Moral Rearmament was his life's foundation. He wanted the children to be brought up with strong moral beliefs and he felt that my influence would undermine those beliefs.

I continued to send love to all the children and to Andrew, and I also continued to write to them, through Andrew. When Jennifer and Richard had passed their 18th birthdays, I wrote to them directly. The child with the deepest resentment and the one I had most difficulty in reaching when sending out love was Jenny, the eldest, because she was the one who had taken on the responsibility of replacing me to bring up the family. I didn't blame her.

I was told in guidance: "The action you took in leaving Andrew was done under My guidance. Without it you would never have been able to do it. Where you went wrong and why things have been held up is the action you took on your own when you went back to them. That hurt Jenny dreadfully. It was like rubbing salt into a wound. But have no fears, that hurt will be truly healed."

I had a photograph of all five children which I kept on the mantelpiece. Day after day I studied the faces of the children I had borne and who were growing up without me. My guidance said: "Spend as much time as you can studying that photograph and get to know the children individually. Keep looking at each one in turn as you radiate love out to them. Jenny is the one to pour out love to unstintingly. Her heart needs to be opened up. Because she is afraid of being hurt any more, she has closed her heart. But she is the key to breaking down all the barriers with the children."

Richard was the first to break the ice. Once he turned 18 in 1960 he wrote to me a very personal and detailed letter about what was happening in his life. It was the first news I had from him in six years. Then followed a long silence. I wrote to Richard:

> My darling Richard, how lovely it would be to hear from you again. I never give up hope and treasure your one and only letter like a priceless jewel.

I sent Jenny a gift by registered post for her 20th birthday but it was returned unopened by the family solicitor. I wrote to her:

> My darling child, when will you ever really learn to forgive and

forget? Won't you ever read what I have to say? Could you not bear to open the envelope and see what was in it? Why is it that other people can forgive and forget and you and Daddy just cannot do it? My heart aches for you both.

May God bless you and may you learn the true meaning of forgiving. Very, very much love, darling, your ever loving Mummy.

I heard not a word. The following year I wrote to Andrew telling him that I wanted to send Jenny a present for her 21st birthday if she would accept it from me. I had a curt reply that she had a mind and will of her own and must speak for herself. I heard nothing, so I sent no gift that year, only a letter via Andrew, as I did not have Jenny's address in France.

My darling Jenny, I did so hope you would soften your heart and write to me. I was so longing to send you a 21st birthday present but I did not want to have it returned unopened again. Jenny darling, is this rift between us going to last for ever? Have you no love in your heart for me? I long to hear from you. God bless you darling.

On her 22nd birthday Jenny accepted a gift from me for the first time. She sent a polite thank-you note. She said nothing about herself or any of the others, but at least she had written. I was thrilled and wrote back to her:

You have no idea how good it was to hear from you. I am so glad you liked the present. You were so much on my heart and mind on your birthday. I honestly find it very hard to believe you are 22. Silly, isn't it, but I suppose we have not seen each other for so many years that the past all seems like a dream. The idea that I have a grown up family just does not seem real. When I feel like that I take your photos out and l study them. You are indeed strangers and yet I know that when we do eventually meet we shall carry on where we broke off, only older and wiser.

I am hoping you will write to me again with news of the family. Is Sue still in the United States? Has Mary Liz passed her exams? How is Penny? I did not forget her birthday but could not write or send anything, as I am not allowed to. I do want you to know that I never forget any of you on your birthdays. You are all on my mind and heart daily. Haw is Daddy keeping? I gather his back is much better. I could go on and on asking for news but I'll pop this into the post and look forward to hearing from you. Very much love to you and the family.

Jenny did write occasionally after that, but her letters communicated nothing of herself and she never mentioned any of the others. Nor did I get any news of the family from Andrew. Still he harboured a terrible resentment towards me and, whenever I thought about the children and sent love to them, I sent love to him as well. I felt he was a deeply unhappy man and I so wanted to clear the air between us. I wrote to him too:

My dear Andrew, I feel l must write to you and yet I do not know what to say, as my last letter you ignored, or perhaps you were too busy to write. Or perhaps you felt there was nothing to answer.

I want you to know that daily not only are the children constantly in my thoughts, but you are as well. Each day my heart calls out to you all. The years slip by with great rapidity. The world situation becomes more and more critical, Every time I pick up a newspaper or listen to the news, I am shocked at the state of the world. It is so easy to see the deadlock in the lives of other people, but what are we doing about it ourselves? I have sought your forgiveness and you say you have forgiven me, but Andrew can you really prove this in your life and your living?

I have had an experience recently where I had to prove by definite and concrete evidence that I could really open my heart wide to let in God's love, to love someone I never thought it was possible to love and forgive. (This was Sheena.) It was one of the most difficult things I have ever done and I shall probably be tested over and over to prove that I really have forgiven and forgotten. But now I know I have overcome what I thought was an insurmountable hurdle.

Surely we are not going to carry on like this for the rest of our lives? If we should come south again this year, would you be willing to see me? I do not want to thrust myself on any of you, but oh how I would love to break the deadlock once and for all.

Then a miracle happened. Some months after I had written this letter, just two days before my birthday, I received a wonderful letter from Andrew, asking me to forgive him for the things he had said and done to me during the years we were married and telling me he had truly forgiven me. I was overjoyed. The very next day I received a letter from Richard saying he would like to come and see me. My cup of happiness was full to overflowing. Joyfully I wrote to Andrew, Jenny and Richard, inviting them to come and stay for a week in August. It was the time when Peter was going south to England to help his parents move house, taking Dorothy and Naomi with him, leaving their rooms free for visitors. I was terribly excited at the prospect and had already started making plans in my mind for this momentous occasion when I received a letter from Jennifer that sent me reeling backwards. It was followed the next day by a letter from my brother Paddy, writing to me on behalf of Andrew, who was so distressed by my letter to him that he was unable to reply to me himself. What on earth had happened?

Evidently both Jenny and Andrew had misinterpreted my invitation to come and stay while Peter was away as a move on my part to reinstate myself with my first family without Peter's knowledge. I couldn't believe it. Nothing had been further from my mind. Naturally I had discussed the plan with Peter before writing to them and had also checked in meditation that it was the right thing to do. Their assumption that things were amiss between Peter and me was far from the truth, as he and I were working in very close harmony at that time, closer than we had ever been. I was astounded that an invitation offered with the purest of motives could have been so misinterpreted, not only by Andrew but by Jennifer as well. I did not hear from Richard.

What concerned me most was the way Jennifer blamed herself for allowing me to leave Andrew. She said she had let me down once, long ago, when she did not help me to hold on to the responsibilities I had taken on for life and she did not want to do so again by coming up to see me while Peter was away. She said she wanted to help me to hold steady in what I have given my last years to, so that Peter's and my sons would know the fullness of our life together and go out into the world happy and fully supported by all I had to give them. My heart ached for the child. Did she not realise that there was no way she could have influenced me all those years ago? Peter and I were destined to be brought together. She went on to say:

> I do not ask you to come back to us all but to go on. You love us
> too, I know and accept, but we ask nothing more from you except that
> you are faithful to the course you have taken.

Jenny's letter also made me realise that she had stayed away from me
to be loyal to the family. She did not want to upset Penny by coming to see
me before Penny was out of the court's jurisdiction, which was two years
away. She felt it would be unnecessarily hard for Penny to take, just because
she was a different age. Of course, I had not thought of all this; I had simply
written what was on my heart. I saw how protective of the family Jenny
was, how she had taken the responsibility of holding them together
without a mother and that she blamed herself for letting me leave. I felt her
anger and hurt, although it was difficult to take, as it came out in such a
judgmental way. That she condemned me for leaving my husband and
children was understandable, as was the fact that she had not forgiven me.
But I could not accept her lecturing me as if I were a naughty schoolgirl.

I tried to write as lovingly as I could of forgiveness:

> How I long for the day when you can really open your heart to
> me. We have not seen each other for over ten years, and in those years
> I have had very few letters from you. Those I have had have been either
> nice, dutiful thank-you letters or lectures. Jenny, I know you have
> been hurt, and because of that hurt you have closed your heart to me
> and refused to be hurt again. But is it necessary for me to be branded
> for life, so all my actions are misinterpreted? Is that absolute love? I
> know you are trying to live up to the MRA principle of the 'four
> absolutes' (honesty, purity, unselfishness and love). But to live is to
> demonstrate, which is one of the most difficult things to do, because to
> demonstrate means one has to forgive and show love. Jesus was able to
> forgive the adulteress. He told her to go and sin no more. Can you not
> try to forgive, darling? Jenny dear, I cannot think why you blame
> yourself for what happened to Peter and me. You were too young to
> realise what was happening, and anyway you could not have changed
> anything. It's up to you if you want to wait for years until Penny is of
> age before seeing me. I hope we are all alive and kicking then, so there

will be no regrets. You know my invitation is open to you at all times;
you know I long to see you, to talk to you, to get to know you again,
but the decision lies in your hands. I pray you will soften your heart
and come.

But it was Richard who broke the barrier in 1968. He had been
working on a farm for two and a half years in South Africa and he wrote to
say he would like to see me *en route* to Sue's Wedding in New Mexico,
USA. He spent three days with us. It had been fourteen years since I had
last seen him and when I opened they door to a charming young man of 27
it was as if we had never been parted. As a child he had always been close
to me and the same love was there, unchanged by the years of separation.
I had been told so often that the time I spent sending love to my children
would unite us, even though we were parted in time and space, and with
Richard this was true. The years simply disappeared.

I remembered the last time I had seen him: we had gone to buy his
school clothes together, as he was about to go to boarding school. He had
been almost as tall as me then, but now he towered above me, a
good-looking, grown-up man. The boys loved their new stepbrother and
Richard related comfortably and easily to Peter and to me. He held no
anger or bitterness towards any of us, and the main reason he had not come
to see me before was that he did not want to be disloyal to the family. It
was a glorious few days, all too short, but the barrier was at last broken and
we kept in touch after he went to South Africa, where he married and had
two children.

The next breakthrough came with Jennifer. She wrote to say she was
touring in Scotland with a friend and wanted to drop in to see me. It was
all very casual, but I knew it was a big step for her. Richard had paved the
way. Of course I was delighted. I fully realised her resentment was still there
but I knew in time it would be resolved. When I looked at this lovely young
woman, I was so grateful to her for caring for the other children so well.
Although we did not speak very much of the past, as I sensed an
understandable reserve in her, we had a wonderful time together and the
boys made a tremendous fuss of her. At last we had come face to face and
our new relationship could go on from there.

Then I had a letter from Mary Elizabeth. She wrote to tell me she was pregnant. The man she had been seeing did not want her to have the baby; he was on the point of going back to New Zealand and felt he was not ready for marriage. Mary Liz was 21 years old. My heart went out to her. Had I not been through the same sense of shame and social condemnation for having Christopher and Jonathan out of wedlock? She was distraught. She didn't want to have an abortion but was getting little support from anyone to keep the baby. It sounded as if her situation had stirred up the family hornet's nest and she had turned to me in desperation.

I wrote to her immediately:

> You have no idea how overjoyed I was to get your letter yesterday and to know that you felt you could write and tell me all about yourself so freely. I feel so close to you, darling, and want to put my arms around you and hold you very tight, to protect you from all those who would judge and condemn you, as so many do when one steps off the beaten track. They never for one moment think that it might have happened to them and that it is at times like these one needs help, love and understanding, not condemnation and judgement. You see, my darling, I understand what you are going through and how you feel. I was the black sheep of the family for so long. I was judged, condemned and put beyond the pale, and yet God's love has carried me through when I was very much alone and out on a limb.
>
> I was wondering if you would like to come up and stay with me and have the baby here? I would simply love to have you. There is plenty to do here to keep you from brooding and perhaps I would be some help to you at a time like this. I know I always longed for my mother when I was expecting my first baby. Please consider this offer very carefully and know that I really do want you. It would be so wonderful to have you with me and to get to know you again. Why not come up for a visit and see what it's like here – and what I am like, for that matter – before you commit yourself?

Mary Liz did come to stay and she was received with absolute love and acceptance by all of us in our still very small community. It was 1969 and there were only a dozen people living with us, although the number of guests was increasing and it was the beginning of the first burst of expansion. I was thrilled to have my daughter with me, the boys loved her and she was kept busy helping with meals and anything else that was going on at the time.

After she had been with us for a while, I decided, with the help of my guidance, to write to Eric, the father of the unborn child:

> My dear Eric, I felt I would like to write to tell you how Mary Elizabeth is getting on. Having got over the initial shock of finding herself pregnant and realising you did not intend to marry her, she has faced the situation very courageously. She has made up her mind she wants to have the baby and keep it, I do admire her, as nothing seems to daunt her and it's not easy for a young girl to do what she is choosing to do. I am sure you will be willing to help her financially to carry the burden of having your child and bringing it up on her own.

> We cannot offer her a home, but she is living in a caravan that was given to the community to be used for visitors and the rent and rates have to be paid. She is contributing her bit and will continue to do so as long as she is able. What happens after the baby is born remains to be seen. She knows she can stay here and bring the baby up here if she wants to, but she must feel free to make her own decisions. She holds no hate or malice towards you. She is bewildered by your attitude but has been able to accept it.

> Mary Liz said you have written to say you'd like to see her before you leave for New Zealand. You are welcome to come and see her here anytime you like. I hope you do come up and we can talk things over.

Eric, or Shack as everyone called him, did come to see Mary Liz. When I opened my caravan door to him, I gave him a warm, welcoming hug which took him by surprise. I was so pleased he had come, I had forgotten that he was probably expecting to be greeted by a wrathful, indignant mother! He was obviously very pleased to be well received and also to see Mary Liz again. It was clear to me that they were still very fond of one another. But I did not expect what followed the next day. They came to me and Shack said, "Eileen, we would like to get married. I've realised that I want to take that step and I don't want to go to New Zealand and leave Mary Liz behind. I'd like to look for a job near here and stay until the baby is born, and then we'll see what we'll do after that."

I couldn't have been more surprised. There had certainly been no pressure from me or my daughter to bring him to this decision, so perhaps just seeing her again in an atmosphere of acceptance without the pressure of obligation had made him realise what he really wanted. I was delighted. Mary Liz wrote to her father telling him they were to be married in the Forres registry office and inviting him to come to the wedding. He accepted, although he made it clear he did not want to stay with us, so we booked him into a small hotel in Forres.

The day Shack and Mary Liz were married was a wonderful one for me. Andrew was very close to Mary Liz but, although her predicament had distressed him beyond measure, he had been unable to embrace it within his strict moral structure. He was pathetically grateful to me for holding out a helping hand to her, and that, more than anything, helped to heal the breach between us. As I pinned a carnation on his lapel, my hand trembled violently. I had an unreal feeling of standing outside myself looking in on this scene, remembering with the greatest difficulty that I had had five children with this man and that we had shared the intimacy of a fifteen-year marriage.

After the brief ceremony in the registry office Andrew, Mary Liz, Shack and I had lunch together at a hotel nearby. The atmosphere was cordial and pleasant. We did not discuss the past but, as Andrew and I walked along the beach afterwards, we talked about the family for the first time in twenty years.

Mary Liz and Shack stayed on with us for fourteen months. Shack worked as a chemist in Inverness and Mary Liz helped around the community, where she was totally accepted as part of the family. And their baby boy, Garvin, gave me my first experience of being a grandmother and an opportunity to start to pay off the debt I owed Mary Liz by helping her all I could. It was a sheer delight.

IN 1970, JUST AFTER Mary Liz's baby was born and she was still in hospital, Penny, my youngest daughter brought her fiancé, Pete, to meet me. She was 20 years old, a beautiful, gentle, charming girl, full of fun and vitality. However, she was tied to Pete's side like a limpet. He would not let her out of his sight, not even to spend time on her own getting to know me again. Pete and I did not hit it off at all well. It was painful to stand back and watch him smother Penny. I knew that, if they were to have true happiness together, he would have to let her go and give her a sense of freedom. They were also very young and I felt strongly that they should wait until they had finished their studies before rushing into marriage.

One day I spoke my mind to both of them. It infuriated Pete and he accused me of trying to split them apart. I wanted him to let Penny stay on for a while to get to know me and to help Mary Liz with the baby when she came home, but Pete would not hear of it. They left with Penny in tears, torn in two. I was sad the visit had been such a disaster and yet, in spite of that, I had felt a natural rapport with Penny, even though I had not seen her since she was a little girl of 5. I knew things would work themselves out in time and could only hope that they would be happy together and prove me wrong.

Penny wrote me a letter that was rather like the bursting of a boil, letting all the poison out. I hoped the core had been removed as well. I replied to her:

> You have your own life to live. If your choice of partner in life is Pete, that is up to you. I am not going to try to stop you. I just hope and pray you will be very happy – indeed prove that I am entirely wrong.
>
> I tried to accept Pete as one of the family but he shied away from me like a frightened pony. I did try to communicate with him but he hung his head and hid behind his mop of hair and I could not get through to him. All I can say, Pen darling, is let him prove himself. I know he is young and has much to learn.

Some time afterwards I heard from Pete as well. His letter was stiff and starchy and a little incoherent – not the sort of letter I expected from a prospective son-in-law. He must have felt very nervous and on edge with me. But I was glad he had at least written and I wrote and told him so. I also reiterated my concern about his over-possessiveness of Penny and again urged them to wait before getting married.

It took some courage to be honest with Penny and Pete in my reservations about their marriage, particularly because I did not want to ruin my relationship with my youngest daughter so early on in our process of reconciliation. I really did not know her at all. I so wanted to love her and feel her love, and yet I couldn't be dishonest for the sake of compromise. I wrote to Andrew of my concerns and just hoped it would all turn out all right. I knew neither Pen nor Pete would like what I had written in my letter to Pete. Pen had said in an outburst that she did not want to have anything more to do with me if I could not accept her fiancé, but I had to say what I felt, even if it was a risk.

Penny took it very well. She wrote that they had fixed a date for their marriage and she asked me whether we could print the invitations on our machine. Unfortunately our printing equipment could not do the job, but I was glad she had asked. Even having set the date, she still wanted my views and opinions about their marriage, which I told her were irrelevant since she'd already made up her mind. I added:

> But I want you to know, darling, that I am always here if you really need me, and I hope one day we shall have the opportunity to get to know each other. I wish you every happiness, darling. God bless you.

It saddened me to see, when the invitation to the wedding came, that Andrew had included me and the three boys but had not invited Peter. The hatchet was not yet buried, in spite of having Mary Liz and her baby with me and the improved feeling between Andrew and me in our letters. As it was, we had an extremely busy Easter and it was easier to let Mary Liz go to the wedding, leaving Garvin with me, so I didn't go. But I sent them my love and knew the power of that love would sustain our relationship and bring us close to one another in the end. I trusted that love now, as I had proof that it worked where all else failed.

JUST BEFORE MARY LIZ and Shack left for New Zealand, they asked Andrew to come up to see them. We booked him in at a nearby Bed & Breakfast house, but made up a bed in the spare room in their caravan just in case he wanted to stay with them. I was glad he had agreed to come at all and wanted him to feel totally free to relate to us however he wished.

After he had arrived, I went over to the caravan to welcome him. He was not feeling well and was defensive and prickly, so I thought it best to stay out of the way until he made the first move. Of his own accord he decided to stay in the caravan with Mary Liz, Shack and little Garvin. Next morning Mary Liz brought him to see me in my bungalow and I casually asked, "Would you like to see around the place?" I took him over to Universal Bungalow, where Anthony Brooke and Monica Parrish were staying, and they discovered they had several friends in common, as Anthony and Monica had connections with MRA. As we wandered through the garden, Andrew was beginning to relax. Then unexpectedly Peter rounded the corner in his usual energetic way. Unable to avoid each other, they did the polite thing and shook hands. From then on the ice was broken. Andrew rediscovered what had originally drawn him to Peter so many years ago and he had a wonderful time meeting people with whom he found he had spiritual views in common. In one week the change in that man was extraordinary.

Andrew and I had a good, open talk about the past and a deep healing took place. He had realised after I took Mary Liz in that there must be some good in me, which helped him to accept me and my way of life. It was a happy and timely reconciliation. We parted with affection and I felt Andrew was grateful that all the animosity of the past was over. I thanked God again and again for bringing about this miracle.

THE LAST OF THE FAMILY to come and see me was Suzanne, my middle child. Although we had been in touch by letter over the years, she had spent much of her time in the United States and Canada, and in 1972 before she emigrated to Canada with her new husband, Alan, she wanted to see me. This was a happy reunion. I liked her husband very much and I felt so proud of Sue. These children, all five of them had grown up into lovely young people. From a detached point of view I could appreciate them all the more, as I could take no credit for who they had become. They had been forced to be independent and at times it had been rough for them, but without a mother they had all learned to stand on their own feet. It filled me with awe to look at these wonderful beings and realise that they were my own flesh and blood.

My ultimate joy came with Jennifer's wedding. This time we were all invited – Peter too – and we drove down to London together and stayed with old friends in a rectory near Andrew's home. I sat in the front pew of the church with Andrew on one side and Peter on the other, watching my first child walk up the aisle with Christopher and Jonathan as her ushers. My eyes filled with tears of joy and gratitude, for here was a public demonstration of reconciliation. Jenny had wanted it that way; she wanted everyone to know that as a family we were now friends. Andrew's family was there, as well as many of our friends from MRA and even the days of RAF. I remembered God's promises over the years that love would win and I smiled.

It was not finished yet. Some years later, when Peter and I were to go to New Zealand on a speaking tour, I went a few weeks earlier to spend some time with Mary Liz, Shack and my two grandsons. While I was there we received news that Andrew was very ill and in hospital. Mary Liz, who had always been very close to him, said "Oh, Mum, how I wish I could see him. I wish I didn't live so far away."

"Why don't you go, then?" I asked.

"It's impossible with the two boys, and Shack working such long hours. But I'd really love to."

I went away quietly and turned to my God within. My immediate impulse was to offer to stay and look after the boys, so that Mary Liz could go. Could I cancel my tour with Peter? Would I be letting him down? Was it right to disappoint all the people who had spent so much time and money to bring us half-way across the world to speak to them about the community at Findhorn? In my heart I knew this was what I had to do to repay part of the debt I owed to Mary Liz and the family. My guidance confirmed my feeling.

"If I stayed to look after Shack and the boys, could you find the money to go to England?" I asked my daughter.

She looked stunned. "Do you really mean it? I'd have to be gone a month at least, Uncle Nick actually said he'd send me a return ticket. . . " She looked enquiringly at Shack.

"Of course you should go," he said. "Take advantage of Eileen's offer. I'd love to have her here if she's willing to stay."

"Why not go for six weeks," I suggested. "You need that time with your father, and you deserve the break. I'll manage just fine, and the boys will help me, won't you?" I hugged young Garvin, whose angelic expression belied his mischievous temperament.

So I stayed and Mary Liz went to Britain. It was a different and challenging experience for me to be caring for two small boys once again, cooking and shopping for the family and being for all the world the normal suburban grandmother! Peter supported my decision without a murmur and I wrote copious letters to all my beloved friends at home, begging for news of them and the community. Although I knew what I had chosen was right, I felt cut off from the rest of my world and living a 'normal' life stretched me to my limits.

Mary Liz returned having had a wonderful time with Andrew and her brother and sisters. Richard had by this time returned to England. The only one she did not see was Sue, who was still in Canada. Only eight days after her return we had a telephone call from Richard to say that Andrew had died. He had been happy and at peace – all the more so for having seen Mary Elizabeth. I breathed a sigh of gratitude and relief that I had not gone ahead with the tour, which at the time had seemed so important. I should never have forgiven myself if I had not enabled Mary Liz to go and see her father before he died. Thank God.

Richard also told me that towards the end Andrew had been of tremendous spiritual help to many people in hospital. He had found his inner serenity and had been able to communicate it to those around him. I had written to him from New Zealand and Richard told me that Andrew had asked him to read the letter aloud over and over. I have no idea now what I wrote, but it must have been very meaningful to him at that time in his life. I realised that a complete healing had taken place between us, and again I thanked God for helping this be so.

When Penny was expecting her fourth baby, I went to stay with her and Pete. I was glad to be able to do that for them, as we all now got on very well together. They had proved me wrong in my misgivings about their marriage, which I gladly acknowledged, and any residual bad feelings about that period of their lives had completely dissolved by the time I left. I found Pete an amusing, bluff character, full of jokes and forever teasing me. Penny was as lovely as ever, a wonderful mother and daughter.

Only a year later, in 1980, I received from them an urgent cry for help. Penny had been taken into hospital with suspected tuberculosis. I dropped everything and went to stay with them for six weeks to take care of my four grandchildren. Catherine was only just a year old and it was quite something to look after a baby again and deal with nappies, bottles and night-time feeds. Fortunately, after extensive tests it was confirmed that Penny did not have TB, only a severe lung infection, and the time she spent recuperating at home gave us the opportunity to get to know and love each other very deeply.

Ten years after her brief visit to me, Suzanne's turn came. I was in Canada, again on tour, and Sue was recovering from a back operation. Alan, her husband, had to fly to Germany on business, so I cancelled my flight home and to look after her and her two boys. Sue, a dynamic, energetic young Woman, combined a busy job with running a home. She was a great believer in liberating women from their downtrodden place in front of the kitchen sink and insisted that the job of keeping a home should be shared by Alan, so that she could do her creative work as well.

Perhaps my views about being a mother were old fashioned, but I felt she was being selfish and putting her needs before those of Alan and the boys. I said as much and Sue flew into a rage.

"I won't be spoken to like that," she exploded. "Leave my house!"

I did just that. We parted on very bad terms and it was two more years before I saw her again. But as with Penny and Pete I felt I had to say what I did, although I didn't know she would react so violently. However, two years later, when she knew I was coming to Canada again, she invited me to spend Thanksgiving with them, because her boys wanted to see me again. From then on, each time I saw Sue, our relationship gradually improved. I stayed in touch with her throughout and finally had a letter from her confiding all her troubles to me and asking for my moral support. She had needed to blow up at me, to set free all her locked-up feelings about me. A few angry words were not enough to send me away for good, however – not after so many years of building up the relationship in my heart.

THE FINAL CATHARSIS CAME with Jennifer. When she had been expecting her second baby, I had been to stay with her and her husband Peter, to help with looking after their 3-year-old Andrew. She had been mild-tempered and chatty with me but I felt there was still a resentment hidden deep down that would eventually have to show itself.

Some time later I went to stay with them for a short holiday.

I thought, "Well, it's time it all came out into the open. I'll ask." So I did.

One morning, while I was meditating, I was told: "Ask Jenny how she feels about your leaving her and the family."

Jenny's face closed immediately. "I'd rather talk about it when Peter is here," she replied stonily.

After dinner that evening she brought up the subject herself. "Peter, Mum asked me this afternoon how I feel about her leaving the family. I wanted to wait until you were home, as I know you have things to say about it as well."

They proceeded to tear me to shreds. "I feel your set of values is entirely wrong," Jenny told me. "Marriage is a sacred act and by leaving your first family you denied God in your life. What you are hearing can't possibly be God's voice. It must be the voice of the devil. When you marry, it's for life, no matter how difficult it might be, and if you break that sacred promise to God you can never be forgiven."

At last they had the opportunity to spill out all the resentment, condemnation and anger that secretly had been building in force for years. It burst out so powerfully I felt I had been struck. And yet I let it come. I wanted it to. By listening to them I was transmuting all that negativity into something positive. It was like a volcano; it had to erupt.

When they had said it all, they waited for my response. "Jenny, Peter," I said, "I am so glad you have let all this out. Our spiritual values are entirely different, and I don't feel I can justify anything. I know how you feel and I know how deeply you both believe in the principles of Moral Rearmament, which absolutely condemn what I did. All I know is that I did what I did under God's guidance and that nothing could have prevented it. I know my guidance is from God, because it works for me. I have put it to the test again and again. I just have to accept that we have different viewpoints and I can't judge which are right or wrong, which are better or worse. I can accept that what you believe is right for you, but I have to do what I have to do, and I still love you. No matter what you say to me, I shall always love you."

Certainly the boil had burst. The hidden tension was gone and Jenny was more herself than I had ever seen her before. No longer was she always sweet and considerate but now she was free to speak her mind. When she did, it was with an honesty that had been missing before.

After I left for home, I fell ill with bronchitis and while I lay for days in my bed I had time to think about what had happened with Jenny and Peter. In spite of the discomfort I experienced, I was deeply grateful that it had all been brought out into the open. It was better this way for Peter and Jenny and better for me. And since then there has never been the same submerged anger, even though they both still disapprove of me and what I believe in and live by. But that doesn't matter as long as we can still feel our love for one another. Our views about how we each should live are unimportant in comparison to that. And I still live by the simple promise I was given so many years ago: love will win. I know it does.

~ 9 ~

In a vision I was shown a man and a woman. On the man were the words 'Light, Intellect' and on the woman, 'Love, Intuition'. I saw there was a great friction between them, even hatred and enmity. Then the woman lay submissively on the ground and the man walked all over her, wiping his feet on her.

I heard a voice say: "Arise, oh woman. Be not subservient to man, for are you not his helpmate? Are you not here to complement each other and so bring unity and harmony and complete oneness?" The man must have heard the voice too, because I saw him kneel down beside the woman and gently pick her up. He removed her filthy garment and put on a pure white one.

Then I saw two great hands take the man and the woman and mould them into one lump as if they were made of clay. The hands placed the clay onto a potters wheel and created a most beautifully shaped pot. I watched the pot being placed into the fire of purification. When it was taken out again, it shone as brilliantly as the sun. It was so beautiful I knew only God's hands could have created it.

I now saw growing out of the pot blooms of every colour and description. I realised that was what could happen when there was no longer any division between man and woman, light and love, intellect and intuition. There will be everlasting peace and goodwill only when they come together as one.

Finally I saw an arrow aimed high into the air, and I heard the words, "Aim high and you will get there."

OUR COMMUNITY AT FINDHORN grew to 150 people in the three years after David Spangler's arrival. Of course, David was not personally responsible for this expansion. However, his presence injected new energy into what had been growing steadily for eight years. He brought an expanded vision of what we were doing and put it into a world-wide context that was even bigger than we had previously imagined. In my guidance I was told: "See your work and David's complementing each other. David is the new age and you and Peter are ones who show the way, leading those who are in the old into the new. You will always work very closely together."

As Peter had been the initiator of the practical, physical expansion of the Findhorn Community, so David was the initiator of ideas – of a deep spiritual, philosophical thinking that had a catalytic effect on people's inner growth. My contribution was my guidance, which formed the foundation stones of the work we were engaged in. I spent long hours in meditation each night, when everyone else was asleep, and whatever I received formed the basis of the morning meditations upon which the life of our group depended. Any problem or decision affecting the community or individuals living in it was checked through my guidance. Having handed over cooking for the whole community to younger members, I now spent most of my days at home in our bungalow, keeping it clean and tidy, mending Peter's and the boys' clothes and sharing my guidance with anyone who came to me for help with their problems. I never offered a personal opinion to Peter or anyone else, but relied totally on the wisdom that flowed so easily through me.

There was so much happening in the community. By now young people – many of them from the United States – outnumbered the older ones by about three to one. Education had become an active, conscious extension of our lives in the form of classes and study groups based on the material David was channelling in a steady and inspiring stream. The performing arts were alive too, with plays, musicals and hilarious skits on community life staged almost every week. The craft studios were busy producing weavings, pottery and candles, while Findhorn Publications had become a thriving little business.

Without Peter's energy and drive, however, little would have been accomplished. I noticed everything slow down when he spent several weeks in hospital having a gall bladder operation. For the first time I was alone with the community, and was forced to come out of my cocoon and spend more time with people. I had always loved people but was afraid to dig too deep in case I ran into something uncomfortable. Now I experienced a new role, which I described in a letter to Myrtle while she and David were away:

> I have always left the dirty work to Peter and just slipped into the background. Now I have to handle it myself, with God's help, and it is most interesting, even having to use the sword of truth, or 'lowering the boom', as you would call it! Now that I don't spend most of my time in the kitchen I find I am getting to know individuals in quite a new way. I can take time with them and find out what makes them tick, hearing about their little gripes and trying to find a solution. You are the one I have to thank for giving me an insight into how to cope with people. I still have a lot to learn.

On Peter's return, however, I slipped back into my old role and left the more challenging part of dealing with people to him. I preferred it that way. At that time there were so many rough corners to be rubbed off those who came to the community. Each one who had stepped into the spiritual path had their own personality to deal with before they blended in harmoniously with the whole. Since Peter had no qualms about being dispassionately honest if he thought someone was putting their own needs or desires before the good of the whole, I was happy to leave that aspect of relating to people to him and return to my role of being a channel for guidance and gently supporting people through their difficulties.

IN OCTOBER 1971 I received guidance that was to change my life: "My beloved, now is the perfect time for a complete change of rhythm for you. It is no longer necessary for you to receive a message from Me each day for the community and for the many. For a long time I have gone on day after day repeating Myself. It is now time that My word is lived and demonstrated. For all those who have failed to take it to heart, for all who need to be reminded, it is there, printed in black and white. Now is the time for living it, and the sooner this is done, the more quickly will changes come. You cannot spoon-feed a child all its life. The time comes when it has to learn to feed itself and you have to let it do so.

"Let go, stand back and allow all those in the community to live a life guided and directed by Me. Let them learn from experience to live positively, demonstrating the laws of manifestation in their own lives. If this means that the work is held up for the time being, let it be held up. Until life is lived, lessons are not learned, and these lessons are far more important than expanding without learning, living on what others have learned."

That message was the last one read in the Sanctuary. Passing on God's word each morning provided inspiration for the community but it also made people dependent. I was reminded of the guidance I had received in 1968 that these messages were necessary only until each person was ready to turn within to find that direct link with God, to become their own channel. David was also aware of this human tendency to rely on an outside authority and was trying to avoid creating a similar dependence on himself.

This was an immense change in my life, which deeply affected Peter and the whole community. It was the beginning of a period during which our relationships, our roles and our work, were to go through a transformation. Even my relationship with God was changing. In the early years I had thought of God as a father. I was a child and God was taking care of me. But gradually the partnership was becoming more equal. It was almost as if I had entered into a kind of marriage with the divinity within, with the Beloved.

Although both my guidance and David's attunement with higher realms had prepared us for this new cycle, we had no understanding as yet of what it might mean. My voice told me: "The community is no longer a slender sapling easily swayed by every wind of change. It is now a sturdy oak with its roots sunk deep within the soil, firmly rooted and grounded in Me. Its trunk is strong, and every bough is perfect. See each new aspect of the work as a new branch growing out of that sturdy trunk. I am the sap, the life force flowing in that tree. The wind may ruffle its leaves, the storms may bend or break the branches, but nothing can now affect the true perfection and beauty of My work."

AT CHRISTMAS THAT YEAR I felt lost and confused about how I fitted into the community now that my guidance was no longer needed. When I mentioned my feelings to Peter, he immediately asked, "Well, what is your new role?

'I don't know," I sighed. "I have no idea at all."

"Well, you still remain the final source of guidance on all community policy matters," Peter said. "If you'd only go out and be with people more, you could be a great help to them, too!"

During the morning the thought came to me, "Why not ask the Beloved?" So I got my book and pen, retreated to the peace of my bedroom and asked, "Beloved, what is my role in your greater work?"

"Be at perfect peace," came the reply. "Your new role will unfold as a flower unfolds its petals in the rays of the sun, so simply and naturally you will not even realise what is taking place. There are tremendous energies being released at this time and you are to absorb them into your being, so that you become part of them. Let go, let go. Let there be no resistance in you. Be afraid of nothing, I am with you always. Open yourself up and let yourself feel very deeply. You need this time of quiet and stillness, of being alone. See only a few people at a time. It is important you are in the Sanctuary during this time, but waste no energy talking to people. There is a reason for all this. That which is empty can now be refilled with My love, My life, and great shall be the overflow."

The following morning I went to the Sanctuary early but not early enough to be alone; David and another person were there before me. As I sat meditating in great peace and oneness, I was jolted out of the quiet by an almighty crash. The lid of the record player had fallen and the shock shattered every nerve in my being. I burst into tears and started shaking all over, and David and Jim came over to comfort me. The events of the next few days made me realise that I had needed that shock to open me up in some way.

Next morning, alone in the Sanctuary, I was told from within to sound an OM, a Tibetan mantra I had used before. I sounded it five times, and as I sat quietly afterwards the top of my head seemed to open up and light poured into my whole being, flowing out of my fingertips as if it could not be contained within my body.

On the third morning the experience was repeated, although this time the power of the light was so great it flowed through every atom of my being. Then all of a sudden I felt suffocated. I couldn't breathe. Something inside me wanted to be released. I started to panic, but then I remembered the words, "Let go, let go. Let there be no resistance in you." It was not easy to do as I struggled for breath, choking and gasping, but as I gradually relaxed I felt something within me come up and up and it seemed that a white dove emerged from the top of my head and flew away. I heard the words, "I am free, free, free!" And I was filled with a wonderful sense of liberation.

I followed the same instructions on the fourth day, and it was clear to me that sounding the OM out loud was to raise my vibrations. Again a tremendous light poured through and out of every part of me, and I seemed to undergo a strange transformation. For a second I became really afraid again, until I was reminded of those words, "Be afraid of nothing, I am with you always." My being seemed to become the earth, battered and bruised, and a terrible pain shot through my body. I thought I was going to die. I tried to let go and trust God but the pain increased until I felt I could take no more.

"Oh God, help me!" I cried out, and as I did so I felt myself very lovingly and gently pushed towards the sun. The nearer I came to the sun, the less I felt the pain, until I entered right into the sun. The pain became nothing and yet it was everything because all was one. Then I heard the words, "The earth and all humanity is made new."

On the fifth and last morning I sounded the OM again and once more I experienced the light pouring through my whole being. It was as if I was being used as a transformer for the pure light to flow through and out to all those not ready to receive it directly. Gradually I became aware of another sensation: it felt as if my skin was being peeled off, from the opening in my head slowly and gently down to my toes. I could see it lying before me, just like the discarded skin of a snake. For a few moments I *knew* how it felt to be a Being of Light. I heard the words, "Go forth and be My Light, be My Love, be My Wisdom."

The next night I awakened at 1.30 a.m. I turned on the light and reached for my blue notebook on the bedside table. The words came, "Now just *be* and let Me use you." So I sat straight up in bed and surrendered my being completely to God. I said, "Beloved, use me in any way. More than anything I want to be of service to you and to all humanity."

The strongest beam of pure light I had ever experienced began to pour into me, flowing in through the top of my head and out through every pore. I sat for a long time just allowing myself to be a transformer. When finally

I was told to turn out the bedside light, I noticed it was 4.30 a. m. I lay very still in the darkness and the light went on pouring through me. Then it switched off. But the light still seemed to shine, generated out of my own being. I lay like this until 8.00 a.m. reverberating from my experience of the past six days. The power I had contacted had been so great that, had I held on to my resistance and fear, I knew I would have been burnt up. And I knew my simple question, so naively asked, about my role in God's work, had most fully been answered: "Be My Light, be My Love, be My Wisdom."

INSTEAD OF SHARING my guidance I now had to learn to be it. This was to prove one of the most difficult challenges of my life. Without my role as the channel of God's word to prop me up I felt weak, ineffectual and worthless. But I trusted God, and my guidance was still there to give me inner strength and support. It was all within now, and there was nothing to turn to outside of me.

The ultimate test came when I was told clearly that I should stop giving my guidance to Peter. Although I no longer shared what I received from my inner voice with the community in general nor with individual members who sought my advice, Peter still came to me several times a day to ask for guidance on community matters and then used this information to confirm his own intuitive sense. Now, however, I was told quite clearly that it was time for Peter to turn within. If I were to go on giving guidance to him, it would hold up his evolution. My job was to support Peter to trust his own inner direction and not lean on the 'higher authority' that came through me. Our old relationship was over.

I was shattered. We had worked together in this way for years and I was comfortable being in the background as a channel for God's word. Weren't Peter and I two halves of a whole, he depending on me and I on him? Why should things change? If I was no longer to give guidance to Peter, what was I to do? Maybe Peter would continue to listen to other sensitives and would start to feel he didn't need me in his life any more. Fear gnawed at my stomach.

Peter couldn't see the point in God's instruction either. He insisted that he was already turning within and following his intuition, and only came to me for final confirmation. About this time David and Myrtle left the community to return to the United States, so another source of higher knowledge that Peter trusted became unavailable to him too. Instead of uniting in our new challenge, we began to move apart.

Soon after that I went into hospital for an operation. The change in routine helped me to break my old habit patterns and by the time I came home again I didn't know where I stood in relation to guidance or even to my life. I was very weak and stayed with Joanie in her bungalow, where she gave me the loving care and attention I so desperately needed. I felt very alone and vulnerable.

Once when Peter came in to see me, he asked for guidance on a problem with a couple he felt ought to leave the community.

"What do you feel about the situation yourself?" I asked.

Peter's face closed and he made an impatient gesture. "I know what I think," he said. "I asked you for confirmation."

"You know I'm not supposed to get guidance for you."

"I don't want guidance," Peter cut in. "I feel I already know. I just want some confirmation on it."

And I longed to give it to him. I could even hear the words of guidance ringing in my ears, but because of the new instructions I was uncertain how much I should say. In the end I told Peter nothing and he left abruptly, his body tense with annoyance.

My fears began to take form. With the community's growing reputation for an awareness of other realms, it was inevitable that a fairly high proportion of those visiting us had their own form of sensitivity. Peter turned more and more frequently to these people for support. It disturbed me to see how some of these 'sensitives', who were often women, seemed to be swept away by the glamour of it all. I couldn't help feeling that having Peter Caddy ask them for guidance swelled their sense of importance. I found it especially difficult when the advice they channelled was not in line with my own guidance which "I still received although now I kept it to myself. What was I supposed to do? Should I speak or remain silent?

Over the next few years this conflict of guidance was to show itself in the building of the Universal Hall. The original instructions I received in 1973 were for a utility hall to be built as quickly as possible to relieve pressure on the community centre, which even with a new extension was already becoming too small for our large group gatherings. The hall was to be a simple structure, completed in a year to eighteen months, while a larger performing arts centre was to be a project for later on. The project attracted intense interest from all quarters including architects and builders. As the plans for the new hall took shape, the creativity and attunement of the many people involved in the process turned the original idea into the beautiful yet complex building that stands at the Park today. It is a tribute to the dedication of hundreds of people who have given their love and their time to create a building of great power and magnificence. And yet during the ten years it took to complete, the community had to put up with over-crowded community gatherings and struggled to raise a great deal of money to finish the building.

Looking at the Universal Hall now, who can say what was or was not right? How could such an achievement be misguided? And yet we never built our utility hall, and along the way there were certainly times when individuals' personal guidance helped to deflect us from our original purpose. All the way through the process I felt my lips were sealed. My voice was one among many, with no more – and quite often less – weight than anyone else's.

In those first years after I stopped passing on my guidance, whenever I voiced my concerns without actually repeating, what I had been given, Peter accused me of being negative or of working from an emotional level instead of from the highest.

In part he was justified, as I felt very vulnerable and emotional about the whole matter, but that did not change what I knew to be right. So, more often than not, rather than cause trouble I kept quiet.

At one point I became so desperate I said to God in meditation, "Couldn't I get guidance for Peter, just when things get confused? I feel we are drawing apart, and he is simply going to others instead of me." The reply was: "Of course you have free will. You can do anything you choose. But if you slip back into that old pattern, you will hold up Peter's evolution. There are tremendous changes taking place and you feel you are living on the edge of a volcano which is ready to erupt at any moment. Do not let this disturb you in any way; every change is for the best. You are moving onto a higher spiral. Know that I am within you."

I loved Peter too much to get in the way of his growth. My refusal to continue giving him guidance was the thin end of the wedge in our relationship and yet there was nothing I could do about it. Having followed that inner voice for so many years, I knew I could not disobey it now. So I continued to keep quiet, or voiced my feelings with such unconvincing timidity that it was no wonder Peter remained unimpressed.

When he came home at the end of a busy day in the community, I'd want to know what he'd been doing. Often he would reply, "I've been talking all day. I just want to relax." And he'd turn on the television. I was incensed. And hurt. I cared deeply about the changes that were happening in the community. It was, after all, our child in a way, and I felt I was being shut out.

AS MORE AND MORE young people joined the community, their energy and enthusiasm demanded that Peter share the responsibility for all the different departments. He formed a Core Group of about ten people to help run the community in addition to their normal work. Although members wanted more responsibility, their standards didn't always measure up to Peter's. He was, and still is, a perfectionist and it drove him to distraction to come back after a trip away to see lights left on, papers in the driveway and tiny bits of evidence of others' carelessness, which was utterly unacceptable to him.

"How can I give people responsibility if they don't take it on one hundred per cent?" he would say. "Nothing less than perfect is good enough for God." He could have added, ". . . and me."

In my guidance in 1972 I received: "The whole community needs to take the whole on their hearts and Peter will help them do this as he relinquishes many of the jobs he has carried on himself for far too long. Let him delegate more responsibilities to others. Let them make mistakes and grow by those mistakes. He can always be there for them to turn to for advice, but it is time he stopped trying to do everything for himself and allowed others to grow. It will not be easy for him, but it will be the best for the whole in the long run. Peter is to look for the very best in everyone and draw it out and cease spotlighting their weaknesses and faults."

I felt compelled to share the gist of this message with Peter. He found it very difficult to accept. "I can only change when the community changes," he protested. "And they aren't ready for me to give up any responsibility yet. Anyway, I have the final responsibility and always will have. It's a spiritual law that what you initiate you are always responsible for."

"But unless you allow others to try taking responsibility, they'll never learn how to do it," I replied. "I think the community will change in that way only when you let go of some things."

"I really can't see it, Eileen. If you were more supportive of me and showed me your guidance as you receive it, I might be able to take it in more easily."

I felt trapped between God and Peter, but I resolved to accept that this was just a phase Peter and I were going through and that in time we would discover a new way of working together.

Dorothy left in 1973 to go to the United States with David and Myrtle but I knew my place was still in the community. Besides, I was discovering a new way of being with people that proved to me that helping them turn within instead of giving them the answers was of value to them. I became more accessible to community members and the many guests who visited us, and began to have a sense of my contribution to their spiritual lives. Sometimes what I had to say was not particularly pleasant for people to hear, as I challenged their commitment to God, putting the emphasis on spiritual growth before their personal desires or attachments. I was gratified, however, to discover that most people took my words to heart because they knew of my own commitment to God.

My feelings of self-worth and usefulness began to grow until I felt I was almost back to normal again. Surely my relationship with Peter would sort itself out too. Throughout the summer of 1974 Peter seemed distant and preoccupied but I didn't worry unduly, as it was an extremely busy time: there were more guests than ever before, Paul Hawken was living in the community writing his book *The Magic of Findhorn*, every caravan was filled to capacity and work on the new Hall had begun. It was a beautiful, warm summer and the community reminded me of an ants' nest, with teams of workers swarming all over the place. I put Peter's preoccupation down to his concern with keeping the wheels oiled and running smoothly.

By this time there were a lot of people for us to deal with, so we formed a Personnel Department which consisted of Peter, myself and Alice, a 22-year-old woman from Sweden with a strong intuitive sense about people. The three of us worked very closely together, talking to everyone who wanted to join the community, and finding somewhere for them to stay and the right place for them to work, not to mention helping them with all their personal problems.

One lunchtime Peter rushed into the bungalow to fetch a rug, "I'm going to have lunch on the beach," he said over his shoulders as he went out the door again. I felt uneasy. It wasn't unusual for Peter to go to the beach at lunchtime; he often went swimming with a group of community members. But this day my intuition told me something was wrong. Suddenly it hit me: he had fallen in love with Alice.

That night Peter took me out to dinner – a rare treat – and I asked him about it. He looked thoroughly uncomfortable at first but finally admitted that this was what had happened. "For the first time in my life I have had my heart opened," he told me. "With you it was always a spiritual union, but I was never in love with you. I knew we were brought together by God but somehow you never opened my heart the way Alice has been able to."

Peter's words sliced into me like a knife. "I don't understand what you mean," I cried. "After all we've been through together, working in such close harmony for all these years . . . I gave up everything to be with you! And even through our ups send downs I've always been convinced God brought us together and nothing could possibly part us."

"Nothing will part us," Peter replied. "We are meant to be together, and I do care about you. But this experience with Alice is so new – and right. I've been told I have to change, and Alice is helping me to do that. I know it's guided by God."

No, no, no! I screamed inside. How can it possibly be guided by God? We are two halves of a whole; we are part of one another. How could this happen to us? I was blind with pain and anger. There was no reason, no value in what Peter was going through. The doors of my heart slammed shut and I was locked inside fermenting with insane jealousy.

Being in such a disturbed emotional state I found it almost impossible to receive clear guidance for myself. I retreated into my shell like a sick animal and barely spoke to anyone for days. The atmosphere at home was deathly and the boys made themselves scarce, sensing that something was amiss. Only Christopher, then 18 years old, asked me what was going on, and I told him. He kept a balanced view and didn't take sides, but even he couldn't prize me loose from my pain.

When finally I could bring myself to be still and listen, this is what I received: "Release, relax, everything is working out according to My divine plan. What is happening to Peter is that he is moving into the universal love pattern. You cannot expect it to happen overnight. Think of a rose bud, how it unfolds imperceptibly, revealing its full wonder, beauty and perfection. Peter is unfolding. At the moment he does not know how to handle the love energy. Be very loving, very patient and know that all is very, very well. His relationship with Alice will level out and she can accept him and help balance him. Trust her completely. She is no threat to your relationship or to your marriage. Remember when the doors of your heart were opened to universal love and you experienced tremendous freedom and love for everyone. If this love is taken for the self it can cause chaos, but when it is used for the highest it is the most wonderful and beautiful thing in the world. This is what Peter is moving into. Try not to react negatively, but simply know that the time is at hand when you will both be functioning the same way and My universal love will simply pour through you both. This is the Cosmic Christ."

This was too much for me! I thought the whole world had gone mad, including my God. Confronting Sheena all those years before had convinced me it was better to face my greatest fear than let my imagination run away with me, so I sat down with Alice and we had a good talk. We were very open with one another, and I began to understand how a young girl might be flattered to have an older man – and particularly such a powerful one – fall in love with her. Alice was clear that she did not intend to embark on a physical relationship with Peter and I found my trust in her growing. I also found that my love for her, which had always been there, grew too.

Even though I was feeling a little more secure, I still couldn't see how to play my part. I didn't feel patient, loving and supportive. I didn't know how not to react negatively, how not to feel what I felt. I hated myself for bursting into tears, for feeling angry and withdrawn, for getting suspicious every time I saw them together, and for closing myself off from Peter. But I felt powerless to change the way I was behaving.

I had a vision at that time of a crumbling building. Its walls were being torn down and all the debris was taken away. In its place, on the same solid foundations, was built a beautiful temple of light. I interpreted this as our relationship and drew strength and purpose from it. It was as if our old way of being together had to be completely smashed in order to make way for something new.

But what was this new relationship? I longed with all my heart to become the kind of woman Peter could fall in love with, and I started to search within myself for the answer. This was new territory for me. Until now my deepest relationship had been with God; all my searching had been in that direction and the human side of me had taken a back seat. For years I had striven to overcome my personality by reaching upwards to something higher, but now the defects in my personality seemed to reach such alarming proportions that they could no longer be ignored. I did not like what I saw in myself at all. The vision I had received in 1969 of a man and a woman being moulded into a beautiful pot out of which flowers of every colour and form began to make sense to me. I realised that there was a great need to bring the quality of balance into each of us so that we could stand together as equals and that I needed to do something about it within myself. But how?

I tried asserting myself by bringing the masculine in me to the fore. I had played the passive, receptive feminine role for so long, with Peter as my masculine balance, that I felt it was time to break out and express another side of myself. To me, Peter was the perfect model of masculine attributes, so I tried to act more as he did – with strength, determination, power. It was a disaster. I joined the Core Group and instead of quietly sitting on my feelings when something arose that I did not agree with, I spoke my mind. It came out with such force and emotion that I turned everyone off completely. I sounded – and felt – aggressive, bossy and totally off balance. The pendulum had swung much too far. It became difficult for people to relate to me, even though they knew what I was trying to do and supported me in it. Peter could hardly stand it. Instead of the meek old Eileen, here was a fierce and outspoken woman. He withdrew even further.

I was told from within to resign from Core Group, which I did amidst protests from the others in the group that I was taking a retrograde step. In spite of the fact that they found my behaviour jarring, they felt I should stay and face myself. But I knew I had more work to do on bringing myself into balance first. I struggled for a while to find an answer and, feeling I was getting nowhere, asked God to send someone to give me a clue.

Soon afterwards a woman called Naomi came to the community. She had been trained in Psychosynthesis, one of the new psychologies that includes the spiritual aspect of the whole person and works with a guided imagery technique. I had a long conversation with Naomi one day and at the end of it she said, "Would you like to try an exercise in visualising your masculine and feminine aspects?"

"Well . . . yes, all right." I replied. I didn't see how it could have any great effect on me but I was willing to try anything.

After getting me to close my eyes and consciously relax my whole body, Naomi told me to visualise my emotions as a large lake. "See the surface of the water gradually smooth itself out until it becomes like a mirror . . .

"Now turn your attention to your thoughts . . . follow any that may be there for a moment or two . . . then just let them drift away . . .

"Allow an image to emerge which for you symbolises the masculine aspect of yourself. Take time to become aware of it . . . what it looks like, its shape, size, colouring . . . and be aware of how you feel about it.

"Now step into the image . . . identify with it. Experience what it is like to be that image . . .

"And now step out of the image . . . have a good look at it."

Naomi went on to ask me to allow another image to surface – this time representing the feminine aspect of myself – and to explore it in the same way.

At this point things began to get difficult. On my first attempt I was given a huge tree as my masculine symbol and a tiny lily-of-the-valley for the feminine. When I tried to bring the two together and blend them, I found it impossible. I just couldn't do it. Naomi very kindly offered to do the exercise again a few days later and this time my masculine symbol was a huge, powerful lion with a great golden mane, while my feminine one was a unicorn-white, pure, delicate and timid. But again when I tried to blend the two together, it wouldn't work. By now I was nearly in tears with disappointment and frustration, so my guide suggested that I let the lion and the unicorn dance together. They began to move round each other, very slowly at first and then faster and faster. Suddenly they became one. At last!

"And now," continued Naomi, "have the two images begin to relate to one another. See them begin to blend together. . .''

The lion was a fairly obvious masculine symbol, but I wondered why I had come up with a unicorn for my feminine aspect. Some days later I happened to pick up an article written by Sir George Trevelyan which shed clear light on the subject. 'The unicorn is a strange and wonderful beast in mythology,' he had written,

> . . . a white horse with great and gentle eyes, gazelle's feet and a shining horn from the centre of its brow. The horse is the symbol of intelligence, very close to man. The white horse thus represents cleansed and uplifted intelligence. The horn from the point of the third eye suggests spiritual knowledge and the faculty of awakened clairvoyance. The gazelle's feet enable it to trip tightly over the morass of materialistic greed and egoism. Legend has it that to find a unicorn a virgin must sit humbly outside the dark forest from whose mysterious depths this wondrous beast will come forth and lay its head in her lap. In the same way, the soul which has cleansed itself and brought itself back to virgin purity is then able to offer itself to be fructified by spiritual knowledge. Thus the unicorn is seen as a symbol of the higher self filled with the Christ Light, which can redeem the mind, heart and will through the inflooding of creative intelligence and love.

I felt this perfectly described my higher self and my real purpose in life. Now I could see the value in working on all the 'lower' aspects of myself. The more I refined them and attained purity, the more would I embody the Christ Light.

Once I realised it was possible to find the masculine and feminine within me, I was able to use these symbols any time I found myself out of balance. When my lion roared too fiercely, my unicorn appeared to bring in gentleness, and when my unicorn was too timid to come out into the open, my lion gave her strength. But I also realised that there was a further step I needed to take on this strange spiritual path – to learn to love unconditionally.

IT'S IMPOSSIBLE TO KEEP anything secret when living in a community. Peter and I shared openly what we were going through, first with individuals and then with the whole group. I felt it was especially important to share my vision of the crumbling building. My inner voice said: "This is the Cosmic Christ energy which has been released here, Universal Love. Now it is a question of learning how to handle this tremendous love energy with wisdom and understanding. It is effecting every soul here in the community and some have been knocked off balance by it." That was certainly true: many couples seemed to be having similar difficulties to Peter's and mine.

There was much discussion about Peter and me being archetypes, and there was an expectation that as we became more whole and clear about our relationship so would everyone in the community become clearer about theirs. Feeling responsible for the whole group was a heavy burden to bear. I didn't want to have to be an example to everyone else.

The instructions to stop giving guidance so that everyone would turn within seemed to bring more confusion than clarity too. People were making sincere efforts to find answers for themselves, but it seemed to me that some 'guidance' was pure selfishness or a justification for following a personal desire. David Spangler wrote an open letter to the community suggesting that the whole matter of guidance had become glamourised and distorted and that it was being used for the self, not for the highest good of all. Since I couldn't share my own guidance, I retreated to the solace of keeping my private journal where I voiced my frustration and bewilderment.

Around this time I was given a vision of Peter's changing role: I saw the whole community becoming very strong and moving into group consciousness, with Peter in the role of counsellor, friend, adviser – a person with great wisdom and understanding to whom people came for help and advice. It was no longer necessary for him to hold all the reins. He was able to release all of them in complete faith and trust, knowing that each individual was responsible for him- or herself for the whole. It was a beautiful vision and I was uplifted by it. Enthusiastically I described it to Peter but he reacted exactly as he had done when I brought the subject up before. He could not accept it. Meanwhile the members of the community were chafing at the bit and almost every group discussion ended up with how to get Peter to let go. I was totally frustrated. Peter wouldn't give my opinion any credit and I couldn't show him my guidance to prove I was right.

I decided the best thing I could do for myself and everyone else was to go away for a while; to have a break, gain some perspective. I went to the south of England to stay with Ross and Aileen Stewart. My daughter Jenny and her family lived nearby and I visited them each day. There I found peace of mind. I was the beloved granny, no matter what, with nothing more expected of me than to be there, read stories and help Jenny about the house.

On the way back to Ross and Aileen's one day I was gazing out of the window of the bus when a thought came into my mind: can I say to you and you say to me, "I love you," without either of us feeling uncomfortable, threatened or that something is expected of us? Can we love one another unconditionally?

I thought about this. Could I say that I loved Peter in that way? I couldn't honestly say yes. I expected him to pay me the same amount of attention he gave Alice or the many psychics who crossed his path. I did feel threatened and uncomfortable. I found it very difficult to be warm and loving to him knowing that his affection was at the very best shared with another woman, or at worst was not there for me at all. On the other hand, could I say that I loved my grandchildren in this unconditional way? Without a doubt, yes. No matter how difficult they might be, I could still love them and, as soon as the tantrum was over, put them on my knee and give them a kiss and a cuddle. So why was it that I couldn't bring myself to sit on the edge of Peter's chair and put my arms around him and say, "I love you"? Somehow I just couldn't until I was sure Peter was willing to love me in the same way. But I wanted to.

When I returned to the community I felt refreshed and ready for a healing to take place. But no sooner had I settled back into my routine than all the wounds opened again. I felt strained, bewildered, unable to see things in their proper perspective. I wrote in my journal:

> I'm afraid, so afraid. It's as if all I have believed in has been an illusion, a dream – and I've woken up to find what? I have this feeling that I am not needed, and a longing to fade away into the background. I don't know what is happening to my relationship with Peter. I feel

miles apart from him. I want to trust him but I'm not sure whether I can. My faith in him has been shattered. He says all he has done regarding Alice has been guided, but I find myself doubting him. I have never doubted him before; I have had complete faith in him since You brought us together. I suppose I feel deep down that, if this has happened once with Alice, it can happen again and again, and he will call it guided each time. That's what hurts. I want to release him completely and not care what happens, but at present that would mean closing my heart to him, and I can't do that. I care so much. I long to be able to leave behind the past and the painful things he has said and live in the now; to be able to start all over again. What is blocking me?

In a vision I was shown a blackboard with a mess of scribbles and jumbled words that made no sense. I saw a hand take a damp cloth and erase all the confusion. I heard the words: "Accept in trust and faith that all is clear and clean, and move into something new. Stroke by stroke see the perfect picture emerge. It is a waste of time looking back. Take that damp cloth of faith, trust and belief and wipe away the past. Start doing it now."

If only it were as easy as that! I tried to wipe the memories out of my mind, but the turmoil persisted. I couldn't seem to do it.

During the summer one of our many visitors to the community, Sandy Mills from Canada, came to see me. In the course of conversation I told him that I had a daughter, Sue, living in Canada whom I had not seen for a long time. To my surprise, a few weeks after he left I received a lovely letter from him inviting me to come to Canada and offering to pay for my ticket. My immediate reaction was: Oh no, I couldn't possibly do that! Have a man pay for me to visit him? My old-fashioned conscience pricked me, and I even wondered whether Sandy had 'designs' on me. I didn't want to be compromised.

I thought about it a little longer and decided that this was a kind gesture from someone who wanted to give to me. I longed to see Sue and her young sons, whom I had never met, and the idea of a holiday did appeal to me. So I accepted. Peter didn't bat an eyelid, so either he knew I was quite safe with Sandy or he simply didn't care. A rebellious little voice inside me said, "Well, Peter has had his fling, so why shouldn't I?"

For the first time in years I travelled alone, flying from London to Montreal. Sandy met me at the airport and took me to his apartment. He had arranged several dinner parties for me to meet his friends, and he took me out to interesting places. He made me feel like a woman again, looking after me, buying me flowers, caring for me in every respect. We drove to Toronto to see Sue and her family, which was marvellous, and all the time he made no demands on me whatsoever. I just had to sit back and enjoy myself.

When my conscience gave me trouble about accepting all this love and attention, I asked for guidance. "My beloved, accept your relationship with Sandy as a gift of love from Me. It is one of love, joy and freedom. Treasure it and nurture it and give constant thanks for it, for it is truly beautiful. He will help to heal the wounds by his love and understanding, so you may know the true meaning of joy and freedom. All the time you are learning to stand on your own two feet so that you are independent. Let it all unfold. You have tremendous work to do; it is only just beginning. The old cycle is finished. Never be tied down by any relationship again."

I just loved Sandy. I could be absolutely myself with him. Just as he asked nothing of me, so could I tolerate his idiosyncrasies with humour and without judgement. I remembered the question I had asked myself on the bus. Could I say to Sandy, "I love you," without either of us feeling uncomfortable or feeling that something more was expected? I tried it. It was wonderful! There was the greatest love between us, and the greatest freedom. How I longed for Peter and I to love each other in the same way. If it was possible with Sandy, then surely it must be possible with Peter, somehow.

I returned home nourished and stronger. For a while I felt an improvement in the atmosphere between Peter and me, but I had the sneaking feeling that he was relieved I had had such a good time with Sandy, as that gave him more licence to do as he pleased. I hated myself for having such an uncharitable thought.

In the summer of 1975 Alice left for Sweden, her home. Anthony Brooke, who was living in Sweden at the time, invited me to visit him shortly afterwards and while I was there I spent a few days with Alice. We talked very openly and I saw clearly she was not the threat to our marriage. It went deeper than that. Peter had needed the experience with her to open up a part of him that he had never permitted himself to express before – indeed had not even known was there in him – and he had been unable to do that with me. I still felt inadequate because of that, but I experienced a deep love and trust for Alice. I was filled with respect for the way one so young had handled a difficult situation with such profound integrity and wisdom.

EVEN THOUGH I HAD been going through some troubled times personally, the community was continuing to flourish and develop. One of the most important milestones was our return to Cluny Hill. Fourteen years previously, at the time of our transfer to the Trossachs, God had told us that we would go back there, but after Peter lost his job with the hotel chain it seemed unlikely. Besides, our lives were so fully taken up by the development of the light centre which became the community at the caravan park that gradually the sadness we felt about Cluny Hill evaporated.

In the years after we left Cluny Hill Hotel it had deteriorated rapidly. No longer was it the clean, light-filled hub of activity it had been under our management; it had become a dilapidated and run-down barn of a place. We had been prompted to visit it in the summer of 1965 and already we could feel a great change. That evening God had said: "You saw for yourself how the very life force has been withdrawn from Cluny Hill Hotel. It is dead. And yet in the grounds you could feel radiations as you walked around the garden. Try to see it as a plant which has finished flowering for the season and is being cut down until there is nothing left on top. To all outward appearances it looks dead, and yet the life force is there in the very roots and at the right time it will once again burst forth and flower and flourish."

By 1975 the Findhorn Foundation, as we were now called, was receiving such a lot of publicity that we were finding it difficult to accommodate all the people who wanted to visit us. But it was only when an American guest pointed out to Peter that the situation was only going to get worse and asked him what plans he had to cope with it that Peter realised Cluny Hill would be the perfect place to accommodate visitors. He made enquiries and discovered that the hotel was up for sale, probably because the owners could no longer make a profit out of running it.

It was important for each member of the community to give their full support to the huge leap of faith that purchasing the hotel would represent, so there were many meetings and discussions, while small groups went over to Cluny Hill to attune to the place. The decision to purchase was finally made on 17 November 1975, the 13th birthday of the community. Significantly, Peter and I were away at the time, so this was one of the first big decisions made by the attunement of the community as a whole rather than based on my guidance or on Peter's intuition.

So Cluny Hill Hotel, renamed Cluny Hill College, became part of the Findhorn Foundation as a centre for our guests and for workshops and classes. We had truly returned – although in a way we had never dreamed of. I didn't really feel any sense of surprise. God had told me we would come back and, even though it had taken fourteen years, I felt a deep sense of gratitude that my guidance had been confirmed.

~ *10* ~

An impulse is moving through you that can be called the School or Ray of Mary. You, Eileen, carry within yourself your attunement to the Mary Principle, which historically invokes and nourishes the Christ energies and helps them to become one with human nature. This principle is neither male nor female in terms of physical gender; it is an embodiment of a feminine principle. It is more than just love. It is an aspect of will and intelligence as well, which permits organisation to take place but from the direction of a consciousness deeply attuned to the subtleties and interplays of the human personality and spirit.

In building the new age, what is ultimately required is an energy that is balanced, that can invoke love and wisdom, with the ability to put this love and wisdom into action effectively, to bring them from the abstract into the concrete realm where the average individual can relate to them.

Transmission through David Spangler

OVER THE YEARS I had had a number of powerful experiences of Mary, the mother of Jesus Christ, beginning with the one while I was making the boys' bunk beds in our old caravan, when I was told, "You are Mary, the mother of Jesus the Christ." When I had questioned that, God had asked me if I could accept it as a Ray of which many people were an expression. That made perfect sense to me, as I had felt an affinity with Mary from childhood. Some time later a woman who came to see me confided with an air of importance that she had received guidance that she was the reincarnation of Mary. I told her my experience too and said I felt there were many souls on the Mary Ray. She found it difficult to accept, as she felt so strongly that she was *the* Mary, so I left it at that, knowing that, for me, sharing that Ray with many souls gave me immense joy and freedom.

One day while meditating in the Sanctuary I suddenly saw myself in a healing sanctuary I knew just outside Glastonbury, sitting in a chair looking at a big fireplace. Mary was standing to the right of it, smiling at me. She held out her hand and I went to her. She said, "Now come and embody my spirit in joy, for this is the new age." As I laid my hand in hers, I disappeared into her.

About three days later Peter received a letter from an old Dutch woman. At the end of the letter she wrote: *Please give my love to Eileen. To me she is the personification of Mary, the mother of Jesus, who to me is Woman in the new age.* I was taken aback. I had met this woman only once for a brief talk and I didn't think she knew me well at all. I certainly had not mentioned my Mary experiences to her.

My next experience of Mary took place in Turkey several years later. In August 1972 we had a visitor who caused quite a stir. His name was Dr Tanman and he was the mayor of Ephesus in Turkey. His visit was, for Peter and me, absolute confirmation that all the years of work sending out love and light on the inner had borne fruit. Dr Tanman stepped off the plane with tears streaming down his cheeks and embraced Peter and me as if we'd known each other for years, which in a sense we had.

Once we were back in the community he told us his story. Years before, in the early 1960s, Dr Tanman had started meeting regularly with a group of businessmen to meditate. Their purpose was to establish telepathic contact with centres of light all over the world, including one in Britain which, they were told, was one of five or seven primary light centres being established. They had no idea where it was or what it was called. In 1972 one of this group of men, who ran a youth hostel in Istanbul, met an airline pilot and during their conversation the pilot mentioned Findhorn.

"Findhorn? What is that?" the hostel keeper asked him.

"Oh, it's a place in Scotland where some people started a spiritual community," the pilot replied, and he told what he knew about it.

The hostel keeper became very excited. "I'd like you to come to a meeting of the group of people I meditate with and tell them all this," he said, picking up the phone.

Very soon the whole group met and their source of guidance confirmed that the Findhorn Community was indeed the centre they had been linking with in their meditations for so long. Arrangements were made for Dr Tanman to come and visit us himself. It was a moving experience for all of us, the culmination of ten years' work – concrete proof that our 'network of light' was real. Others like ourselves had been doing similar work. The group of businessmen I'd seen in a vision did in fact exist!

Dr Tanman's visit led naturally to an invitation to us to visit his group in Istanbul. There I had a moving experience that put me more deeply in touch with the energy of Mary and her role in my life. A few days after we arrived in Turkey we were taken to Selsuk, a small village near Ephesus, to visit Marimana, the House of Mary. As I approached the chapel my shoulders felt heavy, as if I was carrying a burden. I sat down to meditate in this humble place and it seemed that the awful weight of all the grief and sorrow in the world descended upon me, pushing me down into darkness. Tears poured down my face and I sobbed with grief for the world. As I wept, I remembered Mary's words to me in the healing sanctuary: "Come and embody my spirit in joy, for this is the new age." Although this didn't stop the tears, it gave me strength to bear the pain.

I left the chapel still weeping. When I shared my experience with our hosts, they told me that according to legend this was the house where Mary had lived with John after Jesus was crucified. Then I understood. I was at one with the mother who had seen her son die; at one with those in our world who have suffered terribly and been the victims of human cruelty throughout the ages. I found a little spring that bubbled up out of the ground and washed my face and hands in the cool, clear water. Then, without knowing what prompted me, I spontaneously made the sign of the cross on my forehead. The weight of the sorrow seemed to lift from my shoulders and I felt cleansed and healed.

At the end of the week, before we left, I felt I had to go back to Marimana once more. This time my experience was quite different. As I sat in the chapel, a deep peace and stillness washed over me, like balm to a wound. I opened my eyes and for the first time noticed the statue of a black Madonna on the little altar. It was very old and the hands and feet had been broken off, but it had a most beautiful, serene face. I seemed to hear her say: "Now go and be my hands and feet." And I realised that the grief and sorrow had been lifted not only from me but also from this place and from that part of humanity Mary represented. I knew that one aspect of my life's work was to transmute the sorrow and grief of the old world into joy. It was a huge task, but all those on the Mary Ray would do it together.

I came out of the chapel radiant and recounted my experience to our Turkish friends, as well as some guidance I had received for their group while I was in there. It moved us all to tears of joy and our parting was filled with love and a sense of connectedness in the work we were doing together.

PETER COULDN'T RELATE to my experiences with Mary. Nor could he see how my attempts to balance the masculine and feminine within me had anything to do with him, although I felt he too would have benefited from working in this way. The feeling of separateness between us grew. It seemed to me that part of the reason I had been so open to the experience of sadness in Turkey was that it reflected how I was feeling about my own life.

The first tour Peter and I did together was in 1975, travelling from city to city in Europe giving talks and slide shows. I felt I had nothing to contribute. It terrified me to stand up on a platform in front of a sea of strange faces, so I gladly let Peter tell the whole story of how the community had started as he showed the slides. It wasn't so bad talking to individuals afterwards, as then I could relate to them as people, but the thought of addressing them as an audience left me cold with fright, so I just sat there 'being' instead. Peter was impatient with my fears, but since he enjoyed doing the talking he let me be. It was not a happy experience, however, and I decided he could do the tours in future and I would stay at home as much as possible.

Nothing in my life seemed to be going very well. I was so depressed I went to see the doctor. He gave me antidepressant pills, which made me worse to the point where I stayed in my bungalow for weeks seeing no one and going nowhere. I was so low that when a film crew came to make a film of the community I refused to see them. Finally Peter persuaded me to do an interview. A film about the Findhorn Community, he said, would be incomplete without me in it. As I sat talking to the interviewer, I looked down at my feet. I had on two different shoes! – a revealing statement about my confused state of mind.

Even my relationship with the boys took a nose-dive. The middle one,

Jonathan, was emerging into early manhood as headstrong and rebellious as a young colt. He questioned everything: the way I tried to live by faith under God's guidance; the validity of the guidance itself; David Spangler and his work; and even the very existence of a God at all. He believed only in what he could see, feel and understand scientifically. He planned to study Biology and Ecological Science, in which he could concentrate on the facts, not the mystique, of nature. I did not help matters by disapproving of a relationship he was having with a girl in the community who was older than him. When I refused to let them live together, sparks flew, and I lost in more ways than one. Our relationship, which had been very close, was broken. I asked God what to do and was told in no uncertain terms to release Jonathan completely, to take my hands off him and to let him grow. He had lessons to learn on his own and in his own way. So that is what I did, but it took years to mend the rift between us.

When Christopher, the eldest, left home to go to university, my heart sank. I was afraid I had failed him by not giving him the kind of formal spiritual training other children had. I had not taught the boys to say prayers, and we had never read the Bible together. We never imposed our spiritual life on the boys and I hadn't even taught them to meditate, to go within and listen for God's voice. I wrote to Christopher pouring out my heart and sharing my sense of failure. This is the letter I received in reply:

> As always your words choke me, tears come to my eyes and my heart fills with thanks. Very few children are as mightily blessed as we are, and fewer still are brought up under the direct guidance of God. How could you possibly have felt you had failed me? The reason the Bible was not used in my education is many-faceted. Although the Bible contains much truth, it has also become polluted by constant reinterpretation. If one is brought up under the Bible, the time comes when the patterns learned from it have to be broken down and the soul has to turn within. This can be a very painful process for the rigid, orthodox person. So you see, my dear Mum, I believe you did the right thing, and have produced an adult with a broad horizon and an enquiring mind. Rather than being turned away from the Bible, I can now see the wood for the trees and extract the truth from it. Ramming its contents down my throat would only have turned me from it instead of producing an active interest. Just as we should look for the guru within, we must also find the Bible within.

Findhorn and the whole joyous experience of living in a community of spiritual people has had a profound effect on me, much deeper than you or I are aware of. Had you ever forced your work down my throat I dare say I might have rejected it and 'dropped in' on society instead. I have come to see how blessed I am and thank God continuously. Yes, Mum, I thank him especially for you and Dad and the way in which I have been brought up. I know that my life will have a great destiny and I will not fail. All I really want to say is thanks!

When I received this letter, I burst into tears and thanked God for its sheer wonder and wisdom. I realised that children are like pieces of blotting paper: they absorb what you do rather than listening to what you say. It was comforting, at a time when self-doubt besieged me at every turn, to know that I had done something right.

With my self-esteem at its lowest ebb, it was clear I needed help, and sure enough it came – in the form of a visitor to the community who stopped in to see me. We talked and talked about his life and mine. Just as he was leaving, he looked me in the eyes and said seriously, "Eileen, don't you think it's time you started loving yourself? You can only love others to the extent that you love yourself."

What on earth was he talking about? Love myself? That would be egotistical and against the grain of everything I had been taught since I was a child. "You love yourself! Where's your humility?" The schoolgirl taunt rang in my ears. "Always put others before yourself," I heard my beloved auntie say. "Take that make-up off your face, Eileen! It's a sign of your vanity." Andrew. "Everything for the good of the whole. Take nothing for the self." Peter. "If love is taken to the self, it can cause chaos." God.

Oh no, loving myself wasn't right. It couldn't be. I should forget myself and my petty smallness, rise above it all, not wallow in self-pity or self-indulgence.

A few days later I was sitting at my dressing table doing my hair when I caught sight of myself in the mirror as if for the first time. I stared at this person. Do I love myself? Can I love myself? For an instant I saw behind the familiar face, the hair, the eyes, to the divinity within me. 'Yes. I can! I can love the divinity within me. I love God. God is within me. So, yes, I can easily say I love myself, when myself is not just the little personality, Eileen, but is all of me. I was exalted by this revelation and danced for joy inside. I had found the key to unlock a mysterious door, and discovered a wonderful freedom. I could look at myself in the mirror and say, with no hesitation, "You are a wonderful woman."

Then my 'yes, but' voice came in. It's easy to say I love myself when I'm talking about the pure and beautiful divinity within me. But what about the times, so many lately, when I'm negative, angry, sad? When I fall short of who I really am? How can I love myself then? Is that God too?

My true inner voice simply said: "No self-judgement, no self-condemnation. Forgive yourself and move on, for I have need of you. Don't waste time and energy wallowing in self-pity, feeling you are a failure. Learn the lesson each time, apply it and then move on. There is so much to be done."

I WAS BEGINNING TO FEEL better but there was still the situation between Peter and me to work through. We were invited to do a tour in the United States and I agreed to go largely because we would be visiting David Spangler and Myrtle Glines in Belmont, California. They had formed the Lorian Association with Dorothy and a few others who had left the Findhorn Community with them. David and Myrtle and the other Lorians who were there gave us a wonderfully warm welcome. I felt I was home, surrounded by all these dear friends.

Peter and I shared with them what had been happening between us, including his friendship with Alice and the difficulty we were having in establishing a new and independent relationship. We talked long into the night about the community, filling the Lorians in on everything that was happening there, not least the instability in relationships that had resulted from – or at least coincided with – the instability in our own.

Then David asked if we would like to have a session with 'John' ; one of the forms his sensitivity to higher realms took was a relationship he had – and still has – with a higher being calling itself 'John'. The information that came through him was always pure and enlightening. It was also thoroughly objective and Peter respected it totally, which was reassuring to me, since he no longer trusted anything I might say about my own guidance concerning him.

During the session I asked: "How is it that two people who have worked so closely together on a high level can part and go their separate ways, when I have had so many promises regarding the work that Peter and I have to do together in the days ahead? If I know there is a reason for it, I feel I can give my best where I am needed. Otherwise, it appears futile and hopeless."

John's response was complex and extensive, and it took years of deep thought for me to understand it. At one point he said: "God is like a seed within oneself. The future is inherent in the seed. As it grows, other elements enter which pave the way for a new reality and a new future, a new seed. Thus, outwardly, it may seem that prophecy fails, but what is really happening is that a new birth is taking place which was inherent in the older prophecy but which was not foreseen. The promises of God are not broken; but the promises of God which are in the seeds of one level are broken so that the seeds of another level may flourish. That which is essential remains."

He went on: "The voice you hear is an amalgam of your own consciousness and the source. What you hear is not the source but its servant. Now you yourself must expand and grow so that your relationship with your source, a life energy inexpressible in words, can grow. Out of that relationship shall come a new voice, or perhaps a fuller communication. God is not an abstract but a relationship.

"Behind the voice, then, is a source which is your true nature, which you are seeking to grow into ever more fully. For this reason the patterns between you and your partner need to be broken and the energies between you dispersed. This dispersal of energy we do not view as a separation but a necessary growth procedure so that both of you can evolve into deeper levels of attunement."

There followed a full description of the Mary principle, with which I strongly identified. My inner experiences with Mary, as well as the work I had done with the balance of the masculine and feminine, made sense now and had a purpose for my own personal development, for that of my relationship with Peter, and for the community too. For John explained that the elemental, focused, practical energy that had been required to build the foundations of the community was now no longer as important as the need for balance, wisdom and love. Now that the form had been built, it was time to focus on people, bringing clarity into emotions and balancing human needs with getting the practical work done with human needs of relationship.

For this purpose Peter and I needed to balance ourselves, no longer seeing our partnership as two halves of a whole but as two whole beings working together. Although I had sensitivity and attunement to the Mary principle, I had to work to bring out from within me the qualities of will and wisdom, to become more effective and active in the community, and to grow strong in myself and stand on my own two feet. It was time for me to come out from behind Peter's shadow.

About Peter, John said: "Peter has anchored the basic structural energy. Now it must be blended and harmonised with the other aspects of his being which we summarise under this term 'the Mary principle', by which is meant love and the field of understanding on emotional and intuitive levels and in human relationships. Thus he is being moved out of the position of law and leadership. His personal transformation is important to the community, even if he must leave the community to do it. But if he does, then he goes in blessing and in protection and the community will require your presence. You will continue to work with him on the inner, for you cannot affect the energies in the community without affecting his energies as well, so closely are they blended. The two of you together – not together as you have been, but as two wholenesses combining to manifest a greater whole – can help the community to place itself in a more stable position."

John described my role as an educative one, not in the formal sense of giving classes or workshops, requiring special skills or techniques, but just by being available to people and practising living the guidance I had received for so many years. This was exactly what my own guidance had been telling me ever since I had first been told to stop receiving guidance for the community. It helped, somehow, to hear it from another source.

John also talked of a role for me in the world beyond the community. At that time, however, I was fulfiling it by helping to ground the Mary principle within the community through my realisation that the birth of the Christ is in the affairs of everyday life and humanity's challenges; through bringing clarity to human emotions and helping people to realise their deeper potential.

This transmission through David Spangler had a profound effect on our lives and the lives of all who were living in the Findhorn Community at the time. It applied to everyone and we studied it together, discussing the meaning of the changes and how they might look on a form level. Peter and I had the opportunity to make these radical changes within ourselves while continuing to be in a marriage relationship, and I was determined that we would do it. I still believed that was God's plan for us and that somehow we could achieve the miraculous, which was what this switching of roles seemed to require. And for all the talk, the studying, the discussing of archetypal roles, it was in the living of all this that we would be tested.

I FELT LIKE A SMALL child learning to walk, falling down and picking myself up over and over again. I longed to close my heart, particularly to Peter, so that I no longer felt the pain, but again and again God urged me to keep my heart open, to keep the love flowing, and never to build a fence around myself because I was afraid of being hurt.

And the process of growing, of becoming balanced individuals did hurt. I felt prickly, and loving Peter was a supreme effort. He was away on tour increasingly, and more often than not I preferred to stay at home. I did, however, agree to join him on a tour of Australia in 1978, as I could combine it with a visit to my daughter, Mary Liz, in New Zealand.

When we met in Australia, Peter had just come from a month of talks and workshops in Hawaii. I knew intuitively that something had happened, and I felt a tightness around my heart. At the first opportunity I asked him if he had fallen in love with someone. He had. All my good resolutions about releasing Peter to find himself in order to become a warmer, more loving human being went out of the window. The thought of an attractive and apparently psychic young woman luring him away to bask on the beaches of Hawaii was too much for me to take without reaction – and react I did! I had no idea there was such a strong possessive streak in me. I was consumed with jealousy. Sadly, I couldn't contain my anger at all and I let Peter have the full brunt of it. It was not pleasant. But the show had to go on. We had engagements all over Australia for six weeks and somehow we had to come to terms with one another and present ourselves and the Findhorn Community to the Australian people.

I wrote privately in my journal:

> *I feel bewildered and angry because Peter thinks he is always right*
> *in everything he does, and because I feel so strongly that 'whom God*

has brought together, let no man put asunder'. I know Peter and I were brought together by God, but I cannot accept that what is happening right now is right and blessed by God. I do not want to play second fiddle in a relationship because I don't feel this is what God wants. If Peter makes up his mind he needs a relationship to open up his heart, he will go ahead, no matter what I do or feel, which gives me a great sense of inadequacy. Perhaps it would be best to go our separate ways without any further strife, Peter says he is committed to our relationship, but I can't understand that. It doesn't make sense.

Peter loathed my outbreaks of rage against him and did everything he could to avoid them. Although his relationship with the woman in Hawaii came to nothing, he withdrew even further from me and told me nothing about what he was going through, especially in his heart. He knew I would sense if he was involved with another woman, but it was very difficult for him to tell me for fear of making me angry. I got angry anyway, even more so when I thought he was deliberately deceiving me. My inner voice said: "Tell Peter that when he can keep what is happening in his relationships with other women out in the open so there is nothing to hide, tremendous changes will take place in his life. When the relationships open his heart so he can truly love you, his true partner, then he will know he is moving in the right direction. This is what I want to happen. You both need to help to bring it about. I tell you to release him and be at peace, knowing and trusting that the time will come when Peter will recognise you as you really are. When that happens, he will know you as I want him to know you; the love will flow freely and you will work side by side in the most wonderful way."

When Peter and I were in Melbourne, we were taken to William Rickett's Sanctuary, an exhibition of sculptures in a tropical forest. As we walked among the trees and ferns, every now and then we came across a sensitive sculpture of an aboriginal man, child or woman. I was strongly affected by the powerful, earthy vibration of that beautiful place. I couldn't make out what it was, until it struck me that I was feeling the elemental energies ROC and Peter had referred to and which I had always fought against. As I stood in front of a huge statue of the Earth Mother surrounded by her children, I felt myself become one with her. I walked away filled with love and respect for nature. I felt for the first time I could blend those powerful earth energies with the Christ energy and that there was no separation between them. I was also elated to realise that I could now visit Hawaii. Even though I had often longed to go there, I had always felt that I wouldn't be able to handle the primitive elemental energies of the islands to which Peter related so strongly.

Having experienced the elemental energy myself, I had taken a big step closer to understanding and accepting Peter. I smiled to think I had had to come to Australia to recognise something that had been around me in the garden at Findhorn all the time. It was actually a new part of myself I had discovered, and I had travelled a long way to find it.

I RESOLVED TO PUT ASIDE my inferiority complex and travel with Peter more. In working together I believed we would find a new respect for one another and a new purpose. I gave workshops myself, based on my experience with the balance of masculine and feminine energy within. Although Peter didn't think much of this theme, our workshops complemented each other, since his were on the Laws of Manifestation and the principles of starting a spiritual community. He never failed, however, to acknowledge the part I had played in the beginnings of the Findhorn Community. My workshops went well, even though I did find myself in some tight corners at times with the questions people asked. But I found it best just to be myself and not to try to bluff my way through anything, and it worked.

In Sydney I had an experience I shall never forget. Several hundred people came to attend our workshops one weekend at the university. We had four going on simultaneously, led by Peter, myself and two community members, Vance and Helen, who were travelling with us. I had about 150 people in mine. I noticed a man who came in late and sat at the back. He was sending out the most negative vibrations, so I enfolded him in love and carried on leading the group through a guided visualisation on the masculine and feminine. At the end this same man stood up and said gruffly, "It's all a lot of nonsense." He was tall, broad-shouldered and tough-looking, his face burned brown by the sun, in every way a reflection of my image of a typical 'macho' Australian. Peter's apprehensive words flashed through my mind: "You can't do the masculine and feminine workshop in Australia. The men there will never accept what you're talking about."

My heart sank. Perhaps Peter was right, I thought. However, I have to do something, so here goes.

"What made you come to this workshop when there were three others to choose from?" I asked him, all the time sending him as much love as I could muster.

"Well, it was the feeling. . . " he replied uncomfortably.

"Oh, really? What was the 'feeling'?"

"It was – er – feminine." He looked even more uncomfortable.

"Do you know why you stayed?"

"No," he said, "I don't really know why I stayed, but I'm leaving now." He started to move towards the door.

A ripple of agitation swept through the room. People were feeling upset that anyone should criticise. I kept sending out love, and gradually I could feel everyone in the room begin to do the same.

Just as the man reached the door I asked him if he would come up to the platform to talk to me. To my surprise, he did.

"Did you by chance get any symbols during the meditation?" I asked.

"Well, as a matter of fact I did," he replied.

"Do tell me what they were." I was intrigued. "What was your masculine symbol?"

"King Kong."

I smiled encouragingly. The loving support from the rest of the people in the room was tangible.

"That's an interesting one. And did you have a feminine symbol?"

"A little white mouse."

I suppressed a smile this time. The symbolism was so apt!

"And what happened when you brought King Kong and the little white mouse together?"

"To begin with it was difficult. They didn't do anything. But then the mouse ran up his leg and sat on his shoulder."

"Well, that's encouraging," I said. "At least King Kong didn't trample the little mouse underfoot."

We talked a little longer and then I thanked him so much for sharing himself. As I looked into his face I saw that it had softened, and there was a gentleness in his eyes. He gave me a huge bear hug and left, beaming. Later on, when I saw him again, he was quite a different person, friendly, warm and caring. So I was glad I had dared to give my workshop in Australia, even if it was just for him.

PETER AND I TRAVELLED to South Africa, the United States and Canada and back to Australia and New Zealand together in the following few years. Although there was still tension between us, I felt that at least we were developing a working relationship. It was still difficult for me to stand up to his powerful will, and I left all the arrangements to him, especially when we were travelling together. I was feeling more confident and outgoing than before, but I was still under Peter's shadow. Whenever people asked why I didn't say anything about the founding of the community during our presentations, I just said, "Oh, Peter does it much better than I do," and left it at that.

In 1979 I made what was, for me, a major step. I visited Hawaii, by myself. I stayed with a friend and had a most wonderful time relaxing on the beach in the sun and getting in touch with the powerful elemental energies of Hawaii: the warmth, the lush vegetation, the volcanoes which are liable to erupt at any time, throwing the fiery lava from inside the earth into the air. Both the indigenous people of Hawaii and the Westerners who have adopted the islands as their home live an easy-going, relaxed life in harmony with the luxuriance of nature, while their music throbs with an earthy beat like the pounding of the enormous waves breaking on the sands. All this, to me, was what ROC and Peter had described as the 'elemental energies'. At long last I understood what Peter had experienced in Hawaii, for I felt the doors of my heart flung wide open and the true me emerged, relaxed, open and free. As I stood at the edge of the crater of the volcano Haleakala, I said, "With all my heart, I want to learn to love unconditionally. Please God, help me and show me how."

A step in that direction was to confront my jealousy and meet the woman who had been involved with Peter. To my surprise, and hers, we discovered a great love for one another and developed a deep friendship that has lasted for years.

I left Hawaii in high spirits. I was relaxed, slim and suntanned and felt on top of the world. I thought to myself, "This is the sort of woman Peter really wants, one full of life and vitality." I looked forward eagerly to seeing him in Edinburgh, where we were to meet for the graduation of our eldest son, Christopher, from Medical School. For the first time in a long while Peter and I and our three sons would be together. It would be a wonderful reunion, the happiest day in our lives.

We met in the boys' flat. I couldn't stop talking about my time in Hawaii and how much it meant to me. "Peter, at last I've seen the light. Now I know what you're experiencing and I feel we should go and spend a few weeks there together. I feel like a new woman. I've promised to go and stay with Penny until her baby's born and they're out of hospital, but I'll be free after that, so perhaps we could go to Hawaii in September."

Peter had gone very quiet. He was standing with his back to me, looking out the window. Then he turned round and said, "I'm going to Hawaii in July."

"Oh Peter," I said, "couldn't you wait until September so we can go together?"

"I'm going in July, Eileen, and this time I'm going with a new partner, a woman I met in California."

For an endless moment my mind went completely blank as if I did not comprehend his words; then the thoughts came, tumbling over themselves. But this is the morning we were all going as a family to watch Christopher graduate. Why tell me now? How can I get through this day knowing this? Who is she? How could he? And now, of all times, when I'm ready to change and be the kind of woman he's been looking for?

We went to the graduation and then had a picnic at the Botanical Gardens. I was seething inside myself. I felt hurt, angry and above all utterly rejected. Peter just looked blank, showing no feelings at all, and carried on chatting with the boys as if everything were normal. In the end my rage overwhelmed me and I tore my wedding ring off my finger and threw it at Peter as he lay on the grass.

"You can have a divorce right away," I said bitterly. "I shall see a lawyer as soon as possible." And I stormed off to be by myself in the gardens. I found a quiet spot on a bench under a huge spreading tree and asked for guidance. The only thing I received was: "You cannot divorce Peter in anger." Why the hell not? And yet I knew it was true.

Somehow I survived dinner with Peter and the boys that night. I slept in a separate room and didn't see Peter the next morning, as I left early to catch a train to be with my daughter in Devon. I thanked God that I had somewhere to go and plenty to keep me occupied, as I could not face going back to the community.

At my daughter's house I was kept busy with three small, lively grandchildren during the day, but at night it was sheer hell. I could not sleep for wrestling with all the negative emotions inside me. I tried to be sensible and come to terms with the situation, but it was as if I was in the pitch dark of an endless tunnel. I felt a complete failure as a wife and as a woman. My children no longer needed me now that they were grown up with their own lives to live. Now Peter had no more desire or use for me. There wasn't even a role for me in the community any more, as they were working things through themselves and did not need my 'parent' image. I didn't want to go back there.

My guidance was, however, very clear. God kept telling me I was not to divorce Peter. I was to wait. There was so much in the melting pot, I needed to be patient. I was to go back to the community, even though I didn't want to. I was to release Peter completely. I didn't always like what I heard, but those times of stillness, listening to God, were a kind of life-line, and I clung to it.

I had not written to anyone at home since I'd seen Peter in Edinburgh so it came as a shock when I started receiving a great number of letters from people in the community that read like messages of condolence. I rang Peter. To my astonishment he told me that he had shared with the whole community that we were parting, and that he was releasing the community into the hands of François Duquesne who had worked with Peter for years and who, he felt, was the perfect person to take on the mantle of leadership. Peter was leaving the Findhorn Community for good.

I could hardly believe Peter had not waited for me to return before announcing all this. It was all so cut and dried. Now I really couldn't return to the community. I wanted to be left alone to sort this out myself.

Nevertheless, my guidance was firm and clear. I had to go back. If I did not do it now, I would have to do it later when it would be even more difficult. So I asked for God's grace to enable me to return to face 200 kind, loving people and accept their support and love for me. Oh God, what would they think of me? – after all the support to help us sort ourselves out, all the hopes that we would make a breakthrough, all these souls looking to Peter and me for the successful outcome to an age old problem. And I had failed to do my part.

~ 11 ~

In a vision I saw myself as a caterpillar. I was eating everything in front of me and the material things in life meant so much. Then something began to happen deep inside me. I felt a divine discontent which made me want to change. I turned within, into a chrysalis, and prayed and meditated in the stillness.

Then came the time when the grub longed to be something more. I wanted to change again, to move out of my dark, confined space into the light, to become a butterfly. The time of isolation was at an end. I began to wriggle and squirm until I broke out into the sunshine. At first my wings were stuck together, but the warmth of the sunlight soon dried them off. I shook my wings and then I began to fly. I was free! Life was filled with harmony, love, light and the joy of the Spirit.

I asked what was my purpose on this planet. I was told I was here to serve God and humanity, to sow the seeds of Love, Joy and Peace all over the world, to be what God is and to turn others within to live and move and have their being from that divine centre.

NEVER FOR ONE MOMENT had I thought Peter would leave me. In all our ups and downs I always believed we would move through our difficulties and emerge the other side a strong and balanced couple able to help others who were dealing with similar adjustments in their relationships.

I had prayed earnestly to be shown how to love all humanity unconditionally. In my meditations I offered myself to God in service, willing to do anything to learn to love in this way. I had not realised, when I invoked such a powerful energy, that I would have to take the consequences.

When Peter left me, I protested to God: "No! I didn't mean this to happen!" But my inner voice said: "You said you wanted to learn to love unconditionally. This is a perfect opportunity to learn to love Peter without expectations or demands." The time had come for me to release my dependence on Peter and become my own person. I prayed for God's grace to help me through it.

The first hurdle to overcome was my return to the community. I longed to hide away in a dark corner to lick my wounds, and I dreaded receiving sympathy even more than the judgement I expected would greet me. However, my guidance was clear that I should return to face everyone. How glad I am that I did. I was lovingly welcomed back as part of the family, and left alone as much as I needed to be. Everyone seemed to accept that it was indeed time for Peter to leave and let the community take responsibility for itself. In their loving detachment I found strength, and learned the difference between compassion and sympathy: the one offers love and strength, the other a reinforcement of self-pity and weakness.

In spite of my initial impulse, I curbed my desire to divorce Peter right away. My guidance continued to state firmly that I should not divorce him in anger. It would be a long time before I felt no anger towards him, so rather than make a mistake I did nothing about it.

Soon afterwards a dear friend and therapist came to Findhorn especially to see me and help me through my many tears. I had so much to face in myself. I was exhausted, but she was relentless as time was short and much work needed to be done. She said I was bleeding etherically and offered to do a guided healing meditation with me. This is the meditation Barbara led me through:

> *Visualise yourself in a meadow – a beautiful, green meadow where you feel happy and at home . . . In the distance you notice a high mountain and begin to move towards it . . . You see a spiral pathway leading to the top and you start to walk up it, quite easily . . .*
>
> *Without any effort you reach the top of the mountain where you find a temple . . . Inside the temple is an altar . . . Now lay everything in your life upon the altar, and give it to God.*

In my mind I laid Peter on the altar, with all my anger, jealousy, frustration pain and hurt pride. I gave it all to God.

Barbara continued:

> Now visualise an angel standing beside the altar, holding a pair of golden scissors . . . Take the scissors and, of your own choosing, cut the psychic umbilical cord that has linked you and Peter through the years.

I cut the cord with the scissors the angel gave me, then I tied a knot and placed it in my solar plexus. The angel told me not to worry about Peter's end of the cord – it would be taken care of. Then I came out of the temple and went into a silent meditation.

During the meditation I found myself standing before a silver dome. I went inside and stood in the middle of the dome. The inside was silver as well. As I stood there, I heard the words: "Now accept the Freedom of the Spirit, the Joy of the Spirit." Then it was as if the top of my head opened up and the silver from the dome poured into and through my whole being. It poured into every cell and atom until there was nothing left of me but pure silver.

After Barbara left for the United States, I asked God what the experience of that weekend had been all about. I was told I would feel the benefit of it in time. About two days later I realised that I felt free. I no longer felt the same attachment to Peter, nor the pain that went with it. Even more wonderful, I found that I could send him love and blessings. I thanked God for the glorious feeling and hoped it would last. However, it was to take me years to work through my feelings about Peter. Every time I thought I had succeeded, something would happen to throw me off balance and I'd fall flat on my face again. And I'd realise I still had little hooks attached to Peter that I had to release before I could truly say I was free.

I got so angry and frustrated with myself, I had to remind myself constantly of those words of wisdom I had been given in guidance: "No self-condemnation, no self-judgement. Forgive yourself and move on, for I have need of you. There is so much to be done." And I'd pick myself up and try again to love without conditions. I did my best to look for the lesson in the situation, so that I could learn it and move on without wasting time and energy being sorry for myself or feeling a failure.

About a week after Barbara left God said to me: "Now I want you to lay the community on the altar and give it to me." I couldn't understand why I needed to do that. I didn't feel attached to the community. My inner voice said: "As you have had to give up your children, and then Peter, now it is time for you to give up the community, which is your biggest child." I have to admit that I cried and cried. But then I laid the community on the altar and gave it to God, and as I did so I realised it was the last thing I had. I no longer had anything to hold on to or be dependent upon. In future my security would be in God alone. I had put God first in my life and now I accepted the freedom of the Spirit.

It was painful for me to release the community, not least because it was going through a difficult stage of adolescent rebelliousness, rejecting advice from any parent figure, including me. I stood back and watched as things happened that I didn't like, and I spent much time in meditation, where I was encouraged to build a good strong bridge of love with the community which I could walk across at the right time.

I was also given a vision of the community. It was of a beautiful, tall, strong tree. I heard the words: "The leaves will change with the seasons, like people coming and going, and some of the branches will even break off in a storm, like Peter leaving; but the trunk is strong and true, and the roots go deep, deep down. They are rooted in Me, and the sap flows freely. I am the sap. Be not disturbed."

Remembering that vision helped me many a time, for I could see that those spiritual roots were indeed grounded in God, and that even if we had to go through some drastic changes, the community would pull through, no matter what happened. How grateful I have been for that reassurance, for we have been through some very big changes and upheavals indeed.

I WAS BEING FORCED to change. All my life I have had change thrust upon me and I have resisted it to the end. I once was given the very apt image of a pot-bound plant: with my roots bulging over the sides of my little pot I have no room to grow and my roots are desperate for more space. But I feel secure in my little pot. It's snug, if a little tight, and I don't want to change.

When a plant becomes pot-bound, it has to be transferred to a larger pot if it is not to die. To do this the pot has to be turned upside down and given a sharp tap to loosen the soil. If, however, the plant is too firmly stuck, then the pot has to be smashed. Once the plant is in its new, roomy container, though, it quickly begins to flourish again. My fear of change and of the unknown has often got me stuck in my secure little pot and it sometimes takes quite a blow to release me from it. But always, once I have moved, I breathe a sigh of relief that I can grow again. I look back and see the valuable lessons I have learned, and the next time moving is a little easier.

My relationship with Peter simply had to change to let me grow. My life had been completely wrapped up in him, very much like my mother's was with my father. I thought the world of Peter and depended on him for everything. I loved his vitality, his boundless energy and his positivity, even though that was hard to deal with when I felt low. I liked our teamwork, the way we had always worked in such close harmony, and even though his coming to me for guidance annoyed me at times, it gave me a sense of purpose and importance in the larger scheme of things. And although there was not much tenderness between us, we had been brought together by God for a purpose; we were two halves of a whole.

During the first few months after Peter left, I did some deep thinking and began to piece together various experiences that seemed to be connected. I recalled a vision I had been given back in 1974 just when the first cracks were appearing in my relationship with Peter: I was taken to the beginning of time when humans were etheric beings with bodies of light. Peter and I were in one light body. Then I saw us split in two, and Peter wandered his way and I wandered mine. My being became denser and denser, and I lived through lifetime after lifetime of tremendous suffering, pain and anguish. I wandered searching for something I had lost but I did not know what it was. I was a lost soul. Peter and I may have been brought together from time to time, but we did not recognise each other. Then I was brought into this lifetime and God said: "Now is the time. I have brought you together to do a very specific work for me. You are to bring Universal Love to the many. As one you can do it. You are to help anchor the tremendously powerful cosmic Christ energies which have been released at this time."

Then I was shown a great ball of light in the sky with many cords hanging from it. Holding on to each cord was a being helping to anchor this great ball of light. The light poured through the cords into the beings, fusing them with the earth, and I heard the words: "The redemption of the Earth. This is the work of the Brotherhood."

And I saw our higher selves, which were incredibly beautiful. But they were two. I saw the two meet, come together and become one, as it was in the beginning. And I heard the words: "The redemption of mankind."

I remembered that soon after experiencing this vision I came across a description of 'cosmic ties' in a book on Tantra Yoga[1]:

> Cosmic ties evolve out of service, may lead to love and probably will, but are consummated . . . for the purposes of performing certain hierarchical work that can only be performed by two people or initiates of the opposite sex, functioning in polarity. The partners do not select each other but are drawn together according to their several abilities and qualities to carry out a spiritual assignment of considerable importance and delicacy. The selflessness of this arrangement can be seen to be on a higher level than 'twin soul' marriage, although it partakes of its values. The cosmic tie begins at the highest level and works its way down to the physical plane where the rapport becomes complete.

Something about this description rang true for the relationship between Peter and me. I recalled our conversation on the verandah of my home in Habbanya so many years before when he told me excitedly about his revelation that we were 'two halves of a whole'. I also remembered Peter's distress when he came for me after I returned to my children, his insistence that I was creating 'karma' for us both, and that without me he could not fulfil God's plan. Ours had never been the classic love affair. In fact, Peter has always maintained that he never fell in love with me at all, that until I actually went away with him he had only once felt the briefest flash of emotional and physical attraction for me. This had always irked me, as I had fallen head over heels in love with him and would never have left Andrew and my children had my passion for Peter not been so

---

[1] ' Howard, John Zitko, *New Age Tantra* (World University Press, Tucson, Arizona), page 27.

all-consuming.

It made sense that our coming together had been arranged on higher levels. It was true – we had completed the work we had been brought together to do, and the Findhorn Foundation was on its feet and flourishing. I began to see that the next step was indeed for each of us to develop our individual selves, to find the balance within our own being which the other had provided for so long. And as much as we both may have wanted to achieve this individuality within our marriage, it seemed that our patterns were too strong and interlocked and we had to be split apart.

I had the opportunity to repeat the masculine and feminine meditation exercise which had helped me so much when I first became aware of the need to balance those two aspects within myself. Again my masculine symbol was a great golden lion and my feminine symbol a pure white unicorn. This time Mary, the community member who was leading me through the meditation, suggested I allow a third symbol to emerge. "Whichever way it comes," she said, "whether out of the merging of the two or as something separate from them, this third image represents the blending of the masculine and feminine aspects within yourself."

In my mind I saw a fully blown pink rose with a golden centre. It was the symbol of pure love, Unconditional love. An unexpected joy grew within me. For the first time in my life I felt absolute love for both my masculine and my feminine aspects. Now I understood why it was so important for me to bring the two sides of myself into balance. Only out of that perfect harmony could unconditional love be expressed.

How in the world would I ever learn to love Peter unconditionally? In spite of being able to release Peter in meditation and temporarily attaining a taste of calmness and freedom of spirit, I still felt rejected and sorry for myself most of the time, and what's more, I still often churned with anger, jealousy and resentment. I was tempted so many times to close my heart to Peter, to protect myself from the pain by becoming bitter and withdrawn. But I had asked to learn to love unconditionally, and I had to keep open and change and grow.

PETER HAD BEEN LIVING in Hawaii for about six months when I was told from within to write to him there to keep the doors of communication open and the love flowing. I resented having to do it, but I managed to swallow my pride.

We wrote back and forth and in one of his letters he mentioned meeting someone who had received a transmission from Quan Yin. I had no idea who or what Quan Yin was. Three days later I was polishing my dressing table mirror when a small card slipped down from the back. It was a picture of an Eastern female figure. I turned it over. On the back I read:

> *Quan Yin is the ancient Chinese symbol of the World Mother, and is representative of the feminine principle of creation; the Mother aspect of Deity. The feminine principle has been represented throughout history by many names . . . Mother Kundalini, Isis, Sophia, the Virgin Mary. The unfolding 'new age' foretold by prophets has as its keynote the conscious restoration of the Golden Balance between the masculine and the feminine principles. This Golden Balance is to be found in the hearts of all people; and is none other than the True Self. Know the balance by honouring its source which is the True Self. Love is your very nature. God dwells within you, as You.*

I had a strong feeling I should send this card to Peter, so I put it in an envelope and posted it that very day. I was intrigued by the connection between Quan Yin and Mary, with whom I had had such a long relationship. Soon after that, in meditation, I saw myself entering a shrine or chapel. It was quite dark inside. At the other side of the room I saw the figure of Quan Yin. As I came closer, she said, "I have been waiting for you." I sat down cross-legged in front of her, and milk was poured all over me. Then Quan Yin blessed me and said: "Go out onto the highways and byways and into the market place, and know that you are fully protected." She blessed me again, and I thanked her and left. Ever since, I have felt fully protected in all my travels.

I wished I had a small figure of Quan Yin to carry with me when I travelled. I had one of Mary. Then one day my grandson, Jason, rushed up to me in great excitement and dragged me into his room. He handed me a very small figure of Quan Yin and said it was for me.

"Where on earth did you find this, Jason?" I asked him in delight.

"I found it in my toy box," he replied.

I asked my daughter-in-law about it but she said she had never seen it before. So where it came from I shall never know, but it travels everywhere with me in my purse.

I feel the presence of Quan Yin and Mary overlighting me, giving me great strength and courage to persist on my path towards inner balance and the expression of unconditional love. In my travels all over the world they have appeared to me in visions, as well as in a more concrete form. Once I was in New York visiting a friend. After we had meditated together, I felt powerfully drawn to a little roof garden adjoining the apartment. When I stepped outside, there sitting on the parapet, was a huge statue of Quan Yin. Right behind her was the Empire State Building. My friend told me he had known Quan Yin for many years and he shared with me how much she meant to him.

As I continued to wonder about the connection between Quan Yin and Mary, I was reminded of a vision I had had in 1969: I had seen myself as half-male and half female, half Eastern and half Western, and I was sitting cross-legged on the ground. Just in front and a little above me were two incredible Beings. One called himself Confucius and the other said he was to be known as the Ancient of the East and Far East. They began expounding with great wisdom on the brotherhood of mankind, unity between the East and West, and many things I could not understand. I sat and absorbed it all. They then showed me a heavy door which was bolted and locked on the inside and the outside. They indicated it should be unlocked. I asked how it could be done. The Ancient of the East and Far East plunged his hand into me and drew out my heart. I saw it lying on his hand, beating. Then I saw it begin to enlarge and become filled with light. I thought to myself, "If he doesn't put it back soon, it will be too big to fit!" But that was of no consequence. Then I watched myself being drawn into the heart until I was no longer just me; I was all heart. He indicated to me that this was the way the East and West would be linked together, and the brotherhood of all humanity would come about – through love.

At the time I had not understood the meaning of this vision at all, but now it made perfect sense. It gave meaning to my connection with Quan Yin of the East and Mary of the West and fanned my enthusiasm for learning to love unconditionally. I thought about love in all its aspects. Unconditional love became the central theme in my life. I meditated on love, read about it, talked about it to everyone I met. I pondered again on the question I had received while travelling on the bus before Peter and I had parted: can I say to you and you say to me, "I love you," without either of us feeling uncomfortable or threatened? I longed with all my heart one day to be able to say, "Yes, Peter, I do love you, just the way you are!"

The more I thought about loving unconditionally, the more questions came to mind. Some related to Peter, others to my children, and others just to people I knew. Each one challenged me either to forgive or let go.

Can I be myself at all times? Can I allow others to be themselves without judging, condemning or criticising them? As long as I judged myself I would judge others. Without learning to appreciate myself and accept myself with all my faults and gifts, I would never even start on the road towards unconditional loving. It had to begin with me.

Can I love and go on loving, asking nothing in return? So hard to do without becoming a martyr. And yet easy with the children.

Can I love someone to the same extent whether we are together or apart? In some ways it is easier to love Peter from afar, but it was not as deep a love. With my dear friend Sandy it was easy to love him wherever he was.

Can I still love someone when I do not like or approve of something they have said or done? That was a difficult one! For a long time I simply couldn't answer 'yes' to that question. I felt that if I loved someone in these circumstances they would think I approved of them and carry on doing whatever they wanted to. After a lot of soul-searching I realised I could say "I love you *and* I don't like what you have said or done."

Can I love someone enough to let them go to grow and mature? Again, with the boys I could happily say 'yes', but if it meant Peter, I wasn't so sure.

Can I love someone enough to stop helping them because I know if I continue to help, I will hold up their evolution? I watched someone in the community struggle with this one.

The love was protective and restrictive, and really not love at all. The greatest act of love was to let go.

The final question was the most difficult one for me at that time: can I love someone – Peter – enough to see him leave me for someone else, and hold no bitterness, resentment or jealousy? Of course I couldn't. At least not without God's help.

My emotions were my big stumbling block. When I asked how to get over these, I was told to look at each one and learn to love myself and the emotion. In doing that, I would transmute the negative into positive. It was very difficult to love myself when I was jealous, angry or resentful. All I wanted to do with those unpleasant parts of myself was tuck them under the carpet and try and forget about them. But I realised that if I wanted to be a whole being, I had to accept all aspects of myself.

The most difficult emotion for me to overcome was my feeling of rejection. I felt utterly rejected as a woman and as a wife. I worked steadily with affirmations to rebuild my sense of selfworth. I looked for and concentrated on the good in me, and gradually as I began to love more of myself, my resentment of Peter began to fade. I could see more of his point of view without feeling it was a reflection of inadequacy on my part.

Many opportunities arose to test my ability to love Peter unconditionally. When he wrote in 1982 to tell me that he wanted to remarry, I reacted with disapproval. Paula was only 33! However, after asking for God's grace in meditation, I was able to bless Peter in his new life with absolute sincerity. I was glad I had not divorced him in anger as I had initially wanted to do; now we were divorced with the minimum of ill feeling.

However, when Peter informed me that Paula was going to have their child, that stuck in my throat. "You've already got three sons," I grumbled to myself, "and you've never taken the time to get to know them properly, so why do you need any more?" I was surprised when Peter invited our two younger sons to spend a holiday with him in California. Although mollified, I was also jealous. The grumble continued: "For all their growing up years he left the children up to me, and now they're grown up he thinks he can buy their love with an exotic holiday!" These thoughts gave me plenty to work on in my journey towards unconditional loving. In time I did forgive Peter and was glad he had at last the time to spend with his sons before he became a father again.

After their baby was born, I wrote to Paula. I have learned to face difficult situations head on, as mountains invariably turn out to be molehills. I was going on tour in the United States, so I asked if I could visit them at Mount Shasta, where they were living. They were delighted. To face Peter, his new wife and new baby was a big hurdle to overcome. I prayed a lot and in my mind surrounded them with love every day, and to my surprise, when I got there, it was remarkably easy. I felt detached from the life Peter was leading, and found that I could love Paula and the baby, Daniel, without difficulty. In fact, I was delighted to play Granny and felt very relieved it was Peter and not I who was embarking on the beginnings of a new family again. As I sat in the back seat of the car with Daniel, a year younger than our first grandson, Jason, on my knee, I marvelled at the irony of it all – at 65 years old it was I who was travelling the world giving talks and workshops, while Peter was at home changing nappies and getting up at 3 a.m. for the baby!

I was put to the ultimate test of accepting Peter and his new life at the time of the community's 21st birthday in 1983. Everyone felt Peter should be invited and I was very happy about it. However, when he wrote to say he wanted to bring his wife and child with him, I reacted like an angry little robin defending her nest. It was one thing for Peter to come – in fact I wanted him to – but I did *not* want all three of them. This was *my* territory! But when I took it into meditation, I was told very firmly that they were all to come, so I asked for help to be close at hand.

I awaited their arrival nervously, meditating on unconditional love every spare minute of the day. I visualised them walking into the community centre and surrounded each of them with love and acceptance. When they finally did arrive, I was amazed to find I had no reaction at all. The old niggling feelings I had had over the years were miraculously gone, and I found I could love all three of them quite unconditionally. And with this love I rejoiced in the freedom and joy of the spirit. It was then that I fully realised for the first time that only good had come out of Peter's leaving.

FOR A LONG TIME I WONDERED why Peter and I had to be parted to learn our lessons, but gradually, as time went on, I began to see that I would not have grown spiritually had we not finally separated. I needed to learn to stand in my own light. All the years Peter and I were together I was happy to be in his shadow. I had no identity of my own. I was God's channel, Peter's wife, and the mother of his children and his community.

Building my new identity involved more than just learning to love Peter in a new way. I also had to be willing to grow, to learn to be independent and to stand on my own feet. I had to find ways of dealing with the challenges that all these changes would present. One form these took was a number of invitations to give talks and 'workshops' in this country and abroad. Now I no longer had Peter to shield me, I had to do it myself.

I had received a vision in 1975 which helped me to be myself out in the world: I had seen myself with a leather bag full of tiny seeds tied around my waist. I heard the words: "Go forth throughout the world and sow my seeds of Love, Peace and Joy. When the ground has been prepared, I will open the way for you." Then I asked: "But surely the idea of going out and meeting people is to tell them about Findhorn and what is happening here?" Then it came to me very dearly: "What is Findhorn? It is a state of consciousness, and that consciousness is of Love, Peace and Joy. Those are the seeds that are to be sown all over the planet, and the harvest shall be tremendous. Be what I am. Live My life. That is all you have to do. Be at perfect peace. All is unfolding."

In 1980, the year after Peter left, I was invited to do a tour of Britain which even included a television interview. I don't think anyone could ever fully appreciate my fear of appearing in public, even though I had someone from the Findhorn Community with me to support me and help me answer questions. I was in the limelight and it terrified me. It didn't even help when people who had seen me on television told me I looked calm and peaceful, the very embodiment of the inner stillness I was supposed to represent. I had been frozen with fear! Calling on God for help before facing an audience or a TV camera was in fact the only way I got through such experiences at all.

By 1985 I had travelled all over the world – to the United States and Canada several times, to New Zealand and Australia, to South Africa, to several countries in Europe and Scandinavia, and even to the Yukon and Alaska.

In spite of my fears, miracles began to happen to me – an affirmation that God was helping me to stand on my own two feet. I began to see God's hand in everything, and I found that when I lived in this close contact with God, I had the most wonderful, joyous experiences.

One time when I was travelling across the United States on my way home to Scotland and all my flights were changed due to aircraft being grounded, I got as far as Chicago, where I was stuck for several hours. I had somehow to get to Washington DC in time to catch my flight to London, or I would lose my ticket. I managed to stay calm and relaxed, putting my trust in God, until I was on a flight to Washington with just enough time to make the connection. Imagine my panic when I discovered that the plane had landed at a different airport! I had very little time to transfer, and only $5 in my purse, far too little for a taxi. Someone directed me to the Greyhound bus depot, but said he did not think I could possibly get to the airport in time to catch my plane. I rushed over to a bus and sat in it, praying as I had never done before: "God, you know the situation. You know I simply cannot afford to miss that plane. Please, I need some help."

The black bus-driver poked his head around the door. "What are you doing in my bus, ma'am?" he asked in a strong southern drawl.

Without thinking, I replied, "I'm praying that you will get me to Dulles Airport in time to catch my flight to London at 5 o'clock."

"Sorry, ma'am," he said, "I'm not taking any passengers on this run, and anyway there's no way you can get there in time." Then he looked at me in a strange way. "What did you say you were doing?"

"Praying," I said.

"You know, ma'am, you have good vibes. I'll take you. And he jumped into his seat, started the engine and roared off at top speed down the highway. As we drove along he told me that a few years before he would never have done that, but he had recently given his life to God, and when I said I was sitting praying he knew he had to take me to the airport. What's more, God had told him from within to get me there in time for my flight and to take every short cut possible!

So there I was, the only passenger in a 52-seater Greyhound bus racing towards Dulles Airport, with my driver singing the most beautiful negro spirituals. I was uplifted and my spirits soared higher and higher. It really didn't matter any more whether I caught that plane or not.

We arrived at the airport in the nick of time. "That sure was a wonderful drive, ma'am," he said, beaming. "It was a treat to be able to talk to someone about God like that."

This was just one of so many experiences where I have been

wonderfully taken care of. Gratefully I recognised God's hand in everything that had happened. As I sat in the plane winging my way home, I gave my deepest thanks.

I DIDN'T ALWAYS feel grateful to God. When Peter left I felt let down not only by him but by God as well. Because I had lived 'Thy will be done' for so long there was no room for my own personal will. Peter always expected me to put my feelings aside to do God's work. As soon as I felt this separation between God's will and my own I started to practice the affirmation, "God's will and mine are one – there is no separation." Although I believed this was the truth, I still didn't experience God as all of me but only as the 'higher' part of me.

Soon after I had started to practice this affirmation, I went to London to do a workshop called 'Transformation'. I normally stay away from such workshops, but my inner voice was insistent that I should do this one. I had no idea what I was letting myself in for.

During one of the exercises, to my absolute amazement, the most violent anger overwhelmed me. Unable to control it or suppress it, I burst out with the deep resentment that for so many years I had subconsciously harboured against Peter and against God for using me.

"Be my hands and feet. You are my instrument. I have need of you." How angry those words made me!

How dare you use me like that!" I yelled. "What about me? Don't I matter at all?"

I was so embarrassed at exposing all this ugly emotion that I could hardly face the other people in the workshop the next day. I felt I had let the side down and betrayed myself, God and Peter. But what had really happened was that expressing my anger had released the emotional tension inside me and set me free. For the first time I could truly accept that I was needed as a channel for God's word, that Peter had needed me to be that channel, and that God's will for me and my own will were one and the same.

So why had I resisted Peter and God our whole life? Because I had been so completely reliant on Peter I had never realised how angry I was with him for leading me along the path we had walked together, one that he had chosen and I had not. When things became difficult between us, I wished, deep down, that he would leave me, because I longed to be free. And yet I was terrified of losing the security of our life together and clung on all the more tightly.

I had also felt that I had been asked to deny myself by following God's will. If I didn't I would be punished – by losing Peter, or Christopher, or whatever happened to be important to me at that time. I had resigned myself to accepting that I had to put God first in my life.

After the workshop I no longer felt imposed upon from outside, and I began to experience and accept that God and I are truly one. I discovered that there was nothing to resist. Of course I wanted to do God's will!

As I accepted that my 'little will' is part of God's will, I also came to recognise my 'little self' as part of my 'God Self'. Realising that the emotions of anger, sadness and jealousy are all part of the whole Me allowed me to begin to really understand what loving myself could mean. Just accepting that my anger existed had transmuted it and it disappeared. Suppressing it – pushing it away for years – had kept it festering under the surface, causing unnecessary resistance and pain. The art is to see that everything is there for a purpose and turn it around to see the good that can come out of it.

I began to look for the reverse side of negative emotions to find the positive. Behind rejection I saw self-worth; behind jealousy, detachment, behind anger, power. Looking at emotions in this way seemed to shift something in me and allowed me to feel compassion for myself and others. I realised how hard on ourselves we all are, and how we can all do with a little compassion, not least for ourselves.

As soon as I started accepting responsibility for everything that had happened to me, God and I truly became one. Then with joy and openness I could say, every day, "Here I am. Use me."

Whenever I have invoked a change in my life, I have had to be willing to take the consequences. Saying I was open to being used by God in any way that would serve also meant that I was willing to come out from inside my safe little shell. I would have to change. As soon as I invoked change I was tested. Immediately after I had offered myself in service I was invited to the Peace Conference in India – a bigger event than I had ever been asked to speak at before. And I discovered that once I had broken through my resistance everything fell perfectly into place. It was a most wonderful experience of being overlighted by God. I accepted the challenge to grow and certainly reaped the rewards.

I can only talk about what I know, so I developed a workshop on Unconditional Love and another on The Challenge of Change. Then I was challenged further. I was travelling to South Africa, with Liza as my companion, for a six-week tour giving these workshops. As I had just spent two months touring in the United States and had my workshop format neatly worked out, when Liza started discussing ideas she had for 'our' workshop, I felt myself bristle. I said nothing.

The night before our first workshop I was awakened at 3 a.m. and told from within to write this down:

> Here you are faced with the challenge of change and you are kicking like a mule and fighting against it. Come on! Flow with it and stop resisting change. You had your own format for your workshops in the USA and you were comfortable with it. Now you find that you have to change your format and include Liza in all you are doing, and a part of you is resisting doing it. What a wonderful opportunity to put into practice what you are talking about!
>
> First of all recognise the situation. Then you can see where the resistance is in you. Be grateful you have woken up to what is happening. Use this episode to help yourself to move and change and also to help others to see the value of change clearly. Don't just talk about change, live it! It is the same with loving unconditionally. Because you have been resenting having to work with Liza, you have closed your heart to her. Open your heart and let the love flow freely to her. Again demonstrate what you are talking about and do it now. Change can come in a twinkling of an eye. I am with you always; My help is ever there to use in your everyday living.

At breakfast that morning I shared this guidance with Liza and confessed to my feelings of resistance to her participation in the workshops. The result was an even deeper rapport between us than had existed before, and we also used this story as an illustration in the workshops we were holding.

I FOUND WORKING WITH affirmations an effective way to help me change my attitudes towards myself and other people. From that first time when I looked in the mirror and allowed myself to say, "Yes, I am a wonderful woman; I see the divinity within me and I love myself," I continued to affirm my inner beauty and slowly rebuilt my shattered self-esteem.

I use positive affirmations to help me reach upwards – statements like, "I enjoy perfect peace and well-being" or "God grants me the serenity to accept the things I cannot change." To begin with I find the statement impossible to believe, so I continue to make the affirmation until I reach the point where I am it.

These statements are not mistaken, facetious self-compliments. They are absolutely true assertions, whether I believe them or not; they apply to my whole Self, not just my personality.

I can awaken my Self to its full potential. I can express God's perfection in my life. I can be the joyful, healthful, prosperous, constructively wonderful woman God intends me to be! Of course, all this had been repeated over and over for years in my guidance, and very often I had difficulty in truly believing it. But I kept on with the affirmations and gradually I could see they were making a difference to how I felt about myself and, interestingly, about other people too.

When I was first told from within to affirm, "I am a beautiful Christ-filled being," I was quite shocked. But as I meditated on the concept and made the affirmation every day, I realised that if I accept that God is within me, why can I not accept the Christ within? At first it was words and didn't mean very much to me. Then I found that the words began to live, that I became those words until I knew without a shadow of doubt that I am a beautiful Christ-filled being. That we *all* are.

To me, the Christ is a very powerful transforming and transmuting energy that is within and around each one of us. Therefore, as I see myself Christ-filled, I can feel that transforming power alive within me. I can see and feel every negative thought and action being transformed to the very highest, the most positive. I find myself seeing the best in everyone and in every situation.

To be a Christed being, to fully claim my Christhood, means to transmute the negative into the positive every moment of every day. It isn't something I can do only once a day. I need to open my eyes and my heart and see only the very best at all times. I have to be constantly alert and aware of my thoughts, but that keeps me conscious of the Christ energy working within me like yeast in a lump of dough, lifting the dark, heavy spots into the light. Claiming my Christhood means I have to be willing to see everything with new eyes.

The Christ is pure love. Its transforming power is within each of us. All we have to do is recognise it, accept it and use it for the upliftment of the whole. To me the return of the Christ is not as one single Messiah but as the recognition and nurturing of the Christ spirit in all men and women everywhere.

I feel that my work at this time is to awaken this realisation in more and more people all over the world, and to be fearless about it. Knowing it is the truth sets me free, and this is why I suggest to people that they use the affirmation constantly, as I do, and claim their Christhood now. You take the thought into your mind that you are a Christed being, and from that will come positive feelings of great joy, love, faith, understanding, wisdom, forgiveness and peace. And you will begin to see the Christ in everyone around you.

In one of my workshops there was a person who couldn't resist needling me. I became frustrated and annoyed, although I didn't show it, and privately thought how much easier life would be without this person in my group. Then I decided to try an experiment. Every time I looked at her or felt she was trying to get at me, I said quietly to myself: "I love you. I bless you. I see the Christ within you." At first, nothing seemed to happen. If anything, things got worse. But as I continued, I found that my attitude towards her began to change and it became easier to bless her. Eventually I found that a genuine love started to emerge between us. I didn't try to change her at all. I simply changed my own thoughts towards her, and in so doing drew out the best in her without her even knowing it was happening. Later she shared with me that she had felt jealous of me to begin with, but by the end of the workshop it was all gone.

After I watched the film *The Day After* about a nuclear holocaust, I sat pondering on what I had seen and felt. The fear, hopelessness and helplessness hit me. I thought about the transforming power of love. What if more and more individuals used that power to transform the world? At that time Gromyko from Russia and George Shultz of the United States were meeting to discuss a possible halt to the arms race, so I visualised the Christ within those two world representatives. I saw them transformed, their faces filled with joy and happiness and I saw them taking this change of consciousness back to their respective countries. In my mind the destructive energies changed to positive, constructive ones, and a wonderful healing of the earth took place, filling it with light, love and joy.

Many, many people all over the earth are recognising the transforming power of love. Some call it the Christ, others call it something else. The most important thing is that as more and more people recognise the power of this inner energy, the more we will lift the vibrations of the planet, together.

WORKING WITH THE CHRIST in my life led me naturally to think about forgiveness. Seven years after Peter left me I read a passage in *The Daily Word* on forgiveness which made me realise the meaning of freedom. It said:

> *If I think I have forgiven someone whom I feel has wronged me but now I am indifferent towards that person, I have not truly forgiven. If I think I have forgiven someone who has hurt my feelings but now I avoid seeing that person, I have not truly forgiven. True forgiveness is to feel the same towards that person as I felt before the incident took place.*

I thought about Peter and realised what a long way I had moved towards forgiving him and how much I loved him in a caring, yet detached way. I thought of all I had learned in the years we had been apart. I was a completely new woman! From the depths of my heart I felt a genuine gratitude towards Peter for leaving me, for setting me free to find myself. His path had not been easy either. He had had to struggle to establish himself from scratch in the United States and his relationship with Paula wasn't going well.

I remembered a dream I'd had before Peter left. I hadn't understood it at the time, but suddenly it made sense. In the dream I saw Peter being put into a coffin. Then I was put into the coffin on top of him. I tried to scream but no sound came out. I tried to get out but couldn't move a muscle. The lid was fastened on and I sank into oblivion. It was a ghastly nightmare. But then the scene changed to a lovely tropical garden full of flowers, trees and shrubs. In the garden were two butterflies with rainbow-coloured wings. They were flitting from flower to flower, sipping nectar. Every now and then they would come together and sit side by side on a beautiful lily in the middle of the garden. Then they would go their separate ways again. A gossamer veil was placed over the whole garden but the butterflies were oblivious to what was happening. Then I heard the words: "Your auras are being changed completely. The old has to die before the new can come forth."

In a flash of inspiration I sat down and wrote to Peter:

> I have just read a wonderful piece in The Daily Word on forgiveness, which I will enclose. As I read it, I began to do some thinking, which I will share with you.
>
> Have you ever thought what a wonderful demonstration of unconditional love it would be if you and I were to team up and work together again, in a completely different way? Not as husband and wife, but as partners on the spiritual path able to work together in perfect love and harmony.
>
> I realised when I was with you and Paula that I could love you both, see both sides of the picture without taking sides, and because of this I felt really free and loving with the two of you. It was an amazing experience, and I keep giving thanks for the wonder of it. A few years ago I would never have thought it possible, but more and more I realise that nothing is impossible with God. How many times have I received that in guidance and mumbled 'yes' to myself, not really believing it? But now something has happened to me and I realise that I am the guidance. At long last I know that God and I are one, that I am co-creator with God. All this has helped me to raise my consciousness, to claim my Christhood, so that I can say with conviction, "I am a Christed being." I found this difficult to accept to begin with, but as I affirmed this daily I began to realise I am it.
>
> A number of years ago I had a dream. I wonder if you remember it?

I told him the details of the dream and reminded him that I had been
so excited I woke him up, but he just grunted, rolled over and went back
to sleep!

> *Much water has flowed under the bridge since then, I continued.
> Many times I have thought about that dream and seen us as the two
> butterflies going our separate ways but every now and again coming to
> the glorious lily in the garden, the 'Christ consciousness'. We sit side
> by side sipping the nectar of the Christ and then go our separate ways
> again. In the meantime the veil of unknowing is all around us and we
> are blind to what is going on . . . as our auras are being changed and
> the old is dying so that the new can come forth.*
>
> *Does the dream mean anything to you now, Peter? Are we to
> come together in the Christ Consciousness to work together again?
> I am sharing this with you now because I know I am free and willing
> to flow with the energies, whatever they may be. I feel that at last I am
> a whole being, that God, the divinity within, is my All in All; therefore
> I am not dependent on anyone else to complement me or fulfil me in
> any way. I wonder if you understand what I mean. It sounds as if I
> am self-sufficient. I would like to call it God-sufficient.*
>
> *I am not sure how we would work together now. I know I have to
> stand in my own light and never be overshadowed by anyone. Maybe
> our understanding of loving unconditionally, the challenge of change or
> the balance of masculine and feminine energies within is entirely
> different. We may find that our ideas are so different we would be
> unable to work together in harmony, But then with God all things are
> possible. Why not this? Expect a miracle – accept a miracle!*
>
> *Well, Peter, I will stop and send this off to you. I am not crazy –
> just free to follow whatever the divine plan is.*

To my delight, and astonishment, Peter received my letter with
enthusiasm and we agreed we would arrange to work together as soon as
the opportunity arose. The following year, 1987, Peter came to stay in the
community for three months. He and I were able to sit down and talk, and
I felt a deep unconditional love for him. I felt that anything was possible,
and that we were good friends. I did notice, however, that whenever I lost

touch with my inner connection with the Christ, my old feelings of impatience with Peter and his odd habits would surface, and I would have to remind myself firmly that we could only work successfully together when, like the butterflies in my dream, we sipped from the lily of Christ consciousness.

This spiritual life would be impossible for me without faith, prayer and meditation. It restores me and reminds me of what is important. Not long ago I was searching within myself to find out why I was on earth at this time, what I was supposed to be doing, what I had to give. As I meditated on this, it was made very clear to me that I am here to serve God and to serve humanity. I asked how I could best serve God. By putting God first in everything, I was told, and by giving honour and glory to the divinity within. And how could I best serve humanity? I was told the greatest gift I could give anyone was to turn them within to find their own inner divinity, so that they could live and move and have their being free from that divine centre.

So that is what I am doing now: sharing my life and my experiences to give others encouragement to look inside themselves and discover God within, to find their own form of inner guidance and to live by it. My heart is full to overflowing with gratitude that I am able to offer this priceless gift.

As Peter and I embark on our first tour together, I am reminded of a dream I had many years ago. I leave it with you to wonder, as I do, about its meaning . . .

In the dream Peter and I were brought together not as ordinary people; we were to be crowned king and queen.

We were in a huge, beautiful garden. The trees were old and yet they looked as if they had just been planted. The deer and the stags were old and yet they were as lively as young ones. The flowers and shrubs were breathtakingly beautiful, and yet they too seemed to have been there for hundreds of years.

We were walking very slowly through this lovely parkland, examining every tree, shrub and flower, even every blade of grass. It was all so new and yet so old and beautiful.

We were dressed for our coronation, but that was of little concern. Peter was dressed in dark purple and looked very old and yet very young. I was dressed in a simple, very beautiful, old yet new, cream satin dress. I, too, was old yet young. I wore pearls around my neck and in my ears, and my white hair was piled on top of my head. Peter's hair was white too.

We seemed to spend a very long time walking and absorbing the sheer beauty of nature in its oldness and newness. Eventually we came to a place and were ushered into the dining room where, of all places, we were to be crowned.

When they put the crown on Peter's head, he said it was much too big and heavy, so I told them to cut some of the jewels off the back where nobody would notice and I put a piece of elastic in their place. My crown fitted like a glove.

Our three sons, Christopher, Jonathan and David, were there, looking magnificent. Jason, our grandson, was there as well. I looked everywhere for Paula and Daniel, but an old man with a twinkle in his eyes said they were quite happy elsewhere.

As we were talking, I suddenly realised what had happened, "Oh no," I thought, "do I really want to do this?" I wanted to run away from the whole situation. I did not want to be tied to Peter again, nor did I want to work with him, and yet here we were crowned king and queen. We had a very important work to do and we had to do it together.

All I could hear were the words: "No resistance; flow with the energies."

—*Epilogue written in 2002*—

~ *12* ~

If you think you have forgiven someone whom you think has wronged you, but you are indifferent towards that person, you have not truly forgiven. If you think that you have forgiven someone who has hurt your feelings, and now you avoid seeing that person, you have not truly forgiven. True forgiveness is to release the hurt and wounded pride. True forgiveness is to feel the same towards the person as you felt before the incident took place.

"Today I ask God to help me to forgive completely. Here is my heart God. Cleanse it. Renew my spirit so that it may be loving to everyone. I no longer hold anyone in condemnation. I let God's love work in and through me to forgive and forget completely."

WHEN, AT THE END of the previous chapter, I stopped writing *Flight Into Freedom*, I knew my story was not finished. A new life was beginning, with many new doors opening and many questions yet unanswered. The vision I had been given of Peter and me about to be crowned left me confused and resistant. I had no idea what it meant for the future. And yet I was told from within to "flow with it all". Now at the age of 85, it is time I completed the story.

After Peter and I parted, I had become more actively involved in the running of the Findhorn Foundation. I found that my newly emerging masculine side sometimes came over too strongly, upsetting people. I had had no chance to practice it when Peter and I were together. He was all masculine and was only interested in my feminine, receptive side. Now my self-confidence was growing and, as related in the last chapter, I started to travel, to give workshops and talks all over the world. Peter was living with his new partner Paula and their son in the United States, making a new life. We met from time to time, at Findhorn and in America, and our relationship seemed friendly enough. I felt that I had forgiven him and had accepted the way it was between us, and also felt some responsibility to the world, that somehow we needed to demonstrate, together, the reality of unconditional love that I had been talking about in my workshops.

Accordingly, I had written to Peter to suggest that we try to work together, in a different way. We had both been touring many countries, giving our own workshops (mine, Unconditional Love, and his, the Challenge of Change), and perhaps now we could share about them and demonstrate them together. It seemed to me the perfect outcome if, after all we had been through, we could show people that it was possible to work together in perfect harmony. He had responded favourably to my suggestion, and we were about to embark on a joint tour of Europe in September 1989.

This was the first time that Peter and I had travelled together since we had gone our separate ways several years before. We planned a big tour, accompanied by Loren Stewart, who had lived in the community for many years and had seen us through our ups and downs. He had been through his own changes in relationships, too, and we all thought we understood each other very well.

We were to go first to Ireland, then on to Paris, Berlin, Hamburg, Frankfurt, Milan and Venice. Our workshops and slide presentations were organised by the network of Friends of Findhorn all over Europe, and they were looking forward to hosting us in what would be, really, a momentous occasion. We all had great expectations.

In Ireland everything went very smoothly, the way I had hoped it would, united in the Christ consciousness with unconditional love. Peter and I gave our workshops together, in harmony with each other, and Loren played the guitar, sang songs and danced with the group. We all had a wonderful time together. Then we went on to Paris. To our amazement, 300 people had signed up to do workshops with us. That was far too many to have in one group, so we decided to divide into two groups, one with Peter and one with me, and we'd change over at half time.

That was when everything fell apart. When someone asks me a point blank question, I give a straight answer. A woman in my group asked, "Why did you and Peter split up?" I answered simply, "Because he left me for a younger woman. It was his choice. I wasn't happy about it but there was nothing I could do."

Well! That put the cat among the pigeons. The women in my group were furious. When they changed over to spend time with Peter, he was under attack. His reply to the same question was that he was guided to leave the community and to leave me, and that a new partner had been sent to him to help him to open his heart, not because she was younger than me.

After the workshop was over, we got into the car and Peter confronted me. He was furious and, I suspect, feeling very hurt as well. "You don't trust me, do you?" He challenged.

"No, Peter, I'm afraid I don't." I replied candidly. "How can I? Look at the things you have done."

Peter was frustrated, angry and disappointed. "But I've been guided every step of the way," he said, "Why can't you accept that?"

I had no answer for him. I am a divinely ordinary, divinely human woman. If I had been purely divine, I wouldn't have felt so angry, jealous and rejected for all those years. But each of these emotions is part of me, too, and to accept myself unconditionally was as important as accepting Peter. I had spent all those years thinking to myself, "If only he were different, everything would be perfect!" But Peter wasn't different, and neither was I. And I could go on forever thinking, "If only I had done this, if only he had done that", but the truth was that, after everything that had happened, I didn't trust him, or what he said was his guidance.

Perhaps it was difficult for me to trust him because he didn't seem to trust his own intuitive feeling. He always had to check it with others, usually other 'sensitives' or psychics, as for so many years he had checked with me. I suppose I didn't like playing second fiddle!

Years later, Loren told me, "At one point on the tour Peter fell ill. When I spoke with him, he said he realised that when he was listening to you speak about the early years at Findhorn and how you had left him — at all hours — to get guidance, he had been saddened. He had been upset that you would leave when he wanted you to be near him and he realised how much he had loved you..." Unfortunately Peter never said that to me. In all those years, he never once said to me, as a woman, "I love you."

Whatever the reasons, at the end of the day, I was still hurt. I did not trust Peter and I was not afraid to say so to anyone who asked me about it. And that was terrible for Peter. He wanted me to confirm that his actions had been right, and I simply could not do that. My insecurity wouldn't accept that he had acted rightly. When I married Peter, I made a commitment to God and to him which I thought would take us through all the ups and downs. But through our difficulties I learned that each one needs to be true to him or herself, and that I needed to build my own security within myself, and I did not agree that it was God's Will that we part. I had no answers, only questions. I could only say to Peter, "It's your life, and you have to live it."

However, we had to continue our tour because we had promised people we would come. It was very difficult to go on, but we did. We travelled by car through France to Germany and to Italy, where our car was stolen with our slide projector and all our luggage in it. Of course, the tour was not the success we had hoped it would be. The people who came to our workshops after Paris didn't appear to be aware of the strain between us, and I hoped that the many people we shared with received what they needed from each of us, in our different ways. But it certainly did not turn out as I expected.

I had had very high expectations that, after all the lessons we had learned over the years since we were parted, Peter and I would be able to synthesise. But it was expecting too much, too soon, to demonstrate loving unconditionally in such a public way. So, after the tour was over, we agreed not to do that again.

I released all thoughts of working together. At first I felt sad and disappointed because I thought we could have done it if we had been fully connected in the Christ consciousness, but on the human level it just wasn't possible. I had to accept God's grace and forgiveness. It was an experiment that didn't work out, but it was wonderful that we had tried, and it was useful to discover that this particular form of working together was not to be.

So much has happened over the years since Peter and I made that tour together.

Peter married and then left Paula, and later on married Renata Zürn from Germany and settled in her house by Lake Constance. When I met Renata, I got along well with her, very much as I had done with Paula. In time, with God's help and grace, I was able to release Peter completely. I could love him unconditionally and let him be himself without wanting to change him or demanding or expecting anything from him. Peter made a habit of returning to stay in the community each summer with Daniel, his son by Paula. He would visit me and I often looked after Daniel to allow Peter to go to events in the community in the evenings. We gradually became friends. I was reminded of the powerful dream I once had of two butterflies, dipping in to taste the Christ consciousness of Findhorn, and then moving away. Perhaps this was what Peter was doing? Certainly I was pleased that he returned every year.

In time I understood how Peter's leaving was a gift to me.

This is when I really began to touch in on the Christ energy. The Christ energy is love. It was this love that I had to find in myself. I wasn't getting guidance for Peter or anyone else; my guidance was just for myself. When Peter left it helped me to stand on my own two feet and find my own true self. I was forced to ask, "What is the truth for me?" and to turn within, turn within.

God kept on asking me, "Who is your other half, who is your soul mate?" Eventually I got it! I discovered that Peter wasn't the other half of me. I don't need somebody else to make me whole. Wholeness, the balance of the masculine and the feminine, is within me. Then I realised that God is my soul mate, my other half, my twin soul. It was so wonderful, like a flash of light. God is the wholeness.

For me this was the gift.

Before, I had always felt that we were two halves of a whole that had been brought together. Peter had always said, "I'm your other half, your soul mate." Perhaps that was how we needed to understand it when we first came together, under such difficult circumstances. It was true for that time, but it wasn't the whole truth.

I still feel that Peter and I were brought together so that we could work together and complement each other, which we did very well. That was our work, to create this place, the Findhorn community. But on a deeper, personal level, I had to find my own wholeness, the truth within me. Peter had to do the same, for himself, in his own way. I feel that this is key to the search for the truth within. Very often we look for a partner, for somebody else, for another half, a soul mate, a twin soul, to feel complete. But if we are looking for happiness outside ourselves, instead of seeking to become at one with the divinity within, we will not find it. Finding wholeness within is the kernel, the seed of it, as far as I'm concerned.

Some people don't like to hear this because to them it seems a lonely way to live, as if it substitutes a relationship with God within for the relationship with a partner, something that's second best. But it's not lonely, at all. It's a joyous way to live. But you have to get to that feeling of oneness, of completeness. Now that I can feel this wholeness within, there is no separation. My relationship with God is my life, and I wouldn't have it any other way now. But when I was searching for it, I felt miserable: "Peter's my other half. I'm left alone. What happened to me? Now I'm just going to rot by myself." I had all those feelings. I know how hard it is to understand, but the truth is very important: I am a whole being; I am one with the divinity within.

MY LIFE MOVED ON and became very full. Without Peter to hide behind, I found my own place in the community. I regularly gave week long workshops at Findhorn. These proved to be very popular, and, with the help of others in the community who 'co-focalised' the workshops with me, adding their own skills and perspectives, I learned how to be a workshop leader. I made a practice of inviting small groups to my home to share the spiritual principles of building community and living the spiritual life. I travelled a great deal, always accompanied by a member of the community. I went to South Africa, Spain and Italy. I did two big tours of the United States. I went to Milan and Rome on a book promotion tour, gave several talks and workshops in Northern Ireland and talked to a crowded hall in Dublin. I travelled to Brazil and Argentina and all round Australia, ending up in Perth where we flew to Monkey Mire to visit the dolphins, which was most exciting. Each time a television crew arrived at Findhorn, they insisted on interviewing me, and I became quite used to it although I never really enjoyed it. But it was all part of my service to God and humanity, and I was willing to overcome my resistance to being in the public eye if it would serve people and help them come closer to the God within themselves.

As I was growing and changing, the Findhorn community was growing and changing as well. The idea of the community as an Ecovillage was growing, consistent with my vision many years before: "I want you to see this centre of light as an ever-growing cell of light. It started as a family, it is now a community; it will grow into a village, then into a town and finally into a vast city of light. It will progress in stages and expand very rapidly. Expand with the expansion. The foundations go very, very deep and are built on rock. Therefore it now does not matter how fast the growth takes place. It does not matter how great it grows." The farmland next to the community eventually came up for sale, as my guidance had also predicted. A group of people closely connected with the community bought it and are building ecological houses on it, helping to develop the Ecovillage.

My new home Cornerstone was the first eco-house to be completed in the community. It came about in a wonderful way. I was sitting in my little caravan Crystal one day, and in meditation I received guidance that I was to have a house built for me. I was told that it was to be a cornerstone for something new emerging in the community. I didn't understand what that might be at the time, but I knew exactly where it should be: just at the corner of the path leading from the community centre to the Sanctuary, in the very heart of the community.

When I phoned my youngest son David, who is a builder by profession, to tell him I was going to have a house built, he immediately said he would come from America to build it for me. He returned for nine months with his wife Kacie and my grandson Aron.

Cornerstone became a wonderful community project, the first real house to be built in the community. Half the cost was paid by the community and half by donations from people all over the world who just heard about it and wanted to contribute. The project received tremendous support from everyone and donations came flooding in. Without those, we would never have been able to achieve such a big project. Cornerstone was built to a special environmental design, triple insulated and with attention paid to every last detail. It took nine months to plan and build. The group who worked on it together had so much fun that they didn't want it completed! I would make them flapjacks for tea, and from my little caravan opposite, I watched Cornerstone grow every inch of the way. Finally it was ready for me to move in. It was so exciting! I was like a pack rat, running back and forth from my little caravan at dead of night, carrying all my things over! The circle of people who came to the blessing for Cornerstone completely surrounded the house. I was, and am still, thrilled and grateful and I feel truly blessed to live in such a beautiful house after all those years of being cooped up in tiny caravans.

Then I understood the meaning of my guidance that it was to be a cornerstone for something new. It was a symbol that our mode of living needed to change. The time had come to upgrade our members' accommodation and get rid of the draughty, wasteful and uneconomical caravans. They had served their purpose, but now it was time for us to live in houses that reflect the lifestyle we believe in. As a result there is now a cluster of ecological houses at Pineridge, an eco-house village has been built on the field, and the idea of the Ecovillage has been well and truly established in the community.

ON 18 FEBRUARY 1994 Peter was killed instantly in a car crash in Germany. I heard the news in a very strange way. As I did not have a telephone, whenever someone from the family needed to reach me, they phoned Joanie who lived next door and left me a message. That day, just as I was walking out of her door, the phone rang. I picked it up and it was my son Christopher. He told me that he had received a phone call from America, from David's wife Kacie, to say that Peter had been killed in Germany. That was all the information he had.

The summer before Peter died, he and Daniel had stayed with me in my home at Findhorn for eight weeks. They had been planning their annual visit to the community, but there was no suitable accommodation available for them as it was a very busy summer. Muriel, who was arranging their accommodation, was concerned and came to me to ask what to do. I offered the two of them my big room upstairs in my lovely new house, provided Peter felt happy about it. He did, and he and Daniel lived upstairs in my house for the whole time they were here.

We had such a wonderful time, talking together, being friends. That was the most important part about it. It was a happy, harmonious and uneventful time. We had several family meals together, and I made sure that he did his part and did not just expect to be waited on. I made sure too that I didn't fall back into my old patterns. Whenever he said, "Let's have a meal together", I said, "Right, you do your share and I'll do mine." And I didn't do his washing for him, or his mending. Sometimes we watched television together, and we had some very good talks about what was happening in the community at the time. We talked about everything, about the past, the children, and we talked about the community. I enjoyed being able to talk things over with Peter, as of course he still had a special interest in everything that was happening in the community, our community. Once we made omelettes together for the community kitchen as we used to do long ago. It was comfortable and companionable, and we were simply very good old friends. The last vestiges of anger, antagonism or jealousy on my part had completely and utterly disappeared. I really thanked God for the gift of that time. It was wonderful.

I think that I knew I had found wholeness, that last time he was here. It's something I had longed for. I had longed to find an answer, and I didn't know where to look for it. I kept on praying and meditating. I had to work for it, until suddenly I got it. Then I could feel it. I could feel this oneness within my own being. It was a deep, deep feeling of gratitude and appreciation.

I'm not a misery, not now. I did become a misery, after Peter left. I thought everything had gone, and it took a long, long time to get over it. Now I feel whole, and I am very happy. I am so grateful because I am not looking out there for somebody to fulfil me. I just feel fulfiled. I'm not fulfiled by another person, by the community, by my work, or my position here. I'm fulfiled by this incredible oneness. I feel it most of the time.

That was the last time I saw Peter. When I heard of his death I realised what a great gift God had given us, to spend that time together, because I found that I could love him, my husband and partner for 27 years, unconditionally, as a deep friend and colleague. We were at peace with each other.

Although I was shocked by the news of Peter's sudden death, I was not devastated by it. When I heard the news, my first reaction was, "Why wasn't it me?" I would have preferred it to be the other way around because I longed to be entirely in a higher dimension. I was always more comfortable in the spiritual world than on the physical one, and I was ready to go at any time. Peter had told me on his last visit that a psychic told him that he would live to the age of 120, and now I thought to myself that it must have been a shock to him to die so suddenly! I felt envious that he had been allowed to move on while I had to stay here, tied to this body and to the earth.

But I didn't grieve for him. I didn't feel sad. I didn't miss him. To me death simply means casting off the body, like an old cloak, allowing the spirit to move on into the Light. Some people from the community went to his funeral, but it was not something that I felt I needed to do. Both Paula and Renata visited me after his death, and we shared openly and lovingly with each other. I was in harmony with both of them. I am so thankful. It has helped me to see that my lessons of learning to love unconditionally did work out – but only with God's help and grace.

Only once after his death did I connect with Peter on the inner. It was during the meditation we held for him in the Universal Hall. I saw a pure white dove fly in and settle in the middle of the floor. It took off again and flew up and up towards the glass lantern in the roof. Then it disappeared into the darkness. It had to find its way through the darkness before it found the light, and it flew out straight towards the moon. That was extraordinary. It was as if Peter had to go through a certain darkness before he came out into the light. Why, I don't know.

Two years later my dearest life-long friend Joanie died. After her death my desire to be free became really strong. I wanted to join her. I felt that I had done all that I could, I had given all that I had to give, and that it was time to move on. I was 79 years old. Ten books of mine had been published and that was more than enough. I had stopped giving workshops and travelling on tours. The community didn't need my help to run it; they were doing it perfectly well without me. So what was I doing living in the community? Wasn't I just a bit of dead wood with no function? I felt I had given all I was able to give. I was drifting. This became a very powerful death wish. I longed to escape. I longed to die.

After some time, a year or more, while I was meditating, these words came very clearly to me: "You still have work to do. You need to withdraw your death wish. Put it on the altar and give it to God, and get on and do the work that still needs to be done, until more and more can accept the Christ within." I saw a vision of myself as an anchor and heard the words: "You are an anchor for the Christ energies for the whole community."

So I did exactly that. I withdrew the death wish, put it on the altar and gave it to God. I promised that I would remain here on earth until I have completed my work. Now I know that my work at this time is to encourage more and more people to recognise the God within; and to live and move and have their being from that Divine Centre and become conscious of the Christ energy, the energy of love. I simply accept that I am an anchor at this time, and I know I am in the right place, doing the right thing. I am very happy about serving God within and without, in everyone and in everything. This is my work, my service for the whole. And I know that when I am truly not needed to do this work any longer, when this spiritual energy is anchored enough in others, I will be released.

During this period I picked up the book *Opening Doors Within*, a compilation of messages I have received from God over the years. I found this piece of guidance about growing older very helpful. I read:

> *What does age mean to you? Do you fear growing old? Or are you one who knows and understands that the fountain of youth is in your consciousness? When you keep your mind young, fresh and alert, there is no such thing as growing old. When you have many interests in life, and when you enjoy life to the full, how can you ever grow old? Human beings limit themselves when they think of threescore years and ten as being the fullness of life. It can be just the beginning for many souls when they awake to the wonder of life, and in awakening begin to enjoy it. Banish all thoughts of old age. It is but a universal thought form that has become so strong that it is like a very hard nut, tough to crack. Start readjusting your thinking about age now.*

There are so many wonderful things in my life, so many things I am grateful for. I know what my message is: take time to be still, go within and listen to that still small voice within, then live and move and find joy from that within-ness. Inner listening is my work, turning people within.

Once I had surrendered the 'death wish' to God, I was given the 5 C's in meditation: Commitment, Consistency, Continuity, Communication and Courage.

Why was I given the 5 C's? I feel that I am here to demonstrate them. It requires commitment and dedication to do the inner work year after year with no glamour attached to it, very often with nothing much to show for it. I am one of the 'backroom boys', doing my work silently and quietly and doing it with love and service to the whole.

When I have been asked by God, from within, to do something, I will do it until I am told to stop. That is why consistency and continuity mean so much to me. It is so important to be consistent, and not to do something only when you feel like it. I know how important it is, for myself and also for others, that I am in the Sanctuary every morning, no matter how cold and dark or rainy it is, no matter how much I would like that extra few minutes in my warm bed in the morning.

Communication is important, to share with people what it means to be still, to go within. And it takes courage to stick my neck out and say: "This is the key that opens all the doors". It has made me unpopular at times, but I just had to share what came to me from within, whether people liked it or not.

Soon after this, someone in the community received her own guidance that we needed a group of people who were willing to meditate early every morning to hold the whole community in the Christ energies. My heart jumped with joy. I immediately suggested that they join me at a quarter to five every morning to do it together. I had been praying for a group to meditate with me, remembering the words, "When two or more are gathered together in my name, there I am in the midst of you." The group turned down the early morning hour and suggested we meet at 6.30a.m. instead. I agreed. My cat Crystal and I had been doing it together for many years, so to meditate with a group would be quite wonderful. We started off with a flourish, all 22 of us. But then the group said they could only commit themselves for three months. That was when it was made very clear to me that 'you don't bargain with God'. We needed a group to hold the whole together, not just for three months, not just because we were going through a difficult time, but because there was a deep need for more and more people to become aware of the need for much inner work.

Like so many new things, there was great enthusiasm for a while and then it tailed off. It was too much effort to get up so early. Within a few weeks there was just a handful of the original group meditating at 6.30a.m. Then gradually other, different people started to come at that time, because they were drawn there by the spirit. The number varied from 5 to 15. What was most important was that they came in the right spirit. It was quality not quantity that was needed, and the fact that the group meditated together consistently every day.

I learned an important lesson for myself that was very good for me.

It concerned changing the time from 4 .45a.m. to 6.30a.m. The first few mornings after the decision had been made, I found myself up and dressed and standing at my door at 4.45a.m. I was annoyed that no one else would be in the sanctuary to join me. Then I realised that I had got stuck in a rut and that I needed to get out of it. I had to do some changing. I had become crystallised and I needed to smash the habit of going at my usual time and move on to a new routine. It was very good for me, and I gave thanks for the lesson. So often have I said I want to change and change and keep on changing, and yet how stuck I was in that particular rut!

In my life I have found that whenever I find myself comfortable and complacent, the habit has to be broken, no matter what it is, so that I take nothing and nobody for granted. Tough! Yes, very tough. But I have invoked change, so I must be willing to take the consequences, to accept them and move on. I do not want to get stuck in a rut and I can so easily do so. So even after all these years of practice, I need to watch myself carefully, and when I find any resistance in me regarding some action I need to take, I *know* I need to take it in order to make me grow and expand.

This spiritual life is not an easy one. Somebody asked me the other day, "Eileen, did you always like the guidance you received?" I replied that I certainly did not! It was very difficult at times to follow it, but I always carried it out knowing that no matter what it was, it was for my growth and there was a lesson to be learned. And besides that, I want to keep the door always open so God can work in and through me. I do not want to close that door. We are God's hands and feet. I have surrendered all to God, and when you surrender all, all is used. Yes, we do have free will, but I have accepted, after many inner battles, that God's Will and my will are one and the same. God and I only want the highest and the best for all concerned.

The human state is not about being perfect. We are in this life to learn to grow. We do so best by finding God's plan for us and following it. It is by no means easy. Yet learning, growing, overcoming, and then experiencing transformation, can be one of life's greatest joys. It certainly makes life interesting.

Failure is painful. It hurts the human ego. But the great thing about God's gift to humanity is that our endowment of free choice makes a marvellous provision for ultimate success. We can make mistakes, using our free choice, and then grow from these very mistakes. I always say there are no mistakes, only lessons to be learnt.

I had a lot to learn from the community about communication and courage.

When I joined the Core Group for the first time, I was developing my masculine side. It was very powerful, and it came out in a way that got people's backs up, which is why I resigned at one stage.

I was developing my will, and my power. If someone is making a decision that doesn't ring true to you, it is important to say so. It helps the group to get clear, even if your point of view is unpopular. It very often is, which is what happened when I was in the Core Group. I was very unpopular, but I just had to accept it. This was the vision I had, and I had to share it. They didn't like me speaking with authority, but the main problem was the way it came out. I shared what I felt, I was told from within to do that, but I had to find a balance. I had to learn to communicate with a balance of power and love. That was the most important part of the learning experience for me: to develop the balance of the masculine and feminine within me. If I was coming over too strongly, I needed to develop that balance within myself. I needed to spend time on my own, to be quiet and go within to find out what was happening. I was told from within to leave the Core Group until I could find the balance within me, so I did.

Many years later, on my 81st birthday, I was told from within to join the Findhorn Foundation's Management group, as a silent observer. This was an important part of my healing with the community. I had gone through quite a long a period of feeling rejected, when I felt no one listened to me. When I received guidance, I kept it to myself. I used to say that when I shared it with the community it went in one ear and out the other. The same happened in our Wednesday meditation group. I would share the guidance I received, and after a while I realised that no one was paying attention to it. So I said, it's not good enough, and I stopped going.

When my guidance told me to ask the Management group if I could join them, I didn't want to. That's always the trouble. I have to take the steps, and dear oh dear, I don't want to do it. I had tried Core Group and the meditation group and I just never felt they listened. But I plucked up the courage to ask, and they agreed to let me join them.

This time, with the Management group, it was different. When we had an attunement at the beginning of each meeting, I shared whatever I got in meditation. Even if I only had a small vision, I'd share it. And they listened. But I had to take the first step, to be willing to step forward and be there. I think I had to learn to just be, and to share whatever came to me. It didn't matter who listened. I simply had to share what I got.

I learned so much about the community and it was so good for me, but I didn't get involved with the discussions. I just sat quietly and listened. Many times I had to bite my tongue not to say anything. My purpose was just to be there, to sit and be and learn, all the time. I did the same with the Findhorn Foundation Trustees, who allowed me to sit in on their meetings, and I would simply be there, quietly listening.

God wanted me to know what was going on in the community. Then later, if somebody from the Management group came to me to ask what I thought, as they frequently did, we'd have tea and biscuits, talk things over and I would share what I thought.

I don't feel at all rejected now. I feel loved and appreciated by the community, which is lovely.

MANY YEARS AGO I received guidance that I would be reunited with my whole family at the right time. Little did I realise that I would have to wait until my 80th birthday before the guidance was fulfiled! Over the years my relationship with each of my children from my first marriage became healed and grew richer and more loving. Sometimes there were difficult things to work out between us, but the bridge had been built and the love that was always there proved that it was possible to be reunited, no matter what our differences in philosophy and lifestyle.

On my 80th birthday, for the first time in my life, all my eight children and I were together, under the same roof, in an atmosphere of complete peace, love and forgiveness. It had come about, as God had promised it would.

They came from Canada, New Zealand and the United States to join the others who live in Britain: my four sons and four daughters gathered together for the most wonderful celebration at my eldest son Richard's home in Herefordshire. They brought with them their husbands and wives and 13 of my 19 grandchildren, and were joined by my sister Torrie and my sister-in-law Joan, wife of my brother Paddy who had died soon after my 70th birthday. Sixty members of my family came to celebrate my birthday and to celebrate our family. It was a moment of pure joy for me, and for them too.

The party was held in the Barn on the farm, beautifully cleaned and decorated for the occasion. My daughter Suzanne, a Cordon Bleu chef, prepared the most magnificent dinner with my grandson, Michael, also a chef, and my youngest daughter Penny who had come all the way from New Zealand. Most of them arrived the day before, and there was lots of laughter and high spirits during the preparations, as they also had not seen each other for a long time. Children raced around, and 'Granny' was surrounded by games, jokes and merriment.

The Barn was beautifully decorated, festooned with balloons and flowers, and the tables were laden with delicious food. It was a festive and joyful occasion, with a great buzz of conversation and joking. Then my eldest daughter Jennifer stood up and called for everyone's attention to propose a toast to 'Mum'. Each of my children followed in turn, according to their age. They said some wonderful things about me that I found very moving indeed. I just sat and listened, smiling and crying all at the same time. This is what they said:

Jenny, my eldest, who at the age of 14 took over responsibility for her younger brother and three sisters: "I would like to ask you to raise your glasses to a mother, grandmother, great grandmother, aunt, sister, sister-in-law. Because of her we are all gathered here — to Eileen Caddy." Jenny had been the last of my five children to make contact with me, and I remembered how difficult it was for her to accept me, as she felt a strong allegiance to her father and because her own moral views were opposed to my own. And now here she was, making the first toast to her mother.

Richard, my eldest son: "To an incredible mother who has produced a global family. A toast to a wonderful mother and heaven knows what else! My mum, Eileen." My gratitude poured out to Richard for his level-headedness and openness to me at the time when it was so difficult for the family.

Suzanne, my Canadian daughter: "To an amazing mother, very loved. I'd also like to propose a toast to the very happy memories of Auntie in Ireland, Uncle Paddy and Auntie Joan, and all those who have directly and indirectly affected our lives very lovingly and happily. We love you Mum." Memories crowded in of our times together in her kitchen in Canada, when she was struggling with her life and her marriage, and she had confided her troubles to me, allowing me to be the mother I always wanted to be.

Mary Liz, who came all the way from New Zealand: "I want to toast my Mum, who is a wonderful world traveller, all the way around the world, and a very wonderful mum. To you Mum." Her tears muffled her words. I remembered when she came to me at Findhorn to have her first baby there, and many years later when I went to New Zealand and looked after her boys to allow her to go to England to see her dying father.

Penny, always my baby, now a beautiful, elegant mother of four: "It's thanks to you Mum that we owe a lot of flair and artistic talent that has come out in the whole family and in the next generation. Remember all the fancy dresses and the dressing up? We love you for it — wouldn't you all agree? So here's to my mother who has brought out the creativity in all of us." Penny, who reached out to me as soon as she turned 18, was reminding me of the days in Habbanya making fancy dress costumes for all of them, when she was only 3 years old!

Christopher, the image of his father Peter, our eldest son: "I feel very privileged to be here amongst you all. As has been pointed out already, this is a very special time. Lots of friends, a spider's web that has spread its way all around the planet, and really it's all thanks to one person — Eileen. Here is a lot of history and it all revolves around love. One of Mum's leading philosophies in life is unconditional love, and that is what has brought us all together tonight. I'd like to thank everyone for coming, to thank Richard for hosting us here, and to our sisters for putting on such a wonderful spread. I'd like to thank everyone tonight for creating this environment this evening, and for making us feel part of one family. Most of all, I'd like to thank you, Mum." I remembered being robbed of him when he was a baby, his unorthodox childhood growing up in our crowded caravan, and then in later years his wisdom and support for the work we were doing to create the Findhorn community. My heart was filled with love and gratitude.

Jonathan, the next in line: "I don't have to say anything too deep and meaningful as I have a privileged position as the 7th child! It's really incredible, this gathering. At least I don't have to go all around the world to visit all my relations! It has taken me all my life to see most of the people in this room just once, and now on this occasion I can see you all gathered in one place. It's quite amazing to see the breeding stock! As you know, my mother is a very special woman, and she hears an inner voice – ("We all do!" I interrupted.) Yes, indeed we all do, but when the Bible said, 'Go forth and multiply', she certainly listened! Dear mother..." They all raised their glasses again amidst gales of laughter. I recalled the small boy who kept me sane during my dark night of the soul on the island of Mull, and then his years of teenage rebellion, and my heart went out to my kind, reliable son who had returned to live his own life close by, at Findhorn.

David, the youngest of them all: "I am number 8, so I guess she stopped at perfection! (I smiled indulgently at him.) You see, she even agrees! I just want to say that I've had a wonderful time with you Mum, and I have had the time to repay you for all your time as a mother, and more. I just want you to spend more time on this earth with everyone that's here in this room. It's really important that you stay here. And I can't believe you had eight kids — one is enough for me!" My last child, born at Cluny Hill, who built my lovely house for me. I caught my tears. By now it was all too much to contain.

So I simply said, "Thank you all for everything you've done to make this possible. You've all come from so far and wide; it's simply wonderful. The babies are restless so I won't go on too long. I shall simply say, I love you all." At that moment my life was utterly complete.

After dinner was over, along came the cake. It was made in the shape of a very large boot, the one in the nursery rhyme "There was an old woman who lived in a shoe, she had so many children she didn't know what to do!" There were photos of all my children and grandchildren all over the cake, and before it could be cut, I had to guess who they were. There was much hilarity as I made several mistakes! It was such fun. Then the tables were cleared away, and Jonathan organised Scottish country dancing. I have never laughed so much in my life, as many of them had never done Scottish dancing before and they all got so muddled up, tripping over themselves and each other. The fun and joy was wonderful. And then it was all over.

NOW, IN MY OLD AGE, I feel so very blessed. On 26 August 1999, my 82nd Birthday, I wrote:

> *I give constant thanks for all the many, many blessings God pours down upon me constantly. I am mightily blessed. It is wonderful and amazing to me that I am 82 years old. I am still here in Findhorn, surrounded by a loving family. I sometimes wonder why I am still here, and yet I know deep down I am still needed here in the community. My energy, whatever that means, is needed, and I feel I shall be here until, as a community we have collectively found and grounded unity, harmony, peace and love. Please God help me to keep open to do whatever needs to be done to help bring about what is needed.*

I am living in a loving community with people around me who care for me. I have a lovely home, a very special house, built by my youngest of eight, with so much love. The royalties from my books enable me to live comfortably, and the community meets all my other needs. I am indeed very blessed. I know that for many years I have surrendered my life entirely to God. I have been truly dedicated and committed to God. Each day I offer myself to God to work in and through me as a pure, clear channel, knowing that I will take the consequences, no matter what they are. Whatever I receive in guidance, I always follow through. In this time of so many blessings, I wonder, am I reaping the rewards of long years of faithfully serving God through thick and thin, in the rough times and the smooth times? Whatever the reasons, I give constant thanks for everything all the time, and I never take anything for granted.

Very often people have asked me how to make this inner connection with God. It is as simple as switching on the kettle to make a cup of tea. One morning I awoke and was aware of waves, all around me and in me. My thoughts went to sound waves, picture waves, TV, electricity waves, and I realised they are always there, around me all the time. I cannot see them, but nevertheless I am very aware of them.

These waves need an instrument to enable me to become aware of them on the physical level. When I want to boil a kettle to make a cup of tea, the water won't boil if I just sit there looking at it. I need to stretch out my hand, plug the kettle into the mains and switch it on — hey presto! The water boils and I can have my cup of tea.

It is exactly the same with the God-waves. They are there all the time. They are the Source, the mains grid. This is where prayer and meditation come in. This is the socket. When I pray, I am making the link, the connection with these God-waves. But just to make the connection is not enough. It's useless to plug in without switching on. As long as I sit there hoping something will happen, nothing does. I have to become consciously aware of plugging in and switching on. This is when the seemingly impossible becomes possible, because I have plugged in and switched on the God-source and I am fully aware of what I am doing.

This is something everyone can do. It is not reserved for the few. "Seek and ye shall find. Ask and it shall be given. Knock and the door shall be opened." We have to do it. We have to bring it about by our awareness, by plugging in and switching on. It's as simple as that.

My guidance comes to me in the silence, and I always have a notebook nearby to write it down. Sometimes these words of wisdom have come in response to difficulties in my life, and at other times they come in response to an inspiring thought or idea that I have read somewhere. I like to read the Bible and often return to it for inspiration.

I was re-reading the Psalms and other favourite parts of the Bible, and this is what happened: I call them my Love Songs to God.

Praise the Lord!
Sing to the Lord a new song
His praise in the assembly of the faithful.
Psalm 149:1

My prayers are a song of praise to You God and they sing of my faith in Your goodness.

Even when my prayers seem to have become routine, I know You understand what is in my heart of hearts. Even when my thoughts and words do not reflect my gratitude and love for You God, I know that You understand me. Through this understanding love, You lift me out of complacency and raise my spirits to new heights. I feel secure in my relationship with You, because I know without doubt that I am always enfolded in divine love. Taking time apart from the concerns of the day helps me feel closer to Your sweet spirit. During these precious moments of prayer, I centre myself in Your life, love and peace, and express what is in the depth of my heart. In this spirit of openness, I welcome Your expressions of love into my life. Each day I rise with a new song on my lips and a prayer of praise in my heart for You, God.

Thank you.
Thank you, precious Spirit,
for being the source
of unlimited blessings
within me and my world.

Give me understanding, that I may keep your law, observe it with my whole heart. Lead me in the path of your commandments, for I delight in it.
Psalm 119:34–35

Thank you God for being with me on my journey through life. You have cared for me from the beginning, and I know that your love holds me close and keeps me on the right path with each new step I take. You support and uphold me as I walk with You every moment of the day and night. If my footsteps should falter, You are with me to give me strength and to help me move ahead courageously. Your wisdom lights my path. It gently nudges me in the right direction and steadies me as I journey with You. Your Spirit breathes life into me as I journey, sustains and nourishes me and enables me to grow stronger and healthier day by day. Your love smoothes the way for me and everyone I meet, helping me to live in harmony and peace. I feel loved and secure with You as my guide. How grateful I am for Your presence within me and for the rich meaning You bring to everything I experience.
Thank You God!

Then Jesus said "Father forgive them; for they know not what they do."
Luke 23:34

Often I feel that there is another step to take before I begin a new experience: I feel the need to forgive. Forgiveness is the key to my freedom, the key to my progress. To do this, first I pray. I open my heart to the love of God that transcends events of the past, cleansing me of feelings of guilt or anger. With this cleansing comes freedom of the soul, freedom to be the person I want to be. Then I can begin to forgive others. Enveloped by God's love, I release other people to live their lives freely and in doing so I am again set free. I am renewed by God's love to the depths of my being. I expect love will return to bless me in ways I may not be able to imagine yet. When I look at people around me, I see them through new eyes of love.

> *God, Your love shining through me*
> *allows me to see everyone*
> *and everything with new eyes,*
> *with a spirit of love.*
> *Thank You God.*

ALTHOUGH I PUT MY death wish on the altar many years ago, nevertheless I am of an age when my thoughts naturally turn towards settling my affairs, not in a morbid sense, but in a responsible way. I have no fear of my own death, but I do not wish to be a burden on others when I move on to another dimension. Now I feel very open to think and talk about death and dying, although some people might think I am being gloomy about it. But I look forward to leaving my old cocoon behind and letting the butterfly, the spirit, fly free. I don't feel there is anything to be afraid of. Spiritually, I feel I am prepared to move on with no feeling of fear, only of joy and gratitude. I am indeed very, very blessed.

I shall be in the Light. I know I shall be in the Light. I feel I have been used a great deal by God on this plane, I've touched many people, and I give thanks for that. I just say "Thank you God, that you've used me in this way. It's been a wonderful experience." I have lived a very full life and I feel that enough is enough. That's why I'm ready to go. I'm not in a hurry as before, but I'm ready to go whenever it is time, and I just pray that it'll be an easy passing over.

All I want to do in this last chapter of my life is to make a completion, to become reconciled with everyone.

Reunion and reconciliation is a very important part of the preparation work at the end of my life. My life has been dramatic, one way and another, and I want all my relationships to be absolutely clear before I die. I always pray, "If there is anybody I am still at sixes and sevens with, please God show me so that I can clear it up."

I've written about how I was reconciled with my first husband Andrew before he died. He was in intensive care in hospital in England, and I looked after my daughter Mary Elizabeth's children in New Zealand so that she could go to see him. I wrote him a letter and I sent it with her. It wasn't a very long letter, and I have no idea what I wrote, but when anybody came to visit him, he always asked them to read him this letter. It was a completion, a wonderful reconciliation. Whatever I said touched him, and that was all that mattered. Andrew's brother Nick was at a family wedding recently, and he came over to me and we embraced each other and said how wonderful it was to see each other after all these years. So that was all cleared up.

So the reconciliation with Andrew, with Peter when he came here the last time, and with all my children is complete. I don't think there's anybody left to work things out with. I feel I've gathered them all together. It comes back again to oneness, to wholeness.

I have also made all the practical preparations for my death. I have written a 'Living Will', a legal document that states clearly how I wish to be treated if I become ill and unable to explain. I do not wish to be kept alive artificially by machines, and I want to be allowed to die peacefully and naturally. I have left a letter for my family and close friends explaining how I wish to be treated on my deathbed and after I am dead. It is a very private, personal and individual matter, but I share parts of it here, to share my feeling about how the death of a beloved person can also be a celebration.

I wish my death to be a joyous celebration. I want all of you to know that I have given of my best in this lifetime. For whatever has come through me and has been published and translated into different languages, I give God the honour and glory and feel so deeply grateful that God has been able to work in and through me to help other souls all over the world.

I choose to be cremated in whatever I am wearing at the time.

I'd like my ashes to be scattered around an oak tree planted in the St Barbe Baker's wood, given plenty of space to grow into a mighty oak reaching to the heavens.

I would like a stone with a small plaque on it with my name, date of birth, date of death, nothing more. Simplicity is my hallmark, as God has always reminded me. So keep it simple.

When I go into my dying process, if people want to pray or meditate, this I ask of them: to open fully to Christ, and to embrace themselves, the community and the world with unconditional love.

When I die I would like everyone to give thanks for my release and wish me happy blessings on my journey.

I want my death to be a celebration! I don't want it to be a miserable time. I don't want a time of mourning. I hope you all will celebrate and have a wonderful time. You can always get in touch with me, through meditation. Why not?

I leave you with some thoughts of inspiration that came to me not long ago:

ON LOVE

Love is an inner state of being. It expresses itself in a thousand and one little ways — a look, a touch, an action. Love is the universal language. It can be understood by all, for it is the language of silence.

Love is sharing and sharing is communication. Communication is the lifeblood of Love. Communication is the secret of staying in love. Don't just discuss, but share with love.

Seek unity, not just happiness, because happiness is a by-product. Happiness is like a butterfly. The more you chase it the more it eludes you, but if you turn your attention to other things it will come softly and sit on your shoulder.

Love is everywhere, but you have to be aware of it to appreciate it fully, like the air you breathe. Take nothing for granted, for when you do, it takes all the joy and sparkle out of life.

Life is so thrilling, so exciting. Everything has meaning. There is a pattern and plan running through it all and nothing is by chance.

Always remember that nothing can quench Love, nothing can withstand it. Perfect Love casts out all fear. Love dissolves all guilt. Love makes the world go round. It is Love that will bring peace and unity to the world and nothing else can do it.

Where there is Love there is peace.

Postscript

I met Eileen at a time of crisis in her life when Peter had left her and moved away from the Community. It was 1981 and I had come to Findhorn with my husband and 3 children, at a time when she was being asked to do more of her work out in the world. Eileen was a shy person and did not seek to be in the limelight as a public figure and spiritual teacher, yet she understood this was required of her and, drawing strength from God, she spoke from her own personal experience with simplicity and humility. She would not be drawn into abstract discussions and debates, and replied simply that she could not talk about anything of which she had no direct experience. She spoke of her dedication and obedience to the still small voice, making contact with the God within, and that has been her greatest contribution to the world: Practical Spirituality!

Many times she called me Joannie, after her closest friend who had lived in the community from the early days until her death in 1996. To Eileen I was her Social Secretary, helping her with correspondence, setting up appointments, and keeping her abreast of events in the community. She received letters from people all over the world thanking her for the example she set of putting God first in her life. To the many who found their own spiritual journey a challenging path, her story was an inspiration and Eileen offered them encouragement and validation. She would tune into each writer to find the right words that were thoughtful, uplifting and thought provoking, spurring people to take action, heal, forgive and move forward.

Eileen and I were friends and companions. We talked about a lot of things — life's lessons, love, family, forgiveness, joy, death — and enjoyed our coffees, steaks, wine, shopping trips, and fun times together. We shared an Irish heritage, had attended the same school in Dublin, and both of us wore green on St. Patrick's Day. It was both a pleasure and privilege to work with her, travel together, and pop into her home to see her each day.

Towards the end of her life Eileen wondered if she was talking to the wind. Were we listening to her words? She knew with certainty that her life's purpose was to turn us all within, to go into the silence, listen for our still small voice, trust our inner divinity, and bring more love into the world. She saw her work as 'planting seeds' within hearts and minds — if she could make contact with the God within, then it was possible for us all. She reminded us to balance the busyness of our work here in the community with spending time with God, whether that was in Sanctuary or in nature or alone.

There is no retirement on this spiritual journey and we receive our lessons as long as we are alive. When Eileen was having difficulty with a particular person, or with her own physical dependence, with BEING instead of DOING, she continued to go within, ask for help, listen, and act from the guidance she received. She would say she was in a rut and needed to change her attitude and immediately she would make a 180-degree turnaround. Change did indeed, for her, come in 'the twinkling of an eye' and 'all was very very well'.

On Wednesday December 13, 2006, Eileen died peacefully, at home in Cornerstone. She was in her 90th year. Her mind was bright and alert. A few days before her passing we had discussed the Christmas cards she had received, and those that needed an answer. She was sitting up in her chair eating her lunch. Over the weekend she was sleeping more, and it was obvious, she was 'moving into the light', cared for by family and friends.

Thank you Eileen. You have been a great teacher and inspiration in my life. May your example of attuning to the God within, service, simplicity and love continue to be a guiding light for me, this Community and the Findhorn family all over the world.

BLESS YOU.

—Rosie Turnbull
Findhorn, June 15, 2007

FINDHORN PRESS

Books, Card Sets,
CDs & DVDs
that inspire and uplift

For a complete catalogue, please contact:

Findhorn Press Ltd
305a The Park
Forres IV36 3TE
Scotland, UK

Telephone
+44-(0)1309-690582
Fax
+44-(0)1309-690036
eMail
info@findhornpress.com

or consult our catalogue online
(with secure order facility) on
www.findhornpress.com